ROMANOV RICHES

ROMANOV RICHES

Russian Writers and Artists
Under the Tsars

SOLOMON VOLKOV

TRANSLATED FROM THE RUSSIAN
BY ANTONINA W. BOUIS

ALFRED A. KNOPF   NEW YORK   2011

THIS IS A BORZOI BOOK
PUBLISHED BY ALFRED A. KNOPF

Translation copyright © 2011 by Alfred A. Knopf,
a division of Random House, Inc.

This translation is from an unpublished Russian-language manuscript
by Solomon Volkov, copyright © by Solomon Volkov.

All illustrations are from the personal collection of Solomon Volkov.

Library of Congress Cataloging-in-Publication Data
Volkov, Solomon.
Romanov riches : Russian writers and artists under the tsars / by Solomon Volkov ;
translated from the Russian by Antonina W. Bouis. — 1st ed.
p. cm.
"Translation is from an unpublished manuscript"—T.p. verso.
"Published in . . . Canada by Random House of Canada Limited, Toronto"—T.p. verso.
"This is a Borzoi book"—T.p. verso.
Includes bibliographical references.
ISBN 978-0-307-27063-4
1. Romanov, House of—History. 2. Romanov, House of—Art patronage. 3. Russia—
Kings and rulers—Biography. 4. Authors, Russian—Biography. 5. Russian literature—
History and criticism. 6. Artists—Russia—Biography.
7. Composers—Russia—Biography. 8. Arts, Russian—History. 9. Russia—Intellectual
life. 10. Russia—History—1613–1917. I. Title.
DK37.8.R6V55 2011
700.947'0903—dc22
2010045132

Jacket image: Crest of the Romanov Imperial House, Bettmann / Corbis
Jacket design by Helen Yentus and Jason Booher

Manufactured in the United States of America
First Edition

Contents

Introduction

The Romanov dynasty holds the central place in Russian history. It ruled the country for more than three hundred years, from 1613 to 1917. In that time, Russia became an enormous Eurasian empire, covering a sixth of the world's surface and instilling fear and sometimes awe in its neighbors, who were beckoned by its vast expanses and the exotic mores and costumes of the ethnic groups inhabiting it, and later surprised and delighted by their amazing cultural achievements—Russian novels, music, ballet, and drama.

The majestic and often tragic history of the Romanovs has long attracted historians, and the flood of books and studies keeps increasing. Much has been written as well on the various cultural aspects of the Romanov era, but this book is the first to present an integrated narrative history of the complex and dramatic relations between the Romanov dynasty and Russian culture in all its multiplicity: not only with literature (the most researched theme until now) but also with art, music, ballet, and theater.

In that sense, this book is a "prequel" to my previous work, *The Magical Chorus: A History of Russian Culture from Tolstoy to Solzhenitsyn,* which began where the present book ends; thus, together they form a history of Russian culture from Archpriest Avvakum to the present day.

Many still believe that the Romanovs allegedly "demonstrated an amazing indifference to all the arts except ballet, where their mistresses danced, and Guards military exercises, where their lovers marched."[1]

That is a caricature, of course. Yes, the Romanov men were first and foremost military by profession, which is understandable, but as most of them were people of excellent education, they took a lively interest in literature, architecture, music, painting, and theater, and some of them (especially Peter the Great, Catherine the Great, and Nicholas I) took a hands-on approach to culture building.

For the Romanovs, culture was the political instrument par excellence, and they may not have given much thought to the fact that Russian literature and art were arguably their greatest treasure. History, however, has confirmed the connection between control of the cultural process and stability: the more involvement by a Russian ruler with the culture, the stronger the regime.

In an autocratic state, which Russia was, personal relations between monarchs and the cultural elite inevitably took on greater significance. The rulers listened closely to the counsel of Gavrila Derzhavin, Nikolai Karamzin, and Vassily Zhukovsky—even though their advice often irritated them.

Nicholas I called Alexander Pushkin "the wisest man in Russia" and tried to direct his work, albeit with mixed success. Ivan Turgenev's *A Sportsman's Sketches* are rumored to have given emotional impetus to Alexander II's decision to emancipate the serfs. Alexander III read Fedor Dostoevsky's novels avidly, loved the music of Peter Tchaikovsky, and collected the paintings of the Wanderers, whom he supported as truly national artists.

Created under the aegis of Nicholas I, the ideological slogan "Orthodoxy, Autocracy, and Nationality" became an effective tool for cultural and political control for many years. The unwillingness or inability of the last Russian tsar, Nicholas II, to modernize the cultural policy of his predecessors was, I believe, one of the essential causes of the collapse of autocracy in Russia.

As Ralph Waldo Emerson observed, there is no history, only biography. In this book I describe the relations between the Romanovs and "their" writers, poets, composers, and artists as the interaction of living people— gifted, ambitious, vain, impatient, capricious. Both sides clearly imagined themselves onstage, under the floodlights of world history, and acted accordingly.

Victor Shklovsky, one of the fathers of Russian formalism and biographer of Leo Tolstoy, told me in a conversation in Moscow in 1974 that his circle believed that personal dealings with major creative figures (and Shklovsky had known, among others, Vladimir Mayakovsky, Sergei Eisenstein, and Boris Pasternak) help you better understand the great writers of the past.[2]

When you see for yourself how the private emotions and public statements of cultural leaders correlate, Shklovsky maintained, you can make sounder judgments about the diaries, letters, and reminiscences of years past. Comparing the giants of yore with people you knew, you have greater focus in your perception of the legendary figures (for all the conditionality of such parallels), who are then no longer never-erring cardboard "geniuses" but real characters capable—as we all are—of making terrible mistakes and glaringly unjust statements.

I had many opportunities to see the wisdom of the old paradoxalist Shklovsky's idea. Personal contact with Anna Akhmatova, Dmitri Shostakovich, George Balanchine, and Joseph Brodsky helped me, I hope, to research and interpret historical materials on Russian culture in a less prejudiced way.

Shklovsky's hypothesis applies even more to Russia's leaders. Traditionally they have been considered to be "rulers from God," in the words of Ivan the Terrible. Only members of the inner circle or specially selected and vetted "representatives of the people" could have access to them. What were the chances of a Russian Jewish intellectual like me looking the tsar in the eye, even for a second? None.

In Soviet times, the leaders of Russia managed to retain that aura of inaccessible omnipotence for a long time. Joseph Stalin was extremely successful in this regard (having learned much—especially in the sphere of cultural politics—from Nicholas I). His successors gradually lost that political capital.

There were so many jokes about Nikita Khrushchev in the last years of his reign. And yet . . . I remember the excitement I felt in September 1964 in Leningrad when, as a twenty-year-old conservatory student, I found myself in the crowd surrounding Khrushchev (security in those days was rather lax) as he entered the Kirov Theater on Teatralnaya Square with President Sukarno of Indonesia.

Khrushchev (who would be ousted by Leonid Brezhnev in a few weeks) passed by me just half a step away, smiling broadly; his face, contrary to what I read later about his depressed mood in those days, radiated energy and confidence. I was struck by the contrast between his tanned face and his snow-white short-cropped hair around a large bald spot: it literally glowed in Leningrad's unusually bright autumnal sun, creating the effect of a halo.

Perestroika unexpectedly made contact with Russian leaders more possible, even for outsiders like me. I was lucky: living in America, I could "look into the eyes" (if not the souls) of a past, a future, and an acting president of Russia (respectively Mikhail Gorbachev, Boris Yeltsin, and Vladimir Putin) on their visits to New York.

I intersected with some of their closest comrades-in-arms or most prominent opponents (Yegor Ligachev, Alexander Yakovlev, Anatoly Sobchak, Vladimir Yakovlev, Yegor Gaidar, Grigory Yavlinsky, Boris Nemtsov). Sometimes it was merely a quick question and answer, on other occasions a longer conversation. Each meeting added a new and precious insight into the psychology of the political elite, reinforcing my image of national leaders (professional politicians) as a special—in both good ways and bad—human breed, living within its own moral and emotional realm.

The various aspects of the interaction of one such specific group (that is, the Romanov dynasty and their "inner circle") with another special stratum (the Russian cultural elite) have attracted the attention of many remarkable people, whose writing and opinions have served as a guiding light for me.

I will name only a few here. They are Sergei Averintsev, Naum

Berkovsky, Isaiah Berlin, James H. Billington, Andrei Bitov, Kornei Chukovsky, Leonid Dolgopolov, Natan Eidelman, Boris Eikhenbaum, Joseph Frank, Boris Gasparov, Lidia Ginzburg, Yakov Gordin, Lev Gumilev, Roman Jakobson, Vadim Kozhinov, Jay Leyda, Dmitri Likhachev, Lev Loseff, Martin Malia, Irina Paperno, Boris Paramonov, Richard Pipes, Dmitri Sarabyanov, Viktor Shklovsky, Andrei Sinyavsky, Valery Sokolov, Georgy Sviridov, Dmitri Svyatopolk-Mirsky (D. S. Mirsky), Elizabeth Valkenier, Igor Volgin, Richard S. Wortman, Daniel Zhitomirsky, and Andrei Zorin.

I am particularly grateful to those of the above mentioned who shared their views with me in unforgettable personal conversations.

The informed reader will see that this short list nevertheless encompasses a wide ideological spectrum: it includes liberals and conservatives, Marxists and anticommunists, nationalists and cosmopolites. Their ideas stimulated my work. I have always tried to be free of the ideological constraints that to this day hinder an unprejudiced study and evaluation of the political aspects of the treasure house that is Russian culture.

I am most grateful to Grisha and Alexandra Bruskin, Oleg and Tatiana Rudnik, Vagrich and Irina Bakhchanyan, Alexander and Irina Genis, Alexander and Irene Kolchinsky, Valery Golovitsev, and Yevgeny Zubkov for their support during the writing of this book. The illustrations were, as always, the responsibility of my wife, Marianna. The present book is once again the result of close and deeply satisfying collaboration with my translator, Antonina W. Bouis, and my editor at Knopf, Ashbel Green, whose ideas and suggestions were of immense help.

PART I

CHAPTER I

The First Romanovs:
From Tsar Mikhail to Peter I

On Friday, November 27, 1836, "everything that is the best in St. Petersburg"[1] (as a high courtier noted in his diary) gathered for the first performance of the long-awaited new Russian opera, Mikhail Glinka's *A Life for the Tsar*. The premiere occasioned the opening of the Bolshoi Kamenny Theater, one of the capital's most majestic buildings in those days. After the reconstruction, it held two thousand people, and it was packed; the tickets, despite the gala prices, had been sold out a month in advance.

Intriguing rumors about Glinka's piquant (and, most importantly, "national") music had been circulating in elite St. Petersburg circles for quite a while, and the seats in the orchestra and boxes held the cream of Russian culture—the poets Vassily Zhukovsky and Prince Peter Vyazemsky, the writer and musician Prince Vladimir Odoevsky, and the famous fabulist Ivan Krylov.

Some paid special respects to the man on the aisle seat in the eleventh row: thirty-seven-year-old Alexander Pushkin, the nation's literary lion and trendsetter. An avid theatergoer, music lover, and ballet aficionado (particularly of pretty ballerinas), the usually lively and witty Pushkin seemed to be preoccupied "by a family affair." No one suspected that two months later the poet would be felled in a duel over that family affair. Also in the audience was the as-yet-unknown eighteen-year-old Ivan Turgenev, then a student at St. Petersburg University, a young snob who would find Glinka's music "boring."[2]

The boxes held the important courtiers in splendid uniforms with gold braid and all kinds of orders on the chest and their dressed-up wives wearing diamonds (the same diary entry read: "aristocrats, stars, brilliance and beauty"). But all lorgnettes were fixed on the emperor's box: Nicholas I was expected with his family. It was known that the emperor had approved the opera, attended rehearsals, and accepted the composer's dedication—"To His Imperial Majesty."

When Nicholas I, Empress Alexandra Fedorovna, and the grand dukes and duchesses took their seats, the conductor raised his baton, and the light blue and gold curtain rose after the overture revealing a country landscape in the fashionable "Slavic" style, depicting the village of Domnino, near Kostroma.

It was a performance set in the Time of Troubles, a horrible period for Russia in the early seventeenth century: after the death of Tsar Ivan the Terrible in 1584, his sons died one after the other, ending the Riurikovich dynasty. This dynastic crisis led to Russia's first civil war, peasant rebellions, foreign invasions, famine, and epidemics.

The country lay in ruins, empty, humiliated, and looted. The capital, Moscow, was in the hands of Polish usurpers for two years, from September 1610 to October 1612. Foreign observers were sure that Russia would never rise up from its knees and would simply die off and vanish.

Prerevolutionary Russian historians always attributed the miraculous deliverance from that national catastrophe to the rise of a new ruling dynasty, the Romanovs. It happened in February 1613, when the national Assembly of the Land was convened in Moscow, which had been liberated from the Poles, and after excruciatingly long negotiations elected Mikhail Romanov, sixteen years old, as the new tsar. Young Romanov with his mother and entourage were at the Ipatiev Monastery, near Kostroma, and the delegation of the assembly traveled there in March to anoint him tsar.

The new tsar set off for Moscow a few days later. It was then that the legendary exploit that became the basis of Glinka's opera occurred.

Ivan Susanin, the peasant elder of the Romanovs' ancestral lands, allegedly led Polish troops planning to kidnap the new tsar into impenetrable swamps. Susanin was killed by the enemy, giving his own life to save the young tsar—and, with him, the future of Russia.

That was the official legend, based on Tsar Mikhail's decree, which in 1619 granted tax and other privileges to the relatives of the late Ivan Susanin, who, "suffering intolerable torture from those Polish and Lithuanian people, did not tell said Polish and Lithuanian people about us, Great Tsar, did not tell them where we were at that time, and the Polish and Lithuanian people did torture him to death."[3]

This legend crystallized by the early nineteenth century, when the war with Napoleon aroused patriotic and monarchist feelings in Russian society. When Emperor Nicholas I, an unsurpassed master of ideological manipulation, ascended the throne in 1825, he supported and embellished the legend.

In October 1834, Nicholas I even made a special pilgrimage to the Ipatiev Monastery and Domnino village, where he reconfirmed all the privileges granted by his ancestor to the peasant hero's offspring. Nicholas ordered a statue to be raised to Mikhail Romanov and Susanin in Kostroma, as his imperial ukase put it, for "our descendants to see that in Susanin's immortal exploit . . . in sacrificing his life he did rescue the Orthodox Faith and the Russian Realm from foreign slavery."[4]

At the same time Nicholas I also came up with the idea of creating a patriotic Russian opera in the "folk spirit." That idea was obviously in the air, and it consumed the aspiring young composer Mikhail Glinka. When Glinka approached his friend Zhukovsky, a poet with excellent ties at court, he recommended the Susanin story to the composer as the subject for a "national" opera.

Zhukovsky discussed Glinka's initiative with Nicholas I, who became so interested in the project that he recommended a good librettist, the thirty-four-year-old Baron Georg Rozen, personal secretary to the heir to the throne, the future Alexander II. "Even though he is a German," added Nicholas, "his Russian is excellent and can be trusted."[5]

This was a unique example of direct personal involvement of a Romanov ruler in the creation of one of the milestones of Russian culture, an amazing event. But then everything connected to *A Life for the Tsar* was amazing and even mysterious, starting with its author, Mikhail Glinka.

You could rarely find another case of sheer genius contained in a totally inappropriate vessel. There was nothing to indicate that Glinka, a thirty-year-old musical dilettante from a poor provincial noble family, who was short, ugly, sickly, hypochondriacal, and led a raucous and bohemian life, could become the undisputed father of Russia's music as much as Pushkin was the progenitor of Russian literature.

Moreover, the geniuses of Pushkin and Glinka were equal, with the only difference being that in logocentric Russia the poet stood in the center of cultural discourse while the composer inevitably ended up in the background. And of course, Pushkin's biography was much more dramatic and paradigmatic. (In the West, the esteem for Pushkin and Glinka is still based primarily on respect for their preeminence in Russia.)

Even in his youth Glinka dreamed of writing a "Russian" opera. But how did he move from fantasy to reality? That happened in 1833 in Berlin, where Glinka studied composition for six months. The love-prone Glinka met seventeen-year-old Maria: "She had rather Israelite origins: tall, but not yet formed figure, with a very beautiful face, and she resembled a Madonna" (from Glinka's *Notes*). The easily inflamed Glinka started sketching musical themes (in the Russian national style) that later were used in *A Life for the Tsar*.

When Glinka, prompted by news of his father's death, had to return to Russia, he first longed to return to Berlin and Maria, with whom he was "in constant correspondence," but in St. Petersburg he met Maria Ivanova, "a kind, naïve half-German." Pushkin's sister fumed, "Michel

Glinka has married a certain Miss Ivanova, a young thing without money or education, quite homely, and who to top it off hates music."[6]

But it was this marriage (which ended in scandalous divorce) that encouraged Glinka to finish his opera as if on a single breath: "The weather was beautiful and I often worked with the door opened into the garden, drinking in the pure, balsamic air."[7] As Anna Akhmatova noted in a poem a century later, "If you only knew the rubbish / from which poetry grows, knowing no shame."

As it sometimes happens (but very, very rarely) in these situations, everything around *A Life for the Tsar* moved smoothly. Glinka was immediately accepted into Zhukovsky's circle, which met in the Winter Palace, where the poet lived as Tsarevich Alexander's tutor, "a select company, consisting," as the composer put it, "of poets, literary men and in general refined people."[8] Among the guests were Pushkin, Nikolai Gogol (who read his new comedy, *The Marriage,* when Glinka was there), Prince Vyazemsky, and Prince Odoevsky.

Pushkin and Zhukovsky took a lively interest in the libretto of *A Life for the Tsar,* and the latter wrote verses for the opera's final pro-monarchistic apotheosis and in particular for the concluding march-like chorus, "Glory!," which for many years was considered the unofficial anthem of Russia: "Glory, glory, our Russian Tsar! Our God-given Sovereign Tsar!" In the opera, the people gathered on Red Square in Moscow greet the triumphant entrance of the new monarch, Mikhail Romanov, with this vivid, majestic (but not pompous—it was Glinka at his best) music accompanied by two brass bands.

As Glinka reminisced, "As if by magic I suddenly had the plan for the entire opera and the idea of juxtaposing Russian music to Polish music; and then, many themes and even details of their development—all lit up in my head at once."[9]

The music for *A Life for the Tsar* was composed at a feverish pitch, ahead of the libretto. Baron Rozen often had to submit texts to fit quite complex melodic lines and ornate rhythmical figures. Glinka was satisfied: "Zhukovsky and the others used to joke that Rozen had tucked away already prepared verses into his pockets, and all I had to do was say what sort I needed, that is, the rhythm, and how many lines, and each time he would pull out just as much as was needed of each sort, out of different pockets."[10] It sometimes seemed that Glinka didn't care at all about the words in his opera, as long as they were easy for the vocalists to sing: "Write whatever you want as long as you remember to always go to an 'a' or 'ee' for the high notes."[11]

Assured of his own genius, overly ambitious, and often quite capricious, Glinka was inexplicably offered friendly collaboration at every turn. As a result, Zhukovsky, Pushkin, Prince Odoevsky, Count Vladimir Sollogub, and Nicholas I himself were all involved in the opera's creation. Everyone, it seems, understood the cultural and historical significance of what was happening before their very eyes.

Only stupid and greedy theatrical officials tried to sabotage the work during rehearsals. The director of the theater wrote rude letters to Glinka alleging, as the composer later recalled, "that I was forcing the artists to sing in a room filled with tobacco smoke, which was bad for their voices." But the patronage of Nicholas I protected the inexperienced author, who under other circumstances would have been brought to his knees.

The opera was first called *Ivan Susanin,* then *A Death for the Tsar,* and got its final name, *A Life for the Tsar,* at the wish of Nicholas I: "He who gives his life for the Sovereign does not die."[12] For that title alone, Nicholas I deserves to be listed among the collaborators of Glinka's opera.

At the premiere, connoisseurs were astounded by the opera's innovative style and originality. Prince Odoevsky best expressed that feeling of an avant-garde breakthrough: Glinka was able "to elevate folk song to tragedy."[13] It was done without sentimentality or melodrama, in the Glinka style—lyrical, but pure and restrained.

Gogol, in his influential "Petersburg Notes of 1836," captured the delight of Glinka's fans: "He happily melded in his creation two Slavic musics; you can hear where the Russian speaks and where the Pole: one brings the broad melody of Russian song, the other the rash motif of the Polish mazurka."

The first audience was particularly moved by the scene in which Susanin bids farewell to life and then dies at the hands of the Poles. The choristers depicting Poles attacked the singer "with such frenzy that they tore his shirt, and he had to defend himself for real" (from Glinka's *Notes*). Susanin died with the words "Our Tsar is saved." At the moment even the severe Nicholas I shed a tear, but after the performance he told Glinka, "It is not good that Susanin is killed on stage."[14] Naturally, the necessary changes were made.

In a rare occasion, the praise of the tastemakers coincided with the autocrat's approval; thus, the reaction of the cautious high officials and their wives, who filled the orchestra seats and boxes, was predetermined. They had watched closely to see how the unfamiliar and puzzling music was received in the imperial box. The tsar's demonstrative tear had its magical effect: soon after, the entire theater resounded with the sobs of the fashionable audience.

A special treat highlighted the finale: Zhukovsky had suggested the mind-boggling panorama of Mikhail Romanov in a gilded cart entering Red Square with the Kremlin in the background and being met by the joyous crowd, which was cleverly magnified by cardboard figures that created the illusion of an endless mass of people (the equivalent of today's computerized effects in film).

According to the report in the government newspaper, "at the end of the opera the author of the music was unanimously called out and received a most gracious sign of good will from the Crowned Patron of fine arts accompanied by the audience's loud clapping."[15] Glinka was called into the imperial box, where he was thanked first by Nicholas I and then by the empress and their children.

Soon after, the composer received a royal gift: a ring with a topaz, circled with three rows of "marvelous diamonds," costing 4,000 rubles, an impressive sum in those days.

Glinka's opera was instantly taken to heart by St. Petersburg's educated circles: "In societies of the capital, large and small, brilliant and modest, they discuss that masterly work by our young composer and even dance quadrilles made up of his delightful melodies."[16]

Nicholas I could be pleased: the work created under his auspices and even with his participation had entered life and history. The artistic elite considered *A Life for the Tsar* as entrée for Russian music onto the European stage. But for the emperor it was more important that the opera vividly fixed in the public mind the idyllic and patriotic story of the accession to the throne in 1613 of the first Romanov tsar.

The true events of young Mikhail Romanov's accession were, of course, much more complex and cynical than what Nicholas I wanted to present more than two hundred years later. The person selected to be tsar in 1613 was, in the caustic remark of the great Russian historian Vassily Kliuchevsky, "not the most talented, but the most convenient . . . Mikhail Romanov is still young, his mind is not mature, and he will do our bidding."[17] Many thought and hoped that Tsar Mikhail would not last long on the throne. But he persevered, and reigned for a mostly uneventful thirty-two years.

In 1645, after Mikhail's death, the boyars swore in his sixteen-year-old son, Alexei, who turned out to be a much more significant figure. His contemporaries dubbed Alexei "the Most Gentle," and he is best known today as the father of the reformist Peter the Great.

Compared to his famous son's intense activity, Alexei's thirty-year reign may be seen as a time of stagnation. But it was in that period, which was in fact rather turbulent, that the innovative trends, which became so visible under Peter I, first manifested themselves in Russia.

Alexei was intensely religious, a quality that reappeared in later Romanovs. He prayed first thing in the morning, and as an experienced churchgoer could make a thousand or fifteen hundred bows to the ground in the course of several hours of prayer. (Since the tsar tended to be corpulent, those bows also served as a good fitness workout.)

Alexei was well versed in religious rituals, interfering in church services and correcting the monks. He fasted strictly eight months of the year, during which time he dined no more than three times a week, the rest of the time taking only black bread with salt. (Also a good habit.) Alexei performed these rituals easily, without strain or pretense.

Kind by nature, "with meek features and gentle eyes,"[18] the tsar could still sometimes lose his temper and beat the person who angered him. But he would just as quickly calm down, and people did not bear grudges against him.

Still, the royal piety and kindness did not avert the great church schism, so fateful for Russia, or the cruel conflict between the tsar and the greatest writer of the period, Archpriest Avvakum Petrov (1620 or 1621 to 1682), author of the famous *Life,* the first autobiographical work written in Russia.

Both tragedies were closely related. The church schism was the result of the ecclesiastical ambitions of Tsar Alexei and his "bosom friend" Patriarch Nikon. They both envisioned a universal Orthodox empire with Moscow as its center—the realization of an idea first proposed in 1510 by the elder Filofey (Philoteus) of the Elizarov Monastery, that Moscow would be the Third Rome (after the fall of the Second Rome, Constantinople).

In order to make this dream a reality, Patriarch Nikon started church reforms that would bring the Russian Orthodox ritual closer to the Greek—the Balkans were envisioned as part of the new empire. In particular, Nikon ordered all members of the church to make the sign of the cross not with two but with three fingers, and repeat "Hallelujah" not twice but three times, like the Greeks. The liturgy and the rituals of christening and repentance were simplified and the corresponding changes entered into church books.

As is customary in Russia, this was done hastily and unceremoniously. Nikon's reforms upset and angered many believers, who considered them the work of Satan. The defenders of the old faith, who resisted even after they were anathemized, were branded *"raskolniki,"* "breakers-off," but they called themselves Old Believers.

One of their leaders was a former friend of Nikon's, the young and charismatic Avvakum, who at thirty-one had already been elevated to the rank of archpriest. In Moscow Avvakum, who preached at the important church of the Kazan Mother of God on Red Square, caught the attention of Tsar Alexei, who appreciated his "pure and irreproachable and God-emulating life."[19]

Avvakum later remembered one episode in particular. The tsar came to the Kazan church for Easter and wished to see the archpriest's young son, who was out playing somewhere. Alexei, as Avvakum later recalled, "sent my own brother to bring the child and stood for a long time waiting until my brother found the boy outside. He gave him his hand to kiss, but the boy was stupid and did not understand; he saw that he was not a priest, so he did not want to kiss it; the Sovereign brought his hand up to the child's lips himself, then gave him two eggs and patted him on the head."[20]

But the tsar's goodwill did not protect the archpriest from harm. When the persecution began of Old Believers, Avvakum and his wife were exiled to Siberia. There, under harsh conditions, they lived for eleven years.

In 1664, after ridding himself of the power-hungry Nikon, the tsar returned Avvakum to Moscow. He wanted this outstanding priest as his ally and therefore, according to Avvakum, treated him gently: "When he walked past my yard, he would bless himself and bow to me, often asking about my health. One time, sweetly, he even dropped his hat bowing to me."[21]

Alexei even offered Avvakum the position of royal spiritual adviser. But as soon as Avvakum realized that the tsar had gotten rid of Nikon but had no intention of abandoning his church reforms, he wrote Alexei an angry letter. Their subsequent meeting in church was described vividly by Avvakum: "I stood before the tsar, bowing, looking at him, saying nothing. And the tsar bowed to me, stood looking at me and saying nothing. And so we parted."[22]

Avvakum and three of his friends were exiled to the small town of Pustozersk in the north, in a "place of tundra, cold, and no trees," where they spent the last fifteen years of their lives (1667–1682). In Pustozersk the quartet of disobedient Old Believers unleashed a storm of dissident

writing, sending incendiary letters to their associates that were distributed across the country in specially constructed wooden crosses with
secret compartments. Three of the men were punished, their tongues cut
out and the fingers of their right hands chopped off—so they could not
conspire together or write their rebellious letters, or cross themselves with
two fingers.

The tsar spared only Avvakum, causing him to fall into a deep depression: "I wanted to die, not eating, and I did not eat eight days and more,
but the brothers forced me to eat."[23] Avvakum and his "brothers" were
placed in separate dug-out cells that had only a small window through
which food was thrown down to them.

Avvakum sarcastically described his life in the dugout: "where we
drink and eat is where we defecate, and then put the shit on a shovel and
out the window! . . . I imagine that our Tsar Alexei does not have a chamber like this."[24] So the treasure of ancient Russian literature, *The Life of
Archpriest Avvakum,* was written by the author in proximity to his own
shit—a symbolic picture, to be sure.

Avvakum's fierce energy found an outlet in obsessive writing: of the
nearly ninety works that have survived, more than eighty were written in
prison. The most famous is *Life,* first published in 1861, after almost two
hundred years in secret circulation among the Old Believers. *Life* stunned
Russian readers with its vibrancy, colorful descriptiveness, and bold mix
of Church Slavonic and colloquial Russian, often coarse but always
expressive.

Of course, one of the reasons for the popularity of Avvakum the
writer was Avvakum the personality—the archpriest was a martyr writer,
and that always impressed Russian readers. His oppositionist attitude
toward earthly powers elicited respect and awe in the second half of the
nineteenth century, after the long-awaited repeal of serfdom. Avvakum
referred to the tsar, who was traditionally still called "God's anointed," as
being "anointed with filth."

When Tsar Alexei died in 1673, the triumphant Avvakum thundered
curses from Pustozersk: "Poor, poor, mad little tsar! What have you done
to yourself? . . . where is the purple porphyry and royal crown orna-

mented with beads and precious stones? . . . Go to hell, you son of a whore!"

The final punishment came in response to this and other attacks from Avvakum; the new tsar, Fedor, ordered that Avvakum and his three friends be burned alive in 1682 "for great slander on the Royal House." In the following years, tens of thousands of Old Believers all over Russia, inspired by the example of Avvakum, perished in *"gari,"* mass self-immolations. No writer could have ever dreamed of such grandiose and terrifying fiery memorials.

In the year of Avvakum's horrible death, a lively and intelligent ten-year-old boy named Peter took the throne; he grew up to be a six-foot-six colossus and did not physically resemble his "Most Gentle" father in the least. Peter I was a muscular man with a springy step, and swung his arms so wildly as he walked that he frightened people. The effect was intensified by his huge bulging eyes and the nervous tic that marred his face at the slightest bit of agitation or tension.

Perhaps it was because of this marked contrast with the corpulent and kindly Tsar Alexei that people refused to recognize Peter as his true son: "The Sovereign is not of Russian stock and not the son of Tsar; the real son was switched in infancy with a foreigner in the German quarter."[25]

Another popular legend had the real Peter immured in Riga, his place on the throne taken by a foreign impostor. They also called Peter the Antichrist. There was a death penalty for such talk in Russia, but the rumors did not cease, especially among the Old Believers.

Ironically, for all the external differences, Peter I inherited a lot from his father. Like his father, he had a volatile temper; he loved to read and write; he was curious about foreign marvels; and he also shared Alexei's dislike of overly power-hungry church officials and his love of all things military.

All the Romanovs, without exception, were particularly interested in military issues. That is quite understandable. As leaders of an enormous kingdom, they were obliged to care about its security and interests. Russia was continually defending itself or expanding. A mighty army was necessary, and its preparedness was always the main concern of Russian rulers.

No army exists in a social vacuum. It always mirrors the general state of affairs in the country, its social fabric, and the state of its economy, trade, and education. While examining the Romanovs' attitude toward Russian culture, we should always remember that the majority of the important cultural initiatives of all the Russian monarchs were propelled by interests of state security (and personal security as well).

In that sense Peter's father was no exception. Foreigners reported that "in military matters he is knowledgeable and fearless."[26] Tsar Alexei participated in several military campaigns and saw with his own eyes his army's shortcomings. That led to his attempts to reform it: he invited foreign mercenaries to Russia, and from Europe he purchased cannons with iron cannonballs, thousands of muskets, and tons of gunpowder.

In Alexei's reign, Russia started building weapons factories—and needed foreigners again. A long line of unemployed European masters in the most varied professions made its way to Russia: foundry workers, stonemasons, weavers, clockmakers. And after them came architects, painters, teachers of languages, "politesse," and dance. As Kliuchevsky summarized it, "They started with foreign officers and German cannons and ended with German ballet."[27]

Thus, the famous reforms of Peter I did not come out of thin air, but followed his father's lead. In that sense, Peter can be considered a good son. It is another matter that Peter's reforms took on an incredible acceleration, which created the illusion of a radical break with Russia's past.

Instead of the break metaphor, some contemporary scholars offer another—a single flow, albeit rather turbulent at times. In the framework of that current, both national traditions and European innovations coexisted and interacted in Russia in the seventeenth and eighteenth centuries.

According to the populist critic Nikolai Dobroliubov, Peter I "cast off the ancient, obsolete forms in which the highest authority existed before him; but the essence remained the same even under him . . . In a sailor's jacket, with an ax in his hand, he held his kingdom just as terrifyingly and powerfully as had his predecessors dressed in porphyry and seated on a golden throne with a scepter in their hands."[28]

Peter's attitude toward culture in general, and literature and art in particular, was utilitarian. His main goal was the creation of a strong, modern army and navy. This attitude was reflected in the books of Peter's personal library, in which most of the more than fifteen hundred volumes were devoted to military studies and shipbuilding, followed by historical works and books on architecture and parks.

In his desire to strengthen "order and defense," Peter shook up the country. His radical cultural initiatives were part of that shake-up. Merely a listing of those initiatives is impressive: an unprecedented secularization of culture; the establishment in 1703 of Russia's first printed newspaper, *Bulletin on Military and Other Affairs, Worthy of Being Known and Remembered, Occurring in the Muscovite State and Other Neighboring Countries;* and the expansion of the network of printing presses that began producing "civil" books—that is, set in the new, simplified type.

Later, the great scientist and poet Mikhail Lomonosov drew a parallel between this last innovation and the tsar's enforced Europeanization of his subjects' appearance: "Under Peter the Great not only the boyars and their wives, but even the letters threw off their wide fur coats and dressed in summer clothing."[29]

One of the most notable steps in the change of Russia's political and cultural image was the establishment in 1703 of the city of St. Petersburg in the mouth of the Neva River; it became the official new capital in 1712. The tsar was particularly proud of that action, fantastic in both its boldness and irrationality, and he never failed to include it in lists of his main achievements. In terms of culture, St. Petersburg became a laboratory for elaborating the architectural and behavioral models that Peter wanted to extend throughout the country.

Private brick buildings, European-style parks, and streets paved with stones and illuminated by streetlamps first appeared in Russia in St.

Petersburg. Peter's favorite creation was the Summer Garden, which abutted his summer residence; he had personally drawn the original plans for it. An inveterate teacher, the tsar told his gardener, "I want people who stroll here in the garden to find something edifying."[30]

Rejecting the gardener's suggestion to place books on the benches, Peter ordered sculptural groups depicting the characters of Aesop's fables, which he loved, for the park. The groups ornamented the fountains. A metal sign at each fountain gave the fable's text in large letters. Peter liked to gather strollers and explain the meanings of the depicted stories.

Another educational measure was the installation of a Roman marble statue of Venus, bought on Peter's orders in Italy in 1719. This was a direct challenge to the Orthodox Church, which banned sculptural depictions of people in general (it was considered pagan idolatry), and of naked women in particular.

In Russia, the marble Venus was immediately dubbed the "white she-devil," and of course would have been vandalized if Peter had not prudently posted guards. Bringing stunned (and probably secretly indignant) guests over to his beloved Venus, Peter tried to teach them the basics of mythology, which he knew rather well.

Still, Peter's erudition was basically utilitarian. The great German philosopher and mathematician Gottfried Wilhelm von Leibnitz, at one time Peter's adviser, recalled the tsar's statement that he found more beauty in well-working machinery than in lovely paintings. According to Alexandre Benois, Peter made a great mistake: wanting to reform Russian art, he took as his model provincial Dutch culture, bringing in second-rate masters and thereby slowing Russia's artistic progress.

Benois did not understand that Peter was not interested in importing the most fashionable or sophisticated European art; he wanted what he considered most useful and necessary for Russia's current needs.

What Peter needed most of all were craftsmen who could build and design St. Petersburg; he insisted that the European architects, sculptors, and artists he hired be jacks-of-all-trades. By that time in Europe, the leading artists were primarily narrow specialists: some did portraits, others still lifes, and still others historical paintings.

Peter expected that the artists he brought to Russia would be able to paint formal portraits of the tsar and high officials; capture such amusing curiosities as bearded ladies or two-headed children; restore old paintings; paint palace walls; and depict the parades and festivities marking Peter's victories. In addition, the visiting artists were supposed to train Russian apprentices.

Naturally, well-known and self-respecting artists had no intention of signing such contracts, and mostly craftsmen and hack artists came to Russia. Their students were a rather sorry lot, too: "Peter felt that anything could be learned given willingness and diligence—and therefore the selection for artists was made the way it was for seamen or artillerymen—by force."[31]

And this despite the fact that Russia had its own majestic centuries-old painterly tradition. I am speaking of course about icons (without going into their purely religious significance), those astonishing, magical, and spiritually elevating artifacts of medieval Russian culture. But Peter, even though, like all Russian tsars, he grew up contemplating icons, obviously did not perceive icon painting as useful. It was a reflection of his ambivalent attitude toward the church.

While a believer, Peter nevertheless was deeply suspicious of the church hierarchy. Remembering the conflicts between his father and Patriarch Nikon, Peter eventually did away with the patriarchy, informing the gathered church officials that from that moment on they would be ruled by the Government Synod, appointed by the tsar; that is, Peter placed himself as the de facto head of the Russian Orthodox Church. Among its other goals, this move was an attempt to put Russian culture under the autocrat's direct control and away from the influence of the church—an attempt that succeeded in many respects.

Under Peter, icon painting was downgraded to a level commensurate with carpentry, weaving, and sewing. Since icon painting methods could not be used to illustrate scientific books or execute blueprints and drafts, engravers and their work, which was useful for information and propaganda, came to the fore.

A typical figure in that sense was the engraver Alexei Zubov, a leading master of the Petrine period. His father had been an icon painter in the court of the first Romanov, Tsar Mikhail, and served Peter's father as well. Zubov was sent to study with a visiting Dutch engraver who instructed the Russian youth, "Everything that I see or think about can be cut into copper."[32]

For a hereditary icon master, such ideas must have been heretical—icon painting was not about reproducing life but about executing the traditional painterly formulas that had been perfected over generations. But Zubov quite quickly turned into an able professional engraver. He moved from Moscow to St. Petersburg and became the first inspired portrayer of the new capital; his majestic 1720 composition, *The Triumphal Entrance into St. Petersburg of Captured Swedish Frigates,* preserved for us the vital force and visual charm of the young city.

Peter liked Zubov's work, and he was given important commissions, such as his famous *Depiction of the Marriage of His Royal Majesty Peter I and Ekaterina Alexeyevna* in 1712, where more than one hundred feasting ladies and cavaliers hail the newlyweds, and the face of the future Catherine I is significantly larger than the faces of the ladies around her (a vestige of the icon painting tradition).

Peter was famously tightfisted, but a good professional could count on a tolerable salary. A timely reminder of one's accomplishments could help. Zubov received 195 rubles a year, a good sum, three times more than some of his Russian colleagues but half what foreigners got (a humiliating practice that later Romanovs retained). In 1719, Zubov complained to the tsar that in view of the city's "high cost of all foodstuffs there is nothing to feed my family and pay my debts."[33]

We do not know if the tsar raised his salary then, but it is clear from his petition to Peter in 1723 that Zubov did not live in such constrained circumstances as he tried to portray earlier. Zubov addresses the monarch as "His Most Serene Emperor and Autocrat of All Russia Peter the Great,

Father of the Fatherland and Most Merciful Sovereign." (Emperor and Father of the Fatherland were new titles given to Peter two years earlier by the Government Senate; he was named "the Great" then, too.) After the formalities, Zubov moved on to the point: when the artist was traveling in his own carriage on business to the home of Prince Dimitri Kantemir, he was attacked by two robbers, who tried to steal his horse and beat his servant, "and when they started beating me and my man, I screamed. Hearing my screams, they, the robbers, ran off."[34]

This passage is interesting not only because it reveals that an artist had his own carriage and servant, and not only because it is a vivid description of a typical attack by robbers for that time, but also because it mentions the man Zubov was going to see—Dimitri Kantemir.

Serene Prince Dimitri Kantemir was an exotic figure, yet characteristic of the Petrine era. The former ruler of Moldavia, which was then under Turkish rule, Kantemir spent many years of his youth as a hostage in Constantinople, where the Turks treated him with the greatest respect and allowed him to get a brilliant education.

Dimitri Kantemir became a polyglot, and his *History of the Ottoman Empire*, written in Latin and later published in French and English, received the approval of the philosopher Denis Diderot and Voltaire, who used it as a source for his tragedy *Mahomet* (1739). (And in the early twenty-first century in New York, I witnessed Turkish melodies and marches still being performed in the notation made more than three hundred years earlier by Kantemir.)

In 1711, a year after he inherited the Moldavian throne from his father, Dimitri Kantemir tried to free his country from the Turks, entering into a secret alliance with Peter I. That time, the attempt failed. Kantemir and his family fled to Russia, where he settled.

In Russia, Kantemir, just a year younger than Peter, became his chief adviser on all eastern and Turkish problems. Peter bestowed many gifts on Kantemir, gave him the highest-rank title of serene prince, and supported his historical research. Zubov illustrated one of Kantemir's books, *On the Mohammedan Religion.*

One of Dimitri's four sons, Antioch, was a wunderkind. In 1718, at the age of ten, Antioch gave a public speech in Greek at the Moscow Slavic-Greco-Latin Academy. In 1722 Antioch accompanied his father, who with Peter went on the legendary Persian Campaign, in which Russia tried to push the Ottoman Empire and Iran out of Transcaucasia. Peter's army took Derbent and, later, Baku.

Antioch could observe Peter up close for seven months. The unbearable heat made Peter cut off his hair; it was carefully saved and made into a wig, which to this day ornaments the head of the famous "wax person," the posthumous sculptural depiction of Peter the Great in life size, seated on a throne, created in 1725 by Bartolomeo Carlo Rastrelli the elder and now located at the Hermitage Museum in St. Petersburg.

We can imagine the shock felt by young Kantemir when Peter, fifty-two years old, his health undermined by his tempestuous lifestyle, died unexpectedly in 1725 (it is thought now that he had prostate cancer or an inflammation of the bladder). The tsar's funeral was held in St. Petersburg's Cathedral of Saints Peter and Paul, where Archbishop Feofan Prokopovich, a prolific writer and close comrade-in-arms of Peter's in church affairs, began his speech at the emperor's grave with the emotional words that were memorized by Russian schoolchildren for almost two centuries: "What is this? What have we lived to see, O Russians? What do we see? What are we doing? Burying Peter the Great!"[35]

His graveside sermon was not long; it should have taken fifteen minutes but lasted almost an hour because it was interrupted by the sobs and wailing of mourners. The speech and other panegyric works by Prokopovich celebrating the emperor became the foundation of the myth of Peter the Transformer, one of the most enduring cultural paradigms of Russian history.

Peter the Great was and perhaps remains the most popular Russian political figure of the new era, like Napoleon in France. Everyone agrees that his reforms were extraordinary in scope and significance. The disagreements come in the assessment of those reforms. He has his apologists and many severe critics.

Heated discussions about Peter's role have continued for almost three hundred years, with alternating prevalence of the arguments pro and contra. The emperor's proponents maintain that he led Russia onto the European stage, without which all of Russia's subsequent great cultural achievements would have been impossible.

But at what price? counter their opponents. "The artificial state constructed by Peter moved for two centuries from crisis to crisis, engendering ever greater anger of its citizens, until it collapsed in blood and flames."[36]

It is doubtful that this argument will be resolved any time soon. The point is this: after Peter the Great, all political leaders of Russia, to this day, look over their shoulders at the first Russian emperor, imitating him or rejecting him, but inevitably measuring themselves against him.

This reaction is typical for the great cultural figures of Russia as well. None remained indifferent to Peter's ideas and legacy. In their polemics about Peter the Great, they defined their own place in the continuing cultural and historical debates about Russia's fate and path.

CHAPTER 2

Kantemir, Lomonosov, and Barkov

Antioch Kantemir was one of the first creators of the cultural mythos about Peter the Great. The diplomat, master of political intrigue, and biting satiric poet had as a youngster fallen under Peter's hypnotic charm and remained the tsar's zealous apologist throughout his brief and turbulent life, until his death of stomach cancer in Paris in 1744, where he was the Russian ambassador. He was only thirty-five.

Kantemir's satires mocking the opponents of Peter's reforms were popular in intellectual circles, where copies circulated. But Russian poets, from Vassily Zhukovsky to Joseph Brodsky, were always Kantemir's greatest admirers. In 1810, Zhukovsky noted, "We have in Kantemir our Juvenal and Horace," adding that Kantemir "never uses four words when three will do"[1]—the highest praise a poet can pay another. Brodsky, who compared Kantemir to John Donne, enjoyed reading me his sarcastic lines about a hypocritical monk: "He pities people who died in lust, / But secretly stares at a rounded bust."

Kantemir's satires were paradoxically (but typically, for Russian literature) first published in London in French in 1749 and only printed in

Russia eighteen years after the poet's death, in an edition by Ivan Barkov. Even as late as 1851, Emperor Nicholas I could not accept the audacity of Kantemir's attacks on the clergy: "In my opinion, there is no possible use in reprinting Kantemir's works."[2] Yet Kantemir was the first Russian poet to achieve recognition in the enlightened circles of eighteenth-century Europe.

Sent to the West in 1732 by Peter I's niece, Empress Anna Ioannovna, Kantemir learned only belatedly in Paris of one of the most dramatic episodes in Russian history: on the night of November 25, 1741, a squad of three hundred Imperial Guards led by Peter's daughter, the thirty-two-year-old blue-eyed blonde Elizabeth, burst into the Winter Palace, the imperial residence. The guards bore Elizabeth (who wore a very becoming brass cuirass on her pretty head) on their shoulders and declared her empress.

This brought an end to "the era of palace coups": in the twenty-seven years since the death of Peter the Great the throne had been occupied by Catherine I, Peter II, Anna Ioannovna, and the infant Ioann IV, none of whom played a significant role in the development of Russian culture.

Elizabeth I was a different matter. In the twenty years of her reign (she died in 1761) even the most stubborn foes of Peter the Great had to admit that his reforms had become irreversible: Russia was speeding along the European path. And even more importantly: the Europeanized culture that had been forcibly implanted by Peter had not only taken root among the Russian elite but had begun taking on definite national features, under the clear encouragement of the new empress.

In that sense the figure of Mikhail Lomonosov is symbolic. His multifaceted talents and the wealth of his contributions to culture caused him to be called the Russian Leonardo da Vinci. He was a legend in his lifetime, and to this day there is probably no Russian who does not know a few details of his colorful biography.

Everyone heard the story of the peasant lad who at nineteen, in 1730, ran away from home in a northern coastal village and with a load of frozen fish reached Moscow, where he miraculously got into school and then grew up to be a major scholar and poet, experimenting with electricity, creating mosaics, fighting against the German preponderance in the Academy of Sciences, and founding Moscow University, the first in the land.

Nikolai Nekrasov's tear-jerking poem "The Schoolboy," written in 1856, more than ninety years after Lomonosov's death, was instantly included in Russian textbooks and canonized the legend of "How a muzhik from Archangel / Through his own and God's will / Became wise and great."

A close look at some of the "miracles" in Lomonosov's life yields quite rational explanations for them. Of course, Lomonosov was a man of almost supernatural abilities, but many very "earthly" circumstances promoted his career.

For a start, Lomonosov was lucky to be born to a family of a "state" peasant—that is, a free one, not a serf. His father was prosperous: he owned land and fishing rights and carried cargo (more than eighty-six tons) on his own two-masted boat, *St. Archangel Mikhail.* When the village was rebuilding the church that had burned down, Lomonosov's father contributed more than anyone else to the fund—18 rubles. (For comparison: at that time carpenters in St. Petersburg were paid between 12 and 24 rubles a year, depending on their qualifications.)

The legendary "load of frozen fish," with which Lomonosov traveled for three weeks from Archangel Province to Moscow, is a very exotic stroke. But fishing was the main (and very profitable) business of the coastal peasants. If Lomonosov's fellow villagers had been fur traders, the young man would have reached the capital with a "load of sable," which is not nearly as touching.

The miraculous way Lomonosov got into the Slavic-Greco-Latin Academy (the same one attended by young Antioch Kantemir) was described in his official biography of 1784 this way: in the capital the poor youth "knew not a single person"; after spending the first night in

Moscow in the fish stalls, Lomonosov "fell to his knees, raised his eyes to the nearest church and begged God to have mercy."[3]

So the next morning a majordomo, come to buy fish, recognized Lomonosov as a fellow villager and took him home. Two days after that, the majordomo's friend dropped by—a monk from the monastery where the elite academy was housed. The majordomo interceded on Mikhail's behalf, the monk was willing, and the lad was accepted as a student at the academy with an annual stipend of 10 rubles.

In order to get in, Lomonosov had to say he was the son of nobility, since peasant children were not accepted in seminaries at the time. For some reason the abbot of the monastery believed him—had the monk put in a good word for his friend's countryman?—and things were settled.

Today's skeptical reader is unlikely to see "God's providence" or even good fortune in this chain of events; it is more like the expected result of a network of useful acquaintances, which worked in Lomonosov's day just as it does in ours.

Throughout his life, Lomonosov always found numerous patrons who got him out of situations that would have ruined anyone else's career. Lomonosov, who was big and strong not only mentally but physically, also had a quarrelsome nature and a preference for strong drink that led to brawls, which were not suitable for the scholarly milieu in which he found himself. (Even his surname means "nosebreaker" in Russian.)

In 1736, Lomonosov was sent to Germany to study mining and chemistry at the university in Marburg (where 176 years later another great Russian poet, Boris Pasternak, was to study philosophy). Outraged reports soon flew from Marburg to Russia about his "excessively boisterous life and passion for the female sex." Then Lomonosov got into an argument with his professor: "He made terrible noise, banging with all his might on the partitions, shouting out the window, and swearing."[4]

This habit of blowing up over the least thing, or even without a reason, remained throughout Lomonosov's unfairly short life (he died in 1765 at the age of fifty-three). He left Germany for St. Petersburg, where he was hired at the Academy of Sciences. Here again he behaved scandalously, bursting into a neighbor's house in search of his sheepskin jacket. With bared saber in his hand, Lomonosov threatened the neighbor and his guests and hacked up all the furniture; the innocent neighbor's wife, terrified, jumped out the window. The young scientist, apparently drunk, was pacified by six patrolmen, who dragged him to the police.

And once again, as had happened in Germany, the incident was covered up by someone, even though Lomonosov already had a record of "fighting and dishonorable behavior."

This unusual leniency on the part of the authorities is not difficult to explain. From the moment of her accession to the throne, Empress Elizabeth I made it a policy to promote "national cadres" in all spheres, including science. All her advisers urged this policy; in their opinion, Peter's promotion of foreigners, especially Germans, to positions of leadership had gotten out of control under his successors.

There was no open declaration of "Russia for Russians" under Elizabeth, but things were moving in that direction. Well-built, strong, energetic, and full of ideas, Lomonosov proclaimed that "the Russian land can give birth to her own Platos and quick-minded Newtons." He seemed a convenient symbolic figure (despite the excesses of his character) to Elizabeth's ministers.

The young genius quickly showed what he could do. While still studying in Germany, in 1739 he sent a "Letter on the Rules of Russian Versification" to the academy, elaborating his ideas on modernization of Russian verse. The "Letter" and other important works by Lomonosov— "Short Guide to Rhetoric," "Russian Grammar," and particularly "Preface on the Usefulness of Church Books in the Russian Language," set the stylistic norms for Russian writing for at least the next hundred years. Contemporary literary Russian is in many ways the child of Lomonosov.

Pushkin summed up the achievements of this extraordinary man concisely: "Lomonosov was a great man. Between Peter I and Catherine II he appears as a unique champion of enlightenment. He created the first university. It would be better to say that he himself was our first university."

.　.　.

Lomonosov was a genial host. He received guests in the garden of his house in St. Petersburg, wearing a Chinese robe and seated at an oak table set with an abundance of food and drink, including salted pickles and fish brought by countrymen from Archangel. Perhaps the most curious of Lomonosov's drinking friends was his faithful collaborator Ivan Barkov.

Nothing is clear or reliable in Barkov's brief biography: his father's name, exact year of birth, and circumstances of his death (it is supposed that he committed suicide when he was thirty-six or thirty-seven).[5] For ten years Barkov worked for Lomonosov as clerk and editor. He was also highly regarded as an excellent translator from French, German, and Latin. His edition of the first Russian publication of Kantemir's satires, mentioned earlier, was well received.

But that is not what made Barkov famous in Russia. He is known (for some, just by reputation) as the author of the most indecent poems in the history of Russian poetry. The genre itself—pornographic poetry—is still described as "Barkovism." Barkov's poems were considered unfit to print for more than two hundred years, but were circulated in Russia in numerous handwritten copies and memorized by dozens of generations of students, evidence of their indisputable poetic expressiveness and power.

Some of the greatest Russian poets—Pushkin, Mikhail Lermontov, Nekrasov—were his admirers and imitators; each tried his hand at Barkovism.

Pushkin compared Barkov to François Villon, the notorious medieval French poet and reveler. Pushkin was clearly drawn to the figure of Barkov, who was described by people who had known him in his youth as merry and insouciant—a description that fits Pushkin as well.

For Pushkin, who was constantly searching for the parameters of the place of the poet in Russian society, Lomonosov and Barkov clearly represented the two poles of a possible behavioral model: one proud, even arrogant, overly concerned about his honor and overreacting to criticism from the mighty; the other, liberated and carefree. Pushkin maintained, paradoxically, that "poetry, God forgive me, must be foolish." This claim was later interpreted by Mikhail Bakhtin in his groundbreaking book on François Rabelais: "Barrels of wine will burst if from time to time vents are not opened and air let in. We humans are all poorly made barrels that will burst from the *wine of wisdom,* if that wine is constantly fermenting in awe and fear of God. They need air to keep from spoiling. That is why we permit ourselves certain days of foolishness (stupidity) in order to return with greater ardor to the service of the Lord."

Barkov's parody verses are Rabelaisian in character, and, curiously, he parodied his mentor Lomonosov (who apparently and surprisingly did not take offense). For example, Lomonosov's "Psalm 145" begins thus:

> Praise for the All-High Lord
> Try, my spirit, to send . . .

Barkov's version is almost the same:

> Praise for the almighty hero
> Try, my spirit, to send . . .

However, Barkov's ode is "To the Cock."

In Barkov's funny parody of a typical classical tragedy, Prince Limprick and his brother Fuckalot are rivals for the beauty Pussymila. She complains about Limprick: "He may be a prince in his reason, but in his cock he is a slave." The poem has juicy descriptions of violent sexual acts both hetero- and homosexual, still astonishing in their unrestrained language. At the end, the powerful Fuckalot triumphs.

Ironically, Pushkin predicted that the first book to come out in Russia after the repeal of censorship would be the complete works of Barkov. In that prediction, as in many other things, Pushkin was a true prophet: soon after the fall of the Soviet Union, not just one, but three editions of Barkov's obscene poems appeared.

In fact, 224 years after his death, Barkov became a best-selling author and a timely one, originating the ocean of obscene literature that flooded the Russian book market in the uncensored post-Soviet period.

Thus, in the late twentieth century Barkov turned out to be more interesting for readers and writers than his mentor Lomonosov, whose poetry had become the domain of specialists.

CHAPTER 3

Catherine the Great and the Culture of Her Era

An engraved portrait of Ivan Barkov has survived: a round, youthful face, plump lips, and an open, dreamy gaze—the textbook image of a young poet, brow unmarred by the years of drunkenness, debauchery, humiliation, and punishments that led to his sad end. But there were moments of triumph in Barkov's tragic life.

One of them, if legend is to be believed, was the occasion when Barkov was invited to the court of Empress Catherine II, who was brought to power by the Imperial Guards in 1762. Allegedly, Catherine asked Barkov to say a few lines impromptu. He raised his glass of wine and proclaimed, "To the health of the gates through which all mankind entered life!" The empress is said to have replied instantly, "And I drink to the health of the key that unlocks those gates without a knock!"[1]

Barkov's biography is skimpy on precise information and rich in legend and anecdote. In this case, what is important is not the veracity or apocryphal nature of this story but that the names of Catherine the Great and Barkov are intertwined in historical memory. This probably reflects the attitude toward the empress, in whose lifetime popular pornographic caricatures depicted her in flagrante delicto with her lovers (I saw one at a New York Public Library exhibit in 2003).

The legend of Catherine's debauched ways is very persistent, remaining in the public mind (both in Russia and in the West) for more than two centuries. It is not surprising, since the greatest minds insisted upon it, among them young Pushkin ("The corrupt sovereign corrupted her state") and Alexander Herzen ("The history of Catherine II cannot be read in the presence of ladies").

In Soviet times, she was vilified in serious monographs and textbooks: "depraved and criminal woman" and "semiliterate slut who turned the tsar's house into a whorehouse."[2]

Yet when diligent historians compiled a documentary list of Catherine's lovers, it contained between twelve and eighteen men for the period from 1753 to 1796—that is, on average one affair for every two and a half years.[3] A monastic lifestyle? Hardly. But a promiscuous nymphomaniac? That is not a conclusion that would be drawn either in our day or in the rather dissolute eighteenth century.

There was another widespread charge (both then and now) from the opposite side: Catherine II was a hypocrite, "a Tartuffe in skirt and crown" (Pushkin again). But here this makes no sense at all: it is just as silly to accuse a political figure of hypocrisy as it would be to rebuke a zebra for its stripes; hypocrisy and politics are, alas, inseparable. Catherine was perhaps the first politician in the modern sense on the Russian throne—in any case, the first empress politician.

Her predecessor, Elizabeth I, came to the throne as the legitimate daughter of Peter the Great. Catherine II had to fight for the throne, and she conducted that fight just like a modern political candidate: kissing babies, listening patiently to old people, and saluting the military.

Catherine wrote about it in her memoirs, extremely frank for a professional politician: "I tried to gain the affection of everyone, from young to old; I never overlooked anyone and made it a rule to think that I needed everyone and to act accordingly in order to gain general approbation, in which I succeeded."[4]

Given in marriage on the orders of Elizabeth I to Peter the Great's grandson (and her nephew), the future Peter II, the fourteen-year-old German princess was brought to Russia in 1744, and that homely, ambitious, calculating, and phenomenally gifted young woman eventually took over the throne, realizing her long-held plans.

The future Catherine II put all her prodigious effort into turning from a German into an ultra-Russian: she learned to speak, read, and write fluently in Russian; she converted to Russian Orthodoxy, using every opportunity to show her allegiance to her new faith; and, most importantly, from her early years she surrounded herself with friends who were Russian nobles and officers. She learned much from Elizabeth I, whom she observed closely and patiently, in particular how cleverly she used the institution of favoritism in the interests of strengthening her power.

Elizabeth continued Peter's change of ruling class within the framework of absolute monarchy. Peter the Great had marginalized the boyars and made the military caste the country's new elite. It had its own crème de la crème: two Guards regiments, each with three thousand bayonets. These were the tsar's most loyal people, his favorites, his emissaries in varied fields from industry to culture. And they eventually became the striking fist of the new force—the Russian nobility (*dvoriane*), who placed Elizabeth I on the throne in 1741.

Elizabeth clung to power by using their support. Her favorites were not simply and not only her lovers, they were also her most trusted proponents. Sexual proximity guaranteed political loyalty.

For Catherine, this was one of the most important political lessons she mastered. She used the Guards to ascend to the Russian throne in 1762 and absorbed Elizabeth's method of generous rewards to her favorites, which so outraged not only contemporaries but later generations as well.

Yet it is clear that the shower of gold that fell on lucky lovers created a new power stratum loyal to the empress. "Old money" took generations to accrue, sometimes centuries, while a favorite of Elizabeth I could become a millionaire in a year or two.

Seizing the throne, Catherine reinforced her positions in the same way: she gave away money (hundreds of thousands of rubles at a time), expensive jewelry, huge estates, and serfs—her famous lover Grigory Potemkin received no fewer than 44,000 serfs.

A parallel is obvious with the turbulent 1990s, when the same method was used to create a group of loyal oligarchs who successfully masterminded the reelection of Boris Yeltsin to the presidency. But Catherine II, who reigned for thirty-four years, also managed to create a quiet life for her new elite, without the continual threat of arrest or expropriation of property, and in that sense her reign is comparable to the Brezhnev years.

Obviously, Catherine did not like Elizabeth, who played the role of demanding and unpredictable mother-in-law. In her *Notes of Empress Catherine II,* she describes her as being indolent, messy, and not very bright. Catherine the Great's *Notes* is a malicious, prejudiced, and self-serving book, as memoirs should be, especially political ones. It makes clear that for Catherine, Elizabeth I was too much a "person of the Baroque," while she justly considered herself a leading exponent of the new trend—Classicism.

Elizabeth did not stint on the construction of sophisticated and eccentric palaces. Her favorite architect was the Italian Francesco Bartolomeo Rastrelli, who was brought to Russia when he was sixteen and grew up to be the greatest master of Russian Baroque. Rastrelli designed the enormous light blue palace, sumptuously ornamented in gold, for Tsarskoe Selo outside St. Petersburg, which was Elizabeth's main residence for a while. In St. Petersburg itself, Rastrelli created the marvelous complex of the Smolny Monastery.

His most famous work is the Winter Palace, in its final form, the building in which the Hermitage Museum is now housed. It was begun in 1754 and completed in 1762, under Catherine II. The Winter Palace has more than a thousand rooms, around two hundred doors and as many windows, and more than a hundred staircases.

The facade of the palace, with its complicated, eye-catching design of four hundred columns, which Rastrelli treated as sculptural elements, works magically with the interiors, embodying Elizabeth's idea that her "empire has reached such prosperity as it had never seen before."

But Catherine II, even though she accepted the Winter Palace as a posthumous gift from Elizabeth, which remained the official imperial residence until the end of the Romanov dynasty, looked down her nose at the architectural excesses. For her and her enlightened entourage, the Baroque style was "low, poor taste." Catherine II unceremoniously dispatched the sixty-two-year-old Rastrelli into retirement.

If Rastrelli's Winter Palace may be considered the cultural symbol of Elizabeth's reign, then the symbol for Catherine would be the equestrian monument to Peter the Great by the French sculptor Etienne Maurice Falconet (the Bronze Horseman, as Pushkin later called it). Falconet resembled Rastrelli in his independence, stubbornness, bad temper, and the fact that as a foreigner he obtained immortality through projects realized in Russia.

Denis Diderot, a famous French *philosophe,* had suggested bringing Falconet to St. Petersburg from Paris to Catherine. Diderot maintained a correspondence with Catherine, who considered herself a *philosophe* monarch, for many years and even visited St. Petersburg as her guest.

It was suggested that Falconet was Diderot's greatest gift to Russia. The sculptor, at fifty, came to St. Petersburg with his seventeen-year-old student Marie Ann Collot, spent twelve years (1766–1778) working on the monument, and returned to France, unwilling to wait for its unveiling in 1782. The reason behind his unexpected departure was the conflict of the irritable and self-confident sculptor with Ivan Betskoy, president of the Academy of Arts and de facto minister of culture under Catherine.

This Betskoy was a remarkable man. He spent many years in Europe, where in 1728 he met the beautiful young Duchess Anhalt-Zerbst (the mother of the future Catherine II) and became her lover. Catherine was born a year later; rumor had Betskoy as the father (the husband of the frivolous duchess was twice her age).

Later Betskoy took an active part in the Guards' coup of 1782 that led his presumed daughter to the throne. Catherine treated Betskoy kindly, even tenderly, but with a touch of irony, like a loving daughter who has surpassed her father. She valued his mind and European education and his close relations with the French *philosophes* she so admired.

As a progressive, Betskoy was a fan of Classicism, which should have made him an ally of Falconet's. But no: two powerful personalities clashed, and life in the capital turned into hell for the paranoid Falconet. Betskoy controlled the sculptor's every step, accusing him of being slow (for good reason), of wasting state funds (also not without reason), and even of making serious artistic errors (the most controversial).

In particular, Betskoy maintained that Falconet had overly cut down the huge granite boulder intended for the pedestal, which had taken two and a half years to deliver to St. Petersburg (especially for this project). When the dynamic statue of Peter the Great (his head modeled by Collot) on horseback was placed on the pedestal, wags said it looked like "a small cliff squashed by a big horse."

Still, Falconet's main critic and adviser was, naturally, Catherine II, for whom the project was propaganda of the first order. That would explain the unusual fact that almost the day after his arrival in St. Petersburg, Catherine began systematic correspondence with him, which continued for many years.

In their letters, the empress and the sculptor discussed literally every detail of the monument: from the spot where it would be located to the emperor's costume (a stylized Roman toga) to the character of the horse (Catherine worried it would turn out to be a "dumb animal").

In almost every letter Catherine tried to calm and encourage Falconet, who constantly complained about his real and imaginary enemies: "Just laugh at the fools and go your way. That is my rule."[5]

The sculptor's farewell gift was the inscription he suggested for the pedestal: "For Peter I erected by Catherine II." The empress changed it to: "For Peter I Catherine II," an editing masterpiece of her political and literary acumen. Those words, which subtly but indubitably turned her into the legitimate heir of Peter the Great, should be enough to bury the myth of "semiliterate slut."

.   .   .

Moreover, when everything Catherine II wrote (including the memoirs, historical plays, comedies, opera libretti, stories, magazine articles and pamphlets, philosophical and historical works—for example, "Notes Regarding Russian History," intended for her grandsons—and the numerous translations, personally composed decrees and laws, and her voluminous correspondence, with such international luminaries as Voltaire, Diderot, and d'Alembert) is collected and published, it will run to a long line of heavy tomes.

The empress was a tireless worker, rising no later than six in the morning, and sitting down to writing, writing, writing, using two new pens a day. No Russian monarch before or after covered so much paper: of course she had the right to consider Elizabeth lazy. Yet Catherine was no graphomaniac: she had a self-deprecating view of her literary works.

Catherine, cleverly following in the footsteps of Elizabeth, whom she so disliked, continued to russify Peter's cultural project as much as possible; the poet Prince Vyazemsky later summed up the paradox this way: "The Russian wanted to make Germans of us; the German tried to turn us into Russians."[6]

Still, for Catherine, Peter remained the example and model; how close she measured up to him is subject for debate. But the constant unfavorable comparisons seem unfair now and based on anti-intellectual or sexist prejudices, since, as we know, her workday with paper and pen was no less intense than Peter's celebrated days at the lathe or in shipbuilding, wielding his ax.

Catherine was not a spendthrift like Elizabeth, but she spent more generously on culture than Peter had. A good example is her acquisition of paintings, engravings, drawings, sculptures, and works in porcelain and silver that formed the basis of the Hermitage collections. She often said—coyly, no doubt—that she knew nothing about art. But which great figure with a famed art collection could claim to have done it all to his or her own taste? They all turned to professional advisers.

The appearance of Catherine's agents at Parisian art auctions panicked her competitors: she outbid them for some of the Hermitage's acclaimed Rembrandts, Murillos, and Turners this way. It was the first huge invasion of Russian money into the European art market.

Even the *philosophe* Diderot, who admired Catherine, had doubts at first about the success of her collecting ("It is impossible that Russia would ever accumulate enough painting that could inspire a true taste for art"),[7] but soon he would write from Paris to his friend Falconet in St. Petersburg: "I am eliciting real public hatred, and do you know why? Because I am sending you paintings. The art lovers are howling, the artists are howling, the wealthy are howling."[8]

A comparison of the efforts of Peter I and Catherine II in the area of book publishing and journalism is telling. Peter achieved a breakthrough: in the last quarter century of his life, almost two thousand books and brochures were printed.[9] The problem was that most of these publications lay like rubbish in warehouses: Peter's selections did not excite the reading public. After the emperor's death, the unsold backlog was cut up or burned, and many books were used for wrapping.

Catherine's publishing policy was much more successful. She gave Russians translations of Homer, Cicero, Tacitus, Daniel Defoe, Jonathan Swift, and Henry Fielding.

She also sponsored the satirical journal *All Sorts and Sundry,* begun in 1769, which was modeled on the English political magazines of Joseph Addison and Richard Steele. Catherine wrote articles and allegorical tales for the magazine, expressing her political views and mocking the Russian elite's laziness, dissipation, and kowtowing to the West. She continued to support such magazines; for example, when the Freemason and writer Nikolai Novikov, a shrewd and worldly pioneer of Russian journalism, wanted to start his satirical *The Painter* in 1772, the empress gave him 200 rubles.

The Painter was quite biting. Besides the exposés, so dear to Catherine's heart, of the brainless scions of the nobility and the frivolous fashion plates at court, the magazine raised the painful serfdom issue. An anonymous article, now attributed to Alexander Radishchev, the first radical writer in Russian literature, depicted in grim tones the miserable condition of serfs. (In the beginning, Catherine not only tolerated such attacks, she encouraged them.)

Eventually, even with the moral and financial support of the empress, the satirical magazines began to wither: there were too many of them and not enough readers. Wisely, Catherine did not insist on the viability of her initiative and instead made a bold move in 1783, permitting private publishing in Russia for the first time; the state no longer had a monopoly on the printed word. (Of course, this also relieved Catherine of the financial burden of supporting book publishing and journalism.)

Catherine was right in assuming that the private publisher would be a better judge of what books the people wanted. New publishing houses mushroomed all over Russia. The result was a sharp increase in new books—but even more importantly, the book business became profitable. Novikov's Tipograficheskaya Kampaniya, founded in 1784, had huge revenues, reaching 80,000 rubles a year.

At some point, Novikov became a monopolist: almost half the books in Russia were published by his company. Russian translations of Molière, Beaumarchais, Milton, Sterne, Goldoni, and Lessing were printed in elegant and relatively inexpensive editions. Novikov also published Russian authors, such as Lomonosov, and encyclopedias, reference books, dictionaries, and textbooks, which were sold in Novikov's bookshops.

Novikov created the first ladies' magazine in Russia, which had not only pictures of the latest Parisian fashions, but texts by serious writers. He also founded the first magazine for children, where Nikolai Karamzin (the future historian) made his debut. Karamzin later recalled that Novikov "sold books the way wealthy Dutch or English merchants sell their products: that is, with intelligence, intuition, and long-range planning."[10]

. . .

One would have expected the wild success of Novikov's publishing to please Catherine: it confirmed the wisdom of her decree allowing private printing houses. But the empress was concerned that Novikov belonged to the growing number of Russian Freemasons and published Masonic literature. The Europe-based quasireligious union, with its secret rituals and ideas of universal brotherhood and moral self-perfection, was brought to Russia in the 1730s.

Even though there were many Masonic adepts in her entourage, Catherine did not approve of it: "A small-time, useless pastime that leads to nothing. Does a person who does good for the sake of good really need that foolishness?"[11]

At first "that foolishness," the Masonic lodges and rituals, merely irritated the empress. She mocked the Masons as "monkeys" and "shamans" in her comedy *The Siberian Shaman,* where they were depicted as crooks and extortionists.

Gradually, Catherine began to perceive Masonry as a political threat: she received reports of Russian Freemasons establishing secret contacts with the heir to the throne—her son, Paul—and of their ties with the anti-Russian Prussian Masons.

Soon, Catherine branded Russian Masonry as the "new schism." The government banned one Masonic book after another for heresy, but Novikov did not stop distributing them by underground means. When Novikov was arrested in 1792, many banned books were seized from his stores and warehouses.

Freemasonry was now interpreted as a dangerous religious heresy. Deviations from Orthodoxy were punished severely. Novikov was condemned to death, which Catherine commuted to fifteen years in a St. Petersburg prison.

She had commuted another sentence two years earlier of another seditious writer—Alexander Radishchev, author of the daring anti-monarchic critique *Journey from St. Petersburg to Moscow.* Earnest and incorruptible, Radishchev, who was an early collaborator with Novikov (and eventually became head of customs in St. Petersburg), published his pamphlet in 1790 on a home printing press in 650 copies, of which only twenty-five went on sale. The tone of his work was set by the famous phrase from his introduction: "I looked around me and my soul was wounded by human suffering."

Written in the then-popular genre of travelogue, Radishchev's book was a howl of horror at the sight of the difficult lot of serfs and a "satirical call to outrage" (from a later review by Pushkin) against their masters, the heartless landowners: "The Russian people are very patient, and they suffer to the extreme, but when their patience ends, nothing will be able to contain it from turning to violence." Those words sounded a terrible warning.

It is not often that a work with such limited circulation creates such a fuss. Radishchev's timing was very bad. In Paris the revolutionary "ferocious monsters," as Catherine called them, had stormed the Bastille, which gave the empress a serious fright: it became clear that it was just one step from small books to major upheavals.

Even though *Journey* was published anonymously, Radishchev was quickly identified, arrested, tried, and, like Novikov, sentenced to death, which Catherine commuted to Siberian exile.

The cases of Novikov and Radishchev are usually used as evidence of Catherine's cruelty to Russian writers. A hundred and fifty years after her death, the influential philosopher Nikolai Berdyaev maintained that the martyrology of the Russian intelligentsia began with the persecution of Novikov and Radishchev.

Of course, the treatment of Novikov and Radishchev was harsh. Still, they had knowingly broken the rules. We can denounce the excessive severity of domestic law in the Russian Empire of the period, but it would be unfair to accuse Catherine of personal sadism, as is often done to this day.

Peter the Great personally tortured rebel *streltsy* (members of his Imperial Guards); during his reign, in 1689, the important poet Silvester Medvedev was beheaded, but for some reason Medvedev did not make it into any future martyrologies. The persistent rumors that Catherine's investigator had Novikov and Radishchev tortured are rejected by the most recent archival research.

Pushkin is sometimes used as a reference, since he wrote about Catherine's cruelties in his notes. But Pushkin, as we know, based one of his famous "little tragedies" on a rumor that has been totally discredited in our time: that the composer Antonio Salieri poisoned Mozart. Just as Salieri was not a poisoner, Catherine did not torture her writers.

It was another matter that the empress had no intention of being an obedient student of writers and *philosophes,* be they even such European intellectual superstars as Diderot and Voltaire. Catherine truly was interested in their views and could enjoy endless philosophical discussion with them, but running a huge empire soon taught her a dirty little secret known only by professional politicians: theory, however brilliant, is one thing, and daily political practice is quite another.

When Diderot came to St. Petersburg in 1773 at Catherine's invitation, with the right to unlimited access to the empress, he flooded her with his utopian ideas and proposals: how to emancipate the serfs immediately, how to organize agriculture and the army properly, how to improve education in the schools drastically. Seeing how attentively Catherine listened, Diderot grew extremely animated, gesticulating, grabbing the empress's hands, and thought that she would turn his wise suggestions into reality without delay.

But here is what Catherine said to him one day:

> Monsieur Diderot, I have listened with great pleasure to everything that your brilliant mind has produced; but all your great principles, which I understand very well, while making wonderful books, will not manage a state. In all your transformational plans, you forget the difference in our situations: you work only on paper, which bears everything, it is soft, smooth, and does not stop your pen or imagination; whereas I, the poor empress,

work on human skin, which, on the contrary, is very irritable and ticklish.[12]

These words had a sobering effect on Diderot. From that moment on, the *philosophe* no longer made practical suggestions. Was Diderot disillusioned by the empress? Of course. But should he have had the illusions in the first place? The idea that people of culture "know better" how to run a country is close to the heart of the intellectual elite all over the world and therefore ever fashionable in elevated circles. But is it always correct and applicable?

Let's take a look at the governmental activity of the great poet Gavrila Derzhavin, who became minister of justice. (Only one other Russian poet, Ivan Dmitriev [1760–1837], ever reached such administrative heights.)

Derzhavin's brilliant career is doubly remarkable, because it was truly the result of his literary talents rather than his administrative ones. Derzhavin was born in 1743 in a poor noble family, and was so weak as an infant that his parents followed the folk remedy of wrapping him in dough and putting him in a warm oven so that he would "get a little bit of life" (as the poet recalled in his memoirs).[13] After fifteen years in the army, Derzhavin retired, and published his first book of poems anonymously.

His literary and career breakthrough at the age of forty came with his ode "Felitsa," dedicated to Catherine, which opened the first issue of a new magazine, *Interlocutor of Lovers of the Russian Word* (1783), and began solemnly and resonantly (as do all his best poems): "Godlike Tsarevna of the Kirghiz-Kaisatsky Horde!" Derzhavin used the imaginary Kirghiz Tsarevna Felitsa (from the Latin *felicitas,* happiness) to praise Catherine. "Felitsa" was a daring attempt to combine tribute to the empress with satirical attacks on some of her courtiers.

The publisher of the magazine, Princess Ekaterina Dashkova (the empress's best friend), presented her the freshly printed issue, and the next day, when summoned by Catherine, found her august patroness with the open magazine in her hands and in tears: "Who can know me so well to describe me so pleasantly that it makes me weep like a fool?"[14]

Learning the author's name (Derzhavin's ode was also published anonymously), Catherine decided to reward him. The poet was lunching at the home of his director (he was already a clerk in the Senate) when a messenger brought him a paper parcel with the inscription "from the Kirghiz Tsarevna." Derzhavin's boss grumbled, "What are these gifts from the Kirghizians?" But he quickly caught on once he saw what was inside the parcel: a French diamond-encrusted gold snuffbox and five hundred gold coins. With a forced smile, the man congratulated Derzhavin, "but from that time hatred and anger crept into his heart so that he could not speak calmly with the newly celebrated versifier,"[15] concluded Derzhavin in his frank and stern (as he himself was) recollections of that memorable day.

The ode that so pleased Catherine speeded up Derzhavin's career tremendously: in 1784 he became governor of Olonetsk Province and then, in 1785, governor of Tambov Province. In 1791, Catherine made Derzhavin her personal state secretary, with the special unprecedented right to report to her "whenever he observed any illegal Senate decision."

Derzhavin performed his administrative duties with great zeal and seriousness, wearying Catherine with detailed explanations of confusing and complex judicial cases, while what the empress needed from him was his poetry: she kept hinting that he should write more odes like "Felitsa."

Catherine wanted Derzhavin to be her chronicler and glorifier and not pester her with "such requests as women asked his mother-in-law and wife," as she irritably put it. The direct and intense Derzhavin "often bored her with his truth," and she had to cut him off from time to time.

It is easy to imagine them together: both tall and imposing, but Derzhavin sinewy, thin, and narrow-faced, while the empress was plump, full-breasted, with beautiful neck and arms and an ugly long chin on a high-browed face. He would sit before her on a chair—back straight, his army training—surrounded by piles of papers and reading, reading, reading in a steady voice, while she sat back comfortably on a low down-stuffed chaise, listening while knitting and looking over at Derzhavin with her intelligent blue eyes.

Derzhavin later described (in the third person) these extraordinary audiences as the relationship of two people in love rather than empress and courtier: "It often happened that she grew angry and threw out Derzhavin, and he would get huffy and promise himself to be careful and say nothing to her, but the next day when he entered, she would see right away that he was angry: she would start asking about his wife, his home life, would he like something to drink, and more such gentle and kind talk, so that he would forget all his chagrin and become candid once again."[16]

These cozy, almost family relations continued for some two years: Derzhavin continued to bore the empress with his dreary reports but also pleased her with new poems, and for his ode "On the Taking of Izmail" (an important victory over the Turks) Catherine gave him another diamond-encrusted snuffbox with the generous note, "I did not know all this time that your trumpet was as loud as your lyre was pleasant."[17]

In that brief comment, Catherine, like a perceptive literary critic, captured the most important aspects of her favorite poet's style. Derzhavin was an incomparable trumpeter of Russia, praising her glory with clarity and directness, but at the same time his lyre sang the pleasures of private life—love, friendship, culinary delights, and nature's beauty.

Derzhavin died in 1816, outliving Catherine by almost twenty years. He served her successor, Paul I, and even Paul's son, Alexander I, who came to the throne after Paul was assassinated in 1801. But the new rulers did not love Derzhavin the way Catherine had.

When Derzhavin, sent into retirement in 1812 by Alexander I, decided to remind the emperor of his existence by sending a plan of defense against Napoleon's army, the old poet was ignored. And today his achievements as government figure are forgotten, but not his muscular baroque poetry.

Three days before his death, Derzhavin wrote the beginning of his new (and unfinished) ode with diamond on a slate, summing up his profoundly pessimistic outlook on the vanity of political activity in general and his administrative efforts in particular. Those lines are his political auto-obituary. But many Russians repeat them to this day, which is proof of Derzhavin's poetic grandeur:

> Time's river in its flow
> Sweeps away all human endeavor
> And drowns in the depths of oblivion
> Peoples, kingdoms, and tsars.

PART II

CHAPTER 4

Paul I and Alexander I; Karamzin and Zhukovsky

"Old man Derzhavin noticed us / And blessed us, gravebound..."
There probably isn't a Russian who doesn't know those lines, from Pushkin's *Eugene Onegin*. They've become an aphorism, repeated every time talk turns to succession of generations, the passing of the torch from fathers to sons. And it is somehow accepted that this was exactly the symbolic and historic way that Derzhavin, the greatest Russian poet of the eighteenth century, "blessed" Pushkin, the greatest Russian poet of all time.

It was much more complicated than that. Pushkin was fifteen when he met the seventy-one-year-old Derzhavin at public examinations at the Lycée, the privileged school at Tsarskoe Selo, the imperial summer residence outside St. Petersburg. Count Alexei Razumovsky, minister of education, who personally supervised all the Lycée's examinations, invited Derzhavin.

It was January 8, 1815. Derzhavin sat at the table with the teachers; the students answered questions, standing two feet away from him. Pushkin later described Derzhavin: "Our examination wearied him. He sat prop-

ping up his head. His face was expressionless; his eyes murky; lips droop-
ing . . . He dozed until the Russian language examination began. He
perked up and his eyes sparkled; he was transformed."

Pushkin, who was considered a poetic wunderkind at the Lycée, had
been selected to recite his ode "Recollections in Tsarskoe Selo" to
Derzhavin: "I don't remember how I ended my reading, I don't remember
where I ran. Derzhavin was delighted; he demanded to see me, he wanted
to embrace me . . . They searched for me but did not find me."

Thus, according to Pushkin, Derzhavin did not offer any important
advice then, and the scene became symbolic only later, propped up by
Pushkin's later poetic depiction in *Eugene Onegin*. Actually, Derzhavin
anointed the poet Vassily Zhukovsky as his successor: "To you I leave,
Zhukovsky, / My ancient lyre . . ." In turn, Zhukovsky told Derzhavin,
"Your poems are a school for poets."

Here is what Pushkin wrote to a friend just ten years after the Lycée
exams: "I've reread all of Derzhavin, and here's my final opinion. That
eccentric understood neither Russian grammar nor the spirit of the Russian language (which is why he is beneath Lomonosov) . . . There are only
eight odes and a few excerpts worth saving and the rest should be
burned."

In addition, as friends remembered, Pushkin disliked Derzhavin the
man—allegedly he "acted like a scoundrel" in the affair of the Pugachev
rebellion.[1]

As an army officer, Derzhavin participated in the brutal suppression
of the bloody rebellion started in 1773 by the Cossack Emelyan Pugachev,
which shook the very foundations of Catherine II's empire. Pushkin
wrote down the story he got from the poet and minister of justice Ivan
Dmitriev, describing Derzhavin giving the order to hang two rebels.
Pushkin added indignantly, "Dmitriev insisted that Derzhavin hanged
those two peasants more out of poetic curiosity than actual necessity."

So the whole idea of being Derzhavin's successor was Pushkin's later
poetic invention, and it worked. But there were other writers who were
truly authoritative for Pushkin, whom he idolized. Their names, Nikolai
Karamzin and Vassily Zhukovsky, are little known in the West but revered

in Russia. Both were multifaceted talents, but Zhukovsky was most famous as a translator, and Karamzin as the author of the multivolume *History of the Russian State*. They did not hold any official government position but still managed to play a much more important role in Russia's political and cultural history than the poet-ministers Derzhavin and Dmitriev.

Karamzin was sixteen years older than Zhukovsky. He was a nobleman with Crimean Tatar roots that went back to the sixteenth century, born in the provincial city of Simbirsk (where Vladimir Lenin would be born), where Karamzin was noticed as a cute five-year-old in a silk camisole by eleven-year-old Ivan Dmitriev (who much later was known, according to wags, for noticing cute boys).

Later Karamzin and Dmitriev served together in a Guards regiment in St. Petersburg; Karamzin returned to Simbirsk, where he earned a reputation as a social lion and fervent cardplayer who dreamed, according to Dmitriev, of "winning the heart of a fiery, black-browed Cherkessian girl" and in the meantime indiscriminately read everything he could get his hands on, from German philosophy to the latest French novels.

Karamzin's interest in the recent intellectual fad for Freemasonry brought him to its center in Moscow, to the circle of the Mason Novikov, where to the astonishment of his old friends he turned from a wastrel into a "pious student of wisdom" (while still retaining his cheerfulness) and also made his debut as a writer in Novikov's magazine for children.

The key episode in Karamzin's seemingly uneventful life (he died in 1826, not reaching sixty) was his only trip to Europe in 1789–1790, during which he had a half hour's conversation in Königsberg with the great philosopher Immanuel Kant, "a tiny, thin old man, extremely white and gentle"[2] (they discussed the topical question of the discovery of new lands and exchanged views on China). In Paris, arriving at the right time in the right place, Karamzin listened to the fiery speeches of the revolutionaries Mirabeau and Robespierre at the National Assembly.

Back in Russia, Karamzin published "Letters of a Russian Traveler," based on his European trip, in the magazine he founded, *Moscow Journal*. This catapulted him into the spotlight as the leader of Russian sentimentalism, which arose in imitation of European models: Laurence Sterne's *Sentimental Journey*, Jean-Jacques Rousseau and his epistolary novel *Julie, or the New Heloise*, and Goethe's *The Sorrows of Young Werther*.

Karamzin's most popular work of that period was his novella *Poor Liza*, about a poor peasant girl, seduced and abandoned by a rich young man, who drowns herself in a Moscow pond. Several generations of Russian readers, particularly women, wept over *Poor Liza* and other works by Karamzin, discovering their own spirituality and the value of their inner emotional world.

Sometimes a poet's biography resembles the popular narratives of his era. The true story of the childhood and adolescence of Vassily Zhukovsky could be the plot of a typical Karamzin work, just as capable of jerking tears from sensitive souls. The future great poet was the bastard child of Afanasy Bunin, a wealthy provincial landowner of sixty-seven. His mother was a young Turkish slave, brought to Russia in 1770 as a gift to Bunin from his serfs who had fought in the Russo-Turkish War. She was christened as Elizabeth.

The son of Bunin and Elizabeth was given the patronymic and family name of his godfather, Andrei Zhukovsky, a hanger-on in the Bunin household. Bunin loved his Turkish mistress and his son. He was already married, but according to people who knew, "his wife, having had several children with him, left the marital bed and allowed his freedom of choice in the demands of Hymen."[3]

It became a multicultural ménage à trois. The Turkish woman was installed as the Bunins' housekeeper, coming to the lady of the house, Maria, for instructions, which she received while standing. But when Bunin moved permanently from the big house to the small cottage where Elizabeth lived, his wife broke off all relations with her. Elizabeth took the first step toward reconciliation: she brought her three-month-old son to the big house and placed him silently at the lady's feet. Maria wept and gave in: peace was reestablished.

Bunin had hothouses built on his rich estate and grew lemons and apricots, unknown in Tula Province, as well as exotic flowers. Little Vassily Zhukovsky was another hothouse flower, growing up amid his numerous stepsisters. With his curly hair, dusky skin, and big eyes, he resembled his Turkish mother.

But Maria saw a resemblance to her only son, who had studied at Leipzig University and upon his return to Russia committed suicide over an unhappy love affair, like young Werther in Goethe's novel. She basically adopted Zhukovsky, but he always called her "grandmother," saving "mother" for Elizabeth.

The master of the house loved hunting, feasting, and women, but Maria adored books, receiving the latest works from Moscow and St. Petersburg, thereby acquiring most of the books published by the Mason Novikov. Many of his almanacs and magazines served as abundant food for thought for young Zhukovsky. Maria did not know foreign languages, but her son's governors had taught him to speak, read, and write fluently in French and German (later, he mastered English as well). With time, Russia read the best poems by Goethe, Schiller, Byron, and Thomas Gray in Zhukovsky's translations, which remain exemplary to this day.

Zhukovsky's artistic gifts became evident when he was four. According to family lore, Vassily drew a copy of an icon on the floor with chalk; seeing it, the maid fell to her knees in prayer—it was a miracle! The boy immediately put an end to the religious ecstasy by claiming his author's rights.

Zhukovsky's public literary debut was a performance in a private house of his tragedy *Camillus, or Liberated Rome,* based on Plutarch. The twelve-year-old author was also the director and an actor, appearing in a red cape and a "Roman" helmet of gold paper with ostrich feathers, bearing a big wooden sword.

The audience had to pay a 10-kopeck admission (his "grandmother" was let in for free, as an exception). The tragedy's success inspired a new play, but it was an embarrassing flop. Zhukovsky later claimed that this failure contributed to his lifelong insecurity about his writing abilities.

Zhukovsky tended to be overly self-analytical, dreamy, and absent-minded—the typical hero of sentimental prose. His father died when Zhukovsky was eight, leaving him nothing in his will. His "grandmother" gave him 10,000 rubles—a considerable sum, but Zhukovsky still felt miserable.

He later recalled bitterly, "I took every kindness to me as pity. Yes, I had not been left or abandoned, I had a corner, but alas, I felt no one's love; consequently, I could not repay love with love. "[4]

An exaggeration? Probably. A pose? Unlikely. Pure at heart, Zhukovsky was not a poseur.

The sentimental age in Russia gave rise to the ideal sentimental monarch, Alexander I, grandson of Catherine the Great and son of Emperor Paul I. In the remarkable line of Romanov rulers, Alexander I may be the most mysterious figure. His name is still surrounded by legends.

He was born to be happy but grew up, as Alexander Herzen put it, a "crowned Hamlet"—ambivalent, insecure, and given to mystical urges. His childhood gave no clue to the fateful zigzags and dramatic situations in his adult life.

Catherine adored her intelligent and gentle first grandson. She had hated Elizabeth I for taking away her son, Paul, but Catherine repeated (consciously? unconsciously?) the same stratagem: torn away from his parents, Alexander became the favorite toy of the empress.

There is a great similarity (little noted) between the childhood years of Alexander and Zhukovsky. Naturally, the future tsar and the future poet grew up in quite different conditions, but the psychological situation was approximately the same: the powerful grandmother who did not like the mother; the absent father, temperamental and hysterical; a sense of instability about the world and one's place in it.

Both boys found escape in the theater. Young Zhukovsky performed in his own plays, while eight-year-old Alexander delighted Catherine in a performance of her own anti-Masonic play, *The Deceiver*. They grew up to be magnetic personalities; a courtier once said that Alexander was *"un vrai charmant."* The same could be said of Zhukovsky.

Catherine left detailed instructions on bringing up Alexander and his younger brother, Konstantin. They were forbidden to torment animals, to kill birds, butterflies, and flies, and were trained not to fear mice and spiders, to take care of their dogs and horses, and to remember to water their flowers.

The highborn children were schooled in gymnastics, fencing, and swimming; in the summer they were told not to be ashamed of their tan and in the winter not to fear the cold and to bear pain without medicine if possible. Catherine instructed, "Teach the children not to interrupt, not to rush to express their opinion, not to speak too loudly or persistently, but simply, without raising their voice."

All this was good and reasonable. Yet dreamy and mystically inclined Alexander, like Zhukovsky, acutely sensed the absence of an important spiritual vitamin: "Catherine was a wise and great woman, but as for teaching the heart in the spirit of true piety, the St. Petersburg court was . . . like almost everywhere else. I sensed an emptiness and my soul was tormented by a vague foreboding."[5]

This vague foreboding came true. At the age of twenty-three, Alexander took part in a real tragedy, fully comparable to the grimmest of Shakespeare's imaginings. Catherine intended to make Alexander heir to the throne, bypassing her son, Paul. Both father and son knew this. What could be more dramatic? Catherine's cold-blooded manipulations wounded both.

When Catherine was struck by apoplexy in 1796, Paul, then forty-two, took the throne. Derzhavin described the event succinctly and energetically: "Immediately everything in the palace changed: rattling spurs, jack boots, broadswords, and as if they were conquering a city, army people burst into the rooms with great noise."[6]

The first, quite understandable, impulse of the new emperor was to annul his mother's ukases, which he considered unfair. The persecution of Masons was stopped, their leader Novikov was released from prison, and Radishchev returned from Siberian exile.

But unlike his mother, Paul was an utterly unpredictable ruler. Here is a typical story: on the basis of a denunciation, the emperor sent the well-known playwright Vassily Kapnist to Siberia for his pointed comedy *Chicane*. Then he decided to see the play for himself, in a private setting. The only viewers of the performance were Paul I and his son Alexander. After the first act the emperor decreed that Kapnist be returned from exile immediately. After the second, that the author be rewarded.

Censorship was virulent in Paul's reign: with a general decline in printed matter (almost a third less than under Catherine), the number of banned books grew, including Jonathan Swift's *Gulliver's Travels*, published under Catherine's aegis.

Paul had been terrified by the French revolutionary storm of 1789. He felt that Louis XVI "would still be alive and reigning if he had been firmer."[7] Thus came Paul's notorious imperial decree of 1800: "Since books brought in from abroad wreak the corruption of faith, civil laws and decency, from now on we order that any kind of foreign book, in any language, be seized before entering our state, and music as well."[8] As a result, sheet music of works by Bach, Haydn, and Mozart were confiscated on Russia's borders.

Paul's decrees, regulating things large and small, rained upon the country. He banned topcoats and vests, round hats and wing collars, appearing in public places wearing spectacles, combing hair onto the forehead (it was supposed to be combed back), growing sideburns, dancing the waltz, or applauding in theaters.

No one knew what would be permitted or banned tomorrow, who would be sent to Siberia or for what, or be punished with rods—one could get up to a thousand blows. Everyone trembled in fear. The demoralized and embittered elite started to whisper and then gradually say out loud that Paul was mad.

As Karamzin later summed it up, "Russians regarded this monarch as a dangerous meteor, counting the minutes and impatiently waiting for the last one. It came, and the news of that throughout the land was like emancipation: in houses and on the street people wept with joy, embracing the way they do on Holy Easter."[9]

Karamzin's description of the way residents of the capital greeted the overthrow of Paul's four-year reign was apt. At midnight on March 11, 1801, a group of conspirators burst into the Mikhailovsky Castle, the newly built residence for Paul in St. Petersburg. While the Imperial Guards tried to stop them, their commander, Lieutenant Sergei Marin, a poet and adventurer, unexpectedly switched sides, pointing his pistol at Paul's defenders. Confused, they surrendered; Paul's fate was sealed. Marin was the second poet after Derzhavin (who took part in the "revolution," as he called it, that brought Catherine to the throne in 1762) to participate in a palace coup in Russia.

Paul leaped out of bed in his nightshirt and tried to hide, but the armed intruders caught him, beat him, and then strangled him with a scarf. Their leader, Count Peter Palen, "an enlightened cynic" in Catherine's mode, quickly went to Alexander's rooms. The heir had been warned of the conspiracy, but he had not expected his father to be killed.

Learning of the fatality, Alexander fell to the floor, groaning, "How dare you! I never wanted that and did not order it!" The impatient conspirators found the "despair rather natural but inappropriate." Palen cut off Alexander's moaning: *"C'est assez faire l'enfant! Allez régner!"* ("Enough of this childishness! Go rule!")[10]

That was a rather rude send-off. But perhaps Alexander was stung more painfully by his mother (who at forty-one was suddenly a widow) in the morning, who said coldly and scornfully, "I congratulate you, now you are emperor." Hearing those words, the new monarch, twenty-three, fainted.

Alexander I was tormented by his father's assassination all his life, and it probably hastened his untimely end. Of course, he had not strangled his father with his own hands, but everyone blamed Alexander for the regicide and patricide (or, at least, so it seemed to him). It's not clear what was worse: to feel responsible for his father's death or for the sacrilegious murder of the imperial figure.

In the former, Alexander broke God's commandment and man's laws. In the latter, he violated the principle that was the foundation of the state that he would now lead, that of the sacredness of the divine person of the tsar, which was particularly important in Russia, where the sovereign, especially during the early Romanov reign, symbolized the unity and prosperity of the nation.

Alexander, who appeared in public with red-rimmed eyes, could find some comfort, albeit cold, in Karamzin's description quoted above of the joy of the residents of the capital. This apparent happiness was reinforced also by the stark contrast in physical appearance between the short, hunched, rickety Paul, with a pug nose in the center of his chapped face and always hoarse voice, and his tall, slightly stoop-shouldered, and handsome son, a blue-eyed blonde with polite, gentle manners.

Karamzin published a special edition of his new poem, "To His Imperial Majesty Alexander I, Autocrat of All Russia, on His Accession to the Throne," in which he expressed the emotions and hopes of Russia's cultural elite: "It is spring for us, / We are with You!"

Alexander I hastened to justify the hopes, in the first few days of his rule pardoning twelve thousand people arrested by his father, permitting foreign publications into Russia again, and repealing the limitations on travel to and from the country decreed by Paul I.

Calling in some of his young liberal friends, Alexander started to discuss potential radical reforms: limitations on the autocracy, and abolition of serfdom. Even though things never went beyond loquacious debates, the conservatives of the court grew extremely concerned.

They panicked even more when Alexander I, in an obvious attempt to turn vague talk of reform into concrete action, made Mikhail Speransky, an open liberal, his closest administrative councilor and then secretary of state.

These actions came on top of the zigzags in foreign policy that flab-bergasted Russian public opinion: first Alexander joined the Austrians against Napoleon, but then, after several military failures, the most famous being the humiliating defeat at Austerlitz, he concluded the Treaty of Tilsit with the French emperor, signed in 1807 in a special cere-monial tent on a barge on the Niemen River.

The alliance with Napoleon did not please the Russian elite. The out-rage of the conservative opposition reached the boiling point. Their unofficial leader became Alexander's favorite sister, the beautiful, edu-cated, and energetic Grand Duchess Ekaterina. She was seen as the patroness of Russian culture; Derzhavin, then sixty-four, dedicated elated odes to her.[11]

Russian patriots were particularly pleased by her refusal of Napoleon's hand and demonstrative marriage to Georg Oldenburg, a modest Prussian prince in Russian service. When Prince Oldenburg was made governor of Tver Province, the grand duchess settled in provincial Tver, where her salon became the center of oppositionist intrigues.

Karamzin began visiting, calling her "the demi-goddess of Tver." She saw him as the man best able to formulate a conservative program.

It was at the request of Ekaterina that Karamzin wrote his famous "Memoir on Ancient and Modern Russia," a political manifesto of out-standing literary quality. Through the grand duchess, Karamzin sent the "Memoir" to Alexander in March 1811. It came to be a symbolic moment in the history of Russian culture.

Karamzin's evolution from author of elegant sentimental novellas to energetic and influential political journalist and, later, to the greatest Russian historian was gradual but steady. Karamzin, like Novikov before him, had the personality of a natural enlightener. (This may have been characteristic of Masons; or perhaps people with these qualities were drawn to Masonry.)

In 1802, Karamzin took charge of Russia's first political magazine, *The Herald of Europe,* which quickly grew in popularity: it had twelve hundred subscribers, an impressive number for those days. He was the first Russian editor to draw a salary, a substantial one: 3,000 rubles a year.[12]

In 1803, with the help of his older friend, the poet and Mason Mikhail Muravyev, who had taught young Alexander Russian literature, Karamzin petitioned the emperor to be named official historian of Russia. In principle, this was not an unusual request. In that period, the Russian government was assigning knowledgeable people to research topical military or political issues—embryonic think tanks, without special privileges or the crown's personal involvement.

Karamzin received more attention: Alexander by special decree made him historian of the Russian Empire, with a stipend of 3,000 rubles (had he made inquiries about Karamzin's magazine salary?). Also, Karamzin was not expected to prepare a text by a certain deadline, as were the other advisors. All that was expected—only!—was that one day he would write the first "real" history of Russia.

Thus, Karamzin was charged with the responsibility for a unique national project and fell under the emperor's personal patronage. There had been earlier attempts to write the history of Russia, but they were unreadable. Alexander, who was an admirer of Karamzin's poetry and prose, wanted a work on a European level, a narrative that would combine the seriousness and depth of research with entertaining and elegant style.

Alexander got more than he had expected. In 1811 in Tver, at his sister's salon, the emperor enjoyed the author's reading of excerpts from the first volumes of *The History of the Russian State.* Then, on the evening before his departure, Alexander read the manuscript of "The Memoir on Ancient and Modern Russia." As a result, Alexander was markedly cold in his farewells to Karamzin.

What was the cause of the emperor's overnight reversal in attitude toward his historian?

The text Alexander read by candlelight that night began with a brief outline of Russian history from the beginning until 1801, brilliantly written: an inspired poem in prose. Then came an evaluation of the political achievements of the first years of Alexander's reign and Karamzin's recommendations—the part that upset and angered the emperor greatly.

Never had a Russian writer with access to the court dared to criticize his sovereign so sharply and practically to his face. The paradox was that Karamzin did it in order "to protect the emperor from himself."

Alexander dreamed of reform and with the help of his adviser Speransky explored some possibilities for implementing them, while Karamzin, with the passion of a gifted poet and the skill of a professional political journalist, tried to warn him off.

In small, private conversations, Alexander spoke of the need to limit autocracy, but Karamzin maintained the opposite: "Autocracy founded and resurrected Russia . . . What except unlimited single rule could create unity in this vast country?"[13]

The irony of the situation was that Karamzin, in his heart of hearts a republican (as he himself admitted sometimes), after many years of studying Russian history came to the conclusion of the need and benefit for Russia of an autocratic ruler. It was just the reverse with Alexander I: his long-held ideas of liberal reforms came from his reason, but in his heart he still was an absolute monarch.

That may be why Alexander's autocratic impulses prevailed: in 1812 he suddenly fired the liberal Speransky and sent him into exile. There is no doubt that Karamzin's "Memoir," by its timely appearance, played an important role in this dramatic political turnaround. It is just as obvious that both men—tsar and poet—made a corresponding note in their memory.

At the same time, Alexander's relations with Napoleon—described in Karamzin's "Memoir on Ancient and Modern Russia" as "a genius of ambition and victory"—deteriorated. The short Napoleon somehow always managed to look down at the Russian emperor, which irritated Alexander immensely. He wrote to his smart sister, Ekaterina, "Bonaparte thinks I am nothing but a fool. He laughs best who laughs last."

(Napoleon, in his turn, said in 1812: "In five years I will be master of the world: only Russia is left, and I will crush her.")

On June 11, 1812, the French army of 600,000 men led by Napoleon invaded Russia. The Russians called this the Patriotic War. At first, it went very badly for Russia: its army, forced by the French, retreated toward Moscow. At the very beginning, Alexander personally led the troops, but in the face of failure he turned over command to the old and experienced military leader Mikhail Kutuzov, who fought Napoleon near the village of Borodino on August 26, 1812.

The battle, later vividly portrayed in Tolstoy's *War and Peace*, was a meat grinder, with close to 100,000 men of both armies wounded or dead. It was so confused that both sides claimed victory.

When we think of the Battle of Borodino, we imagine it through the eyes of the fictional Pierre Bezukhov from Tolstoy's novel. But there was a real observer of that clash of two giant camps, a person in many ways similar to Bezukhov, just as much a dreamer with a lofty and pure soul: the poet Zhukovsky. "We stood in the bushes at the left flank, which the enemy was pressing; shells flew at us from an invisible source; everything around us roared and thundered; huge clouds of smoke rose along the entire semicircle of the horizon, as if from a universal fire, and finally with a terrible white cloud enveloped half the sky, which quietly glowed above the battling armies."

Zhukovsky had joined the army as a corporal, serving in the staff of one-eyed Kutuzov and working in propaganda: he wrote leaflets, proclamations, and daily bulletins. That practical activity gave birth to his patriotic verse cantata "A Bard in the Camp of Russian Warriors."

It was a veritable hymn to the might of the Russian army. Zhukovsky mentioned many brave officers by name, finding encouraging words for each one. For that reason, the rather long poem circulated instantly throughout the Russian army in manuscript copies. As one officer noted in his diary of 1812, "We often read and discuss 'A Bard in the Camp of Russian Warriors,' Mr. Zhukovsky's latest work. Almost all of us have already memorized it. What poetry! What an inexplicable gift to rouse the spirits of soldiers!"[14]

Another popular poem in those days was the fable "Wolf in the Dog House." This small masterpiece by Ivan Krylov (1768–1844), whose aphorisms are so ingrained in Russian culture that they are often taken for folk proverbs, described the current military and political situation: after Borodino, Napoleon tried to reach peace with Kutuzov, but was rebuffed.

In the fable, the wolf (Napoleon) sought easy pickings in the sheep manger but by mistake ended up in the dog house (Russia), where he was surrounded by dogs and tried to negotiate with the experienced dog keeper (Kutuzov), who breaks off the clever wolf's entreaties:

> You are gray, and I am gray-haired,
> I know your vulpine nature well,
> And hence my custom:
> I only talk peace with wolves
> After I have skinned them.

There was a story about this fable: allegedly Krylov had guessed Kutuzov's strategy—to exhaust Napoleon's troops—and so Kutuzov liked declaiming it to his impatient young officers who were straining to enter battle with the French again. Reading from the manuscript Krylov had sent him and reaching the words, "You are gray, and I am gray-haired," Kutuzov would stress the words and "remove his cap and point to his hair. Everyone present was delighted by that spectacle and joyous exclamations resounded all around,"[15] a witness recounted. Krylov's short fable was more effective than a long military explanation.

In executing his clever plan, Kutuzov made a great sacrifice—he surrendered ancient Moscow to Napoleon. Going against public opinion and Alexander I's will, Kutuzov declared, "The loss of Moscow does not mean the loss of Russia . . . By yielding Moscow we will prepare the end for the enemy."

Hysterical official propaganda urged the majority of Muscovites to evacuate the city hastily, and Napoleon entered an empty city, which met him with fires that consumed more than two-thirds of Moscow in a few days.

Napoleon blamed the arson on the Russians; the Russians accused the French. In the end, the French army, left without housing and food, abandoned Moscow, with Napoleon cursing "that terrible country" and "those Scythians." As the wise Kutuzov had predicted, it was the beginning of the end of the French emperor.

CHAPTER 5

Alexander I, Zhukovsky, and Young Pushkin

Pursuing Napoleon's vanishing army, Alexander's troops entered Europe in January 1813. Kutuzov died soon after. Napoleon still managed to gather a new force, but it was clear that his star was waning.

The famous "Battle of the Nations" at Leipzig opened the way to Paris for Alexander I and his allies. The day Russian troops entered the French capital, Alexander smugly told one of his generals, "Well, what will they say in St. Petersburg now? Wasn't there a time when they adored Napoleon and took me for a simpleton?"

Europeans, liberated from Napoleon, called Alexander "king of kings," like Agamemnon in *The Iliad*. He also became a patron of the arts throughout Europe: Beethoven dedicated his violin sonatas op. 30 to him, and later the tsar supported young Chopin, giving him a diamond ring.

In Russia, he was deified and the title of "Blessed" was bestowed upon him, which Alexander I modestly refused. Among the chorus of praise Zhukovsky's crystalline and strong voice stood out with his 1814 ode "To Emperor Alexander."

Starting out as a pensive lyric poet, Zhukovsky, to the surprise of many (and perhaps himself), confidently moved to the unofficial spot of number one state poet, replacing the elderly Derzhavin. In his "Bard in the Camp of Russian Warriors," Zhukovsky came up with an apt poetic description of the political and mythos-making role of culture: "Bards are allies of leaders; / their songs give life to victories." In his epistle "To Emperor Alexander" we find another important aphorism, "The voice of the lyre is the voice of the people," which delighted the young Pushkin.

In his verse, Zhukovsky praised "the Blessed" but also gave his monarch bold and unusual advice, all the more prescient because it was later echoed in the thoughts, fate, and posthumous legend of Alexander I:

> Leave for a time your magnificent throne—
> The royal throne is surrounded with unfaithful praise—
> Cover your royal brilliance, alone enter
> The crowd, and listen to the murmur.

Pushkin knew this poem (and many others by Zhukovsky) by heart, and even ten years later proudly commented, "This is how a Russian poet speaks to the tsar."

"To Emperor Alexander" became Zhukovsky's pass into the imperial palace, turning him into "the new state poet, probably the last in the empire's history and certainly the last to be accepted in equal measure by the authorities and by educated society."[1]

It was a remarkably intricate political and cultural dance, with the poet and the court taking careful steps toward each other, wary of appearing vain, silly, vulgar, or insincere. The initiator of the rapprochement with Zhukovsky was the royal family: back in the spring of 1813, the widow of Paul I, Maria Fedorovna, rewarded Zhukovsky for his "Bard in the Camp of Russian Warriors" with an expensive ring and ordered a special edition of the poem.

On his part, Zhukovsky wrote the epistle to Alexander with great care, unlike "Bard," which was written in the field and almost as an improvisation. This time Zhukovsky intended "to add his name to Alexander's monument," as he put it.

The poem was not presented directly to Alexander. First Zhukovsky sent it to his mother, the dowager empress, through his friends at court. Even though at first she had blamed her son for Paul's assassination, she and her circle now acted as the tsar's cultural advisers.

A cautious step-by-step procedure ensued. First Maria Fedorovna heard Zhukovsky's ode in a small family circle (the grand dukes and duchesses), read aloud by one of the courtiers, while she followed along with a copy in her hand. Everyone was delighted: "Marvelous! Excellent! *C'est sublime!*" When the family circle decided that Alexander, "who floats above flattery," would "feel the power of the poet's genius," another copy of Zhukovsky's poem was sent to the emperor in Vienna.[2]

At the same time, the empress invited Zhukovsky to her residence in Pavlovsk, outside St. Petersburg, in order to meet him. He lived there for three days, and on the first he read his ballads to a small circle, while at the next, reading for a larger group, he declaimed "A Bard in the Camp of Russian Warriors" and "To Emperor Alexander."

Zhukovsky and his manner of reading charmed Maria Fedorovna; as a memoirist noted, "to know Zhukovsky and not love him was impossible," he was "a combination of child and angel."[3]

The result was an invitation for Zhukovsky to accept the coveted post of "reader to the empress" (yet another important step up the court hierarchical ladder). This impressed Alexander. He also knew that Zhukovsky had received the rank of staff captain and the Order of St. Anna, Second Degree, for the war against Napoleon: that is, he had proven his loyalty not only in poetry but in action.

An imperial decree on December 30, 1816, was a formal response to the gift edition of Zhukovsky's poems accompanied by a letter from the poet. The decree read: "To the minister of finances. Observing attentively the work and gifts of the prominent writer, Staff Captain Vassily Zhukovsky, who has enriched our literature with excellent works, many of which are devoted to the glory of the Russian forces, I order that as a sign of my good will and to provide him the financial security needed for his work to give him a pension of four thousand rubles a year from the state treasury. Alexander."[4]

There was more. In 1817, Zhukovsky was asked to teach Russian to the bride of Grand Duke Nicholas (the future Emperor Nicholas I), the Prussian princess Charlotte, who upon converting to Russian Orthodoxy took the name Alexandra Fedorovna. Zhukovsky, who spoke German fluently, was expected to work with her for an hour every day on Russian language and literature. The rest of the time Zhukovsky was free, and his salary was 3,000 rubles from Alexander and 2,000 from the duke, as well as a free apartment in his palace.

And then came the crowning achievement of Zhukovsky's service to the house of Romanov: in 1826, Nicholas I officially hired the poet as governor for his eight-year-old son Alexander (later Emperor Alexander II). By that time, Zhukovsky was practically part of the family. He accompanied Alexandra Fedorovna to Moscow, where she bore a son, and commemorated the festive occasion with a special poem, which, in particular, captured for us Nicholas's rare display of emotion at the sight of mother and child (which the poet had witnessed):

> Seeing the child, the young father knelt
> Before the saved mother
> And in the heat of love wept, at a loss for words.

Nicholas I already knew what a perfect pedagogue Zhukovsky could be for a blue-blooded child. There is a lively description of him in action in a letter to Pushkin from his friend the poet Anton Delvig: "Zhukovsky, I think, is lost irretrievably to poetry. He is teaching Grand Duke Alexander Russian, and I am not joking when I say that he is devoting all his time to creating a primer. For each letter he draws a little figure, and for syllables he draws pictures. How can you blame him! He is imbued with a great idea: to educate, perhaps, the Tsar. The possible benefit and glory of the Russian people consoles his heart."[5]

Zhukovsky's friends called him the "children's Aristotle," for he taught the heir not only Russian literature but also geography, history, and even arithmetic. True, Zhukovsky wrote poetry much less, but it sometimes seemed that he did not regret it: "I do know that the *world of children is my world,* and that I can act with pleasure in that world, and that I can find *total happiness* in it."

There was a reason Zhukovsky spoke longingly of "total happiness" in the closed world of the Romanov family, living in their sumptuous residence, the Winter Palace, where he was given a spacious and comfortable apartment. He suffered a painful crisis in 1823, and the wound never healed for him.

In 1805, at the age of twenty-two, Zhukovsky first recorded in his diary words of love for Maria (Masha) Protasova, his stepsister's daughter, aged twelve. It was a passionate but ultimately platonic feeling: despite the grown-up Masha's love for him, her devout mother never gave her blessing for them to marry. In 1823, at the age of thirty, Masha died, after a few years of marriage to another man.

This sad story dominated Zhukovsky's oeuvre for more than thirty years and imbued the poet's worldview with religious and mystical tones. Both he and Masha had always talked and written to each other about "trusting Providence." Zhukovsky's "To Emperor Alexander" was also based on providential rhetoric. Perhaps that was what touched a secret string in the emperor's soul, for he was always in search of trusted advisers and a word of spiritual approval.

This inclination toward mysticism increased sharply after Alexander's victory over Napoleon. Napoleon's fame as military leader was legendary, and so the inexperienced Russian tsar's triumph could easily be interpreted as God's will. The Bible was now always on Alexander's bedside table, and he saw himself as the weapon of Providence. The goal of his state policy became the affirmation of Christian morality in international relations.

As leader of the anti-Napoleonic coalition, Alexander had enough power to attempt bringing those ideas into life. After the Congress of Vienna (1814–1815), on Alexander's initiative, the victorious nations—

Russia, Austria, Prussia, and England—formed the Holy Alliance. Its purpose would be to instill Christian principles in the management of Europe.

We can imagine Alexander's thinking: while the power-hungry Napoleon was celebrated for constant warfare, the pious Russian emperor would be remembered for the permanent peace that would come from following Christian ideals. To achieve this goal, Alexander made substantial foreign policy concessions and was extremely disillusioned by the cynical behavior of his Western partners, who stubbornly refused to be guided by "the commandments of love, truth, and peace," as Alexander dreamed.

The Russian elite, first deliriously patriotic after the victory over Napoleon, sobered up gradually, and some people even began expressing dissatisfaction with their mystically inclined ruler. Reports of such ingratitude drove Alexander to melancholic despair that bordered on clinical depression.

Zhukovsky's melancholy and mystical ballads were balm for Alexander's soul. And the emperor may have appeared as the ideal personage of his poetry and certainly the constant object of Zhukovsky's thoughts. Never before or since had tsar and poet been so close.

"He took Paris, he founded the Lycée." Thus Pushkin summarized the almost quarter-century reign of Alexander I, equating the glorious historical event with the relatively modest educational project, one of many liberal initiatives of the early years of Alexander's rule.

And yet, October 19, 1811, when the Imperial Lycée was opened in Tsarskoe Selo, became a legendary day in Russian culture, first of all because among the thirty boys in the first class of the school, that day standing in three rows in the big, light-filled recreation hall of the four-story Catherine Palace, was the curly-haired, lively, and quick son of a Moscow nobleman, twelve-year-old Alexander Pushkin.

As one of the students recalled, they were presented to Alexander I, who came to the school: "After the speeches, each came up to the table and bowed to the emperor, who regarded us kindly and patiently returned our clumsy bows."[6]

Alexander wanted to create an elite, closed boarding school for "educating youths especially intended for important state service." Originally, the tsar's younger brothers, the Grand Dukes Mikhail and Nicholas (the future emperor), were to be educated there too, but their mother objected. Nevertheless, the royal treasury spent lavishly on the Lycée: the boys had luxurious accommodations and the best professors.

Pushkin, however, was not interested in his studies. In math class, he wrote poetry, brow furrowed and lips pursed. The professor of mathematics let it pass: he enjoyed Pushkin's epigrams mocking the school doctor (who chuckled at Pushkin's jabs at the math professor).

Pushkin was called to the blackboard to work on an algebra problem; the teacher watched compassionately as the young poet shuffled his feet and scribbled formulas endlessly in chalk. When he got tired of waiting, he interrupted Pushkin's suffering: "Well, what did you get? What does X equal?"

"Zero."

"Pushkin, in my class, everything comes out zero for you. Go back to your seat and write poetry!"[7]

Everyone indulged the wunderkind, including the royal patron of the Lycée, Emperor Alexander I. As one of the poet's classmates put it delicately, Pushkin "liked sometimes, secretly from the authorities, to make sacrifices to Bacchus and Venus"—that is, to drink and traipse after maids.

Once Pushkin found himself in the dark corridor of the tsar's palace and grabbed the maid of Princess Varvara Volkonskaya, lady-in-waiting of the tsar's wife. Hugging and kissing her, he discovered to his horror that it was not the maid but the elderly princess—a scene out of a French farce. Pushkin ran off, but the princess complained to the emperor, who scolded the Lycée's director, Egor Engelhardt: "What is happening? Your pupils not only steal apples from my orchard, now they won't even leave my wife's ladies-in-waiting in peace!"

The director pleaded on behalf of Pushkin: "The poor lad is desperate: he came for my permission to write to the princess and beg her pardon." Alexander was forgiving: "Let it be, I'll have a word on his behalf; but tell him it's the last time."

With those words, Alexander hurried to catch up with his wife, whom he saw in the distance, but managed to whisper to the overjoyed Engelhardt: *"La vieille est peut-être enchantée de la méprise du jeune homme, entre nous soit dit"* ("The old maid may be delighted by the young man's mistake, just between us").[8]

Such encounters with the world of the tsar's family—real and potential (after all, the future Nicholas I, just three years older than Pushkin, could have been a classmate at the Lycée)—had to have fired young Pushkin's imagination: next to him, palpably close, personified history took place. This was a heady sensation, whose influence must be stressed also because for more than a hundred years first liberal and then Soviet scholars diligently minimized the significance of young Pushkin's contacts with the court of Alexander I.

For Pushkin's generation, the cult of historical personality was typical—first embodied by the romantic figure of Napoleon, an ordinary Corsican officer who rose to the peaks of fame and power and, in the words of sixteen-year-old Pushkin, destroyed "Europe's divine shield."

The War of 1812, when Guards regiments heading to fight Napoleon passed the Lycée, gave Pushkin and his schoolmates new, more real heroes. Now for Pushkin the "men of history" were the young Russian officers who went for glory. Almost a quarter century later, Pushkin still recalled how hard it was for him to remain in school, "envying those who walked off to die past us."

Dreams of glory and immortality made his head spin. A military career was impossible then because of his age; its surrogate was poetic triumph. A fellow Lycée student, Anton Delvig, published a poem in 1815 in a prestigious magazine, in which he called his sixteen-year-old friend Pushkin "immortal."

That golden ticket, given by a peer, was supported by approval from the professors, older colleagues, and, through them, the court and royal family. The poem "Recollections in Tsarskoe Selo," which Pushkin recited during his examinations in the presence of the old poet Derzhavin, had been commissioned by his professor Alexander Galich; at the examination rehearsal, an important official heard the poem and was delighted—Count Razumovsky, minister of education.

Even earlier, Ivan Martynov, director of the ministry department that oversaw the Lycée (where his own son was a student), asked the young Pushkin to write an ode, "On the Return of the Sovereign Emperor from Paris in 1815." This ode for Alexander I, with an accompanying letter from Pushkin, was given by Martynov to Count Razumovsky, who presented it to the emperor.[9]

Another notable step in the relations between young Pushkin and the royal family was the commission of a poem for the marriage of Alexander's sister, Anna, and the heir to the Dutch throne, Prince William of Orange, who had fought at Waterloo.

This commission came through the court historian Karamzin, who had become the poet's mentor. The performance of Pushkin's poem, set to music, was described in the official communiqué as follows: "Groups of settlers of both sexes performed dances, games, and, united, sang a chorus that expressed their love for the brave Prince, the object of this festivity. After that chorus, couplets were sung in honor of his great successes at the famous victory."[10]

Alexander's mother, the dowager empress Maria Fedorovna, made special note of Pushkin's offering, sending him a gold watch and chain. According to one story, Pushkin lost the watch immediately; according to another, he "squashed it under his heel on purpose."[11]

On June 9, 1817, the twenty-nine graduates of the Lycée were presented to Alexander I in order of achievement, with an announcement of the rank bestowed and awards of gold and silver medals. Pushkin was the twenty-sixth to be called: his successes were very modest, except for Russian and French and fencing. There was no chance of a medal.

The rank he was awarded upon graduation was collegiate secretary, which was part of the tenth class in the official Table of Ranks. Seventeen of his fellow graduates were in the higher ninth class. (Pushkin achieved that just before his death.) Alexander smiled benignly at them all, but for Pushkin, who had enjoyed a personal triumph at the previous examinations in the presence of the great Derzhavin, this ceremony must have been humiliating.

Once Alexander inquired of the students, who was first in the class? Pushkin replied, "We don't have any firsts, Your Imperial Majesty, we're all second." And suddenly it became painfully clear that there actually was a division into first, second, and last, and that the wunderkind poet would have to sign official papers as "10th-class Pushkin."

He had to find his revenge in another field, where Pushkin knew his true worth—poetry. The old and wise Lycée director Engelhardt had written perceptively in his record, "Pushkin's highest and ultimate goal is to shine, with his poetry."[12]

He rarely appeared at the Ministry of Foreign Affairs, where he was assigned after graduation: civil service bored him, and Pushkin, unlike Derzhavin, never did become an official.

After six years of being cooped up at the school, the twenty-year-old poet led a wild life in St. Petersburg: wine, young actresses, all-night orgies. In a letter to a friend, Pushkin described his life in 1819: "Everything goes on as usual: the champagne, thank God, is good, and the actresses, too—the first flows, the latter fuck—amen, amen. As it should be." The letter ends on an amusing note: "I love you—and hate despotism. Farewell, dear one."

Freethinking was fashionable in his circle. In order to be popular, you had to write dissident poems. The social commission was in the air, and at eighteen Pushkin responded to it with an ode "To Liberty." It is a gem of political poetry, containing three exceptionally bold stanzas on a topic forbidden at the time—the murder of Paul, Alexander's father, in 1801.

Only whispers were heard about that terrible episode in Russian history, and suddenly there came this fiery poetry. It is no surprise that the ode immediately became samizdat: it was copied, passed around, and enthusiastically memorized and declaimed at young people's parties.

Inevitably, the poem reached Alexander I. His father's assassination was an unhealed wound, and we can only imagine his reaction when he read:

> O shame! O horror of our days!
> Like animals the Janissaries burst in!
> Ignominious blows fell,
> The crowned villain died.

Pushkin was balancing on a knife edge here. On the one hand, he called Paul I a crowned villain. On the other, he called his murder horrible. As we know, Alexander did not sanction the killing. Still, he felt deep guilt for the crime. Surprisingly, Alexander "did not find reasons for punishment" when he read the ode, according to a contemporary.

A mysterious note has survived, written by Pushkin in December 1824 (a year before the tsar's death), "An Imaginary Conversation with Alexander I." Pushkin has the tsar praise "To Liberty," in words he wanted to hear: "There are three very good stanzas here. While behaving very imprudently, you did not try to blacken me in the eyes of the people by spreading ridiculous slander. You may have unfounded opinions, but I see that you respected the truth and personal honor even in the Tsar."

This text proves how significant the dialogue—actual and imaginary—with Alexander was in Pushkin's mind. The intensity of the dialogue is confirmed by other politically tinted poems of the young Pushkin—for instance, his elegy "The Village" (1819), which was as popular among readers as "To Liberty."

In "Liberty," Pushkin talked about Russia's need for a "reliable roof of law." In "Village," he turned to another urgent theme, serfdom: "Will I ever see, O friends, the people unfettered / and slavery fallen at the Tsar's command."

Once again, Pushkin touched a sensitive string in Alexander's heart;

the emperor was studying a number of projects on emancipating the serfs. After reading "The Village," Alexander had Pushkin thanked in his name "for the good feelings elicited by this poem." Alexander's words went deep into Pushkin: seventeen years later, not long before his death, he quoted them in his poetic testament, "The Monument," a variation on Horace's "Exegi monumentum . . ."

> And long will I be beloved by the people,
> For eliciting good feelings with my lyre.

People who knew him recalled Pushkin's independent, proud character and legendary volatility. Some attributed these qualities to his African heritage: his maternal grandfather, Abram Gannibal, came from Abyssinia, now Ethiopia (although now scholars think that he was from the territory of modern Cameroon).

In Russia, Gannibal became one of Peter the Great's favorites, rising to the rank of general in Elizabeth's reign. Pushkin's mother was a cheerful, insouciant woman "with lovely Creole looks"; Pushkin inherited her curly hair and dusky complexion. Prince Vyazemsky recalled that Pushkin's younger brother, Lev, "resembled a white Negro."

Hot African blood and aristocratic Russian pride (his father could trace his family to the time of Prince Alexander Nevsky—that is, the thirteenth century) made a dangerous mix. But it was not genetics that made Pushkin's relationship with the Romanovs so complex and difficult. He was the right man in the right place at the right time, and he paid dearly for it. Pushkin would conduct a paradigmatic cultural experiment labelled "poet and authority in Russia," in which he himself was the subject. He got the starring role in this symbolic parable that became entrenched as one of the most influential Russian cultural myths. Pushkin lived up to the great role, even if, at the end, it cost him his life. This, and not just his exquisite poetry, is Pushkin's incomparable significance for Russian history.

Of course, Russian poets before Pushkin tried to position themselves vis-à-vis the Romanovs—for example, Lomonosov and Derzhavin (who

both left their own paraphrase of the ode by Horace). Even more important were the later attempts by Karamzin and Zhukovsky. But Pushkin is
the most influential model, remaining the example of dialogue with the
state for many generations of the Russian cultural elite to our day.

By writing the ode "To Liberty" and "The Village," Pushkin basically
"threw stones in the permitted direction," to use Joseph Brodsky's expression about similar liberal escapades of the young Moscow poets in the
second half of the twentieth century.[13] Later scholars, especially Soviet
ones, interpreted those poems as terribly "revolutionary," never mention-
ing Alexander I's benign reaction.

I have already mentioned that the poet and emperor were on the
same emotional wavelength about the need for the rule of law and the
evils of serfdom. This explains in part why Alexander I, upon receiving
denunciations of budding underground organizations whose aim was the
abolishment of serfdom and the introduction of a constitution, reacted
rather indifferently. As he threw one such report into the burning fire-
place, Alexander commented on the republican ideas of the conspirators:
"You know that I once shared and supported these illusions; it is not for
me to punish them!"[14] Three weeks before his death, the tsar admitted in
a private conversation, with a sigh, "And still, whatever people may say
about me, I lived and died a republican."[15]

These musings cannot be dismissed as pure hypocrisy. Alexander
demonstrated this ambivalence at a dangerous time for Russian autocracy. The victory over Napoleon had seismic international effects and
brought about important changes inside Russia. While energizing Russia's educated classes, especially young people, the epic war had wearied
and disillusioned Alexander I.

The emperor returned to Russia gray-haired, heavier, and suddenly
aged. His irritability had increased sharply, and his reactions were unpredictable. He became much more conservative.

By contrast, the young Russian officers who had picked up revolutionary ideas in Europe had become radicalized. Many of them were

friends and acquaintances of Pushkin. They saw that the poet shared many of their views, but they refrained from inviting him to join any of their organizations.

Later, a beautiful legend took root that the revolutionaries did not bring Pushkin into their plans because they wanted to protect his genius from possible repercussions. But Prince Vyazemsky, who knew them well, quite reasonably noted that some of the conspirators, poets themselves, did not rate their own literary potential lower than Pushkin's; they simply did not trust him. In their opinion, he was merely "the Aeolian harp of liberalism at the feasts of young people, responding to any which wind."[16]

It didn't matter. Pushkin was starting to claim the role of poetic spokesman for the political opposition to Alexander I. Finally, he wrote a satire that managed to insult the emperor personally. In the satire, Pushkin has Alexander returning from Europe (he calls him the "nomadic despot") and declaring,

> O be happy, people: I am well fed, healthy, and fat;
> The newspaper writers glorify me;
> I drank and ate and promised—
> And I'm not exhausted by work.

Pushkin's frequent jabs at Alexander spread through the capital instantly. One of them was particularly popular. After a tame bear cub escaped its chain in the park at Tsarskoe Selo and attacked the emperor, Alexander ran away. The poor bear cub was put down. Acerbic Pushkin quipped, "Finally one good man was found, and even he was a bear!"[17]

Angered, Alexander ordered the military governor of St. Petersburg, Count Mikhail Miloradovich, to start a dossier on Pushkin. We know the tsar's stated intentions: "Pushkin should be exiled to Siberia: he's inundated Russia with outrageous poems; all the young people know them by heart."[18]

Count Miloradovich called in the poet. Pushkin showed up, and when Miloradovich announced that he was sending a police officer to Pushkin's apartment to seize all his manuscripts, the poet quickly responded, "Count! All my poems are burned! There is nothing in my apartment; but if you wish, everything will be found here," and he pointed to his head. "Better give me pen and paper, and I will write everything down for you."

Sitting at the table, Pushkin filled an entire notebook, pleasing Miloradovich with his spontaneous frankness. The governor shook the poet's hand and cried, "*Ah, c'est chevaleresque!*" The very next day he reported to the tsar and handed him Pushkin's manuscript with the words, "Here is everything that is spread to the public, but you would be better not to read it, Sire!"

Alexander asked, "And what have you done with the author?" Hearing that the governor had pardoned Pushkin in the emperor's name, Alexander frowned and grumbled, "Isn't that premature?"[19] He still wanted Pushkin sent to Siberia. But Karamzin was already petitioning on the poet's behalf.

In the end, Pushkin was not sent to Siberia, but he was exiled from St. Petersburg and dispatched to the south of the country. Liberal St. Petersburg society perceived this imperial act as "a declaration of war against freethinking," meant "to strike horror" in real and potential oppositionists. The consequences were predictable: "What has happened to liberalism? It vanished, went underground; all grew quiet. But that is when it started being dangerous."[20]

There was something providential in Pushkin being the first victim ("you could say, the only martyr then," as an observer put it) of yet another switch in Alexander's domestic policy. The man who liberated Europe from Napoleon's rule and who had once been beloved by all was once again feeling alone, misunderstood, and deceived, as he had in his youth.

Not a single one of his ideas—constitutional reform, abolition of serfdom, or the ideal pan-Christian alliance of European monarchs—had come to pass. Alexander I lamented that people "had forgotten him, like an abandoned fad," feared that he would die at the hands of conspirators, as had his father and grandfather, and concluded bitterly, "I no longer have any illusions about the gratitude and loyalty of people and therefore have turned all my thoughts to God."[21]

The dénouement of this quasi-Romantic drama, which could have been written by Friedrich Schiller, was swift—in fact too fast and sudden for some of his contemporaries, and therefore mysterious. Unexpectedly, Alexander announced that he would take his ailing wife for treatment to the remote town of Taganrog in the south of Russia. (Anton Chekhov was born there thirty-five years later.)

In a modest one-story house in that provincial town, the emperor and his wife lived for some two months, filled with spiritual talk, prayer, and, as far as we can judge, quiet family joys. Not long before his forty-eighth birthday, Alexander, who had been known for his robust health, caught a chill, which quickly turned into a fatal fever.

On November 19, 1825, the emperor died, far from the capital, the court, and his beloved army. (His wife died, just as suddenly, six months later.) This quick death on the outskirts of the empire stunned contemporaries and gave rise to instant rumors and legends. Alexander was said to have been murdered, or to have committed suicide, or to not be dead at all. The last version gained some credence and has its adherents to this day.

According to this version, Alexander traveled to Taganrog in order to fake his death. This was to be his chance to realize his dream, which he had shared with people close to him: to abdicate from the throne and live a private life. Proponents of this theory argued that a different person was buried in March 1826 in St. Petersburg, which was why it was a closed-coffin funeral, which is against Orthodox custom.

There are numerous historical works seriously debating the question of whether the holy man Fedor Kuzmich, who appeared in Siberia ten years after Alexander I was declared deceased, was in fact the emperor, who had fulfilled his longing for a different kind of life.[22]

The mysterious elder Fedor Kuzmich, who had resolutely refused to tell anything about himself and was buried in Siberia in 1864, had a remarkable resemblance to Alexander I: the same height, slightly stooped, and with blue eyes; he spoke several languages and had undoubtedly belonged to higher society in his past.

In fact, the story of Fedor Kuzmich being Alexander was taken seriously at court and even in the Romanov family. Grand Duke Nicholas (the future Nicholas II) stopped in Tomsk on a return trip from Japan in 1891 to visit the elder's grave at a local monastery.

But the greatest memorial stone for that legend is Leo Tolstoy's short novella *The Posthumous Notes of the Elder Fedor Kuzmich,* written in 1905 but published only in 1912, after the writer's death (and even then over ferocious objections from the tsarist censors).

When younger, Tolstoy had been very skeptical of Alexander, as can be seen in *War and Peace,* his epic novel about the War of 1812 against Napoleon. But Tolstoy became involved in the story of the monarch's rejection of fame and power and his flight to the people when the topic started to be acutely relevant to the writer's own situation.

In 1905, while working on the novella, Tolstoy made a notation in his diary about the way he saw his own life: "A mass of people, all festive, eating, drinking, demanding. Servants run and obey. And it is more and more painful for me to participate in this lifestyle and not condemn it."

In *The Posthumous Notes of the Elder Fedor Kuzmich,* narrated by Alexander I, Tolstoy endows the emperor with his own thoughts and emotions: "I was born and lived forty-seven years of my life amid the most terrible temptations and not only did I not resist them, I relished them, being tempted and tempting others, sinning and forcing others to sin. But God looked down at me. And the vileness of my life, which I had been trying to justify to myself and to blame on others, at last was revealed to me in all its horror."

Tolstoy's Alexander I looks at things just the way the writer was thinking in 1905 as he prepared to run away from his family estate, Yasnaya Polyana. "I have to do what I've long wanted to do: abandon everything, leave, vanish."

Pushkin in 1829 said that Alexander was "a harlequin in person and in life." The skeptical and rational Pushkin did not believe in the emperor's mystical moods or his presumed repentance. Seventy-five years later, Tolstoy, tormented by his own moral dilemma, was inclined to believe in Alexander's "desire to leave everything, brought on by repentance," and in his escape, which Tolstoy tried to emulate in 1910, "without vanity, without thought of human fame, but for myself, for God."

Would Pushkin have agreed with Tolstoy's passionate idea? He never did forgive Alexander I for his persecution. But Tolstoy's assumptions about Alexander might easily have struck a chord with the poet Zhukovsky. The early-nineteenth-century mystic and the early-twentieth-century Christian anarchist would probably have had much food for spirited conversation.

CHAPTER 6

Nicholas I and Pushkin

Emperor Nicholas I called December 14, 1825, the "fateful day." It became one of the most famous dates in Russian history: three thousand rebels—soldiers and sailors, led by several dozen officers, who came to be known as the Decembrists—came out onto Senate Square in St. Petersburg, to keep Nicholas, the younger brother of Alexander I, who had died less than a month previously, from becoming the new monarch of Russia.

The Decembrist uprising was like a sudden lightning bolt, and could have destroyed the empire. Part of the blame for this catastrophe was Alexander's: he ignored reports of growing conspiracies, and his instructions on succession were exceptionally befuddled. (Many thought that the next tsar would be his brother Konstantin, next in age. Only a select few knew Alexander intended to make Nicholas his heir.)

The Decembrists took advantage of the confusion. They told the rebel soldiers that they would swear allegiance to Konstantin, while their real goal was the introduction of a constitution and the repeal of serfdom.

The soldiers on Senate Square shouted, "Constitution, hurrah!," believing it to be the name of Konstantin's wife.

Most of the Decembrists were noble and courageous men, but they acted foolishly. The rebels who assembled around the Bronze Horseman, the monument to Peter the Great, had no idea what to do, their leaders vacillated, and their plans changed. Nicholas, displaying determination and firmness, surrounded the mutineers with troops loyal to him.

At first Nicholas had hoped to avoid bloodshed. But the rebels responded with bullets when ordered to give up, fatally wounding Count Miloradovich. It grew dark. As Nicholas I later recalled, "I had to put an end to this, otherwise the rebellion could spread to the rabble." A loyal general said, *"Sire, il n'y a pas un moment à perdre; l'on n'y peut rien maintenant; il faut de la mitraille!"* ("Sire, there's not a moment to lose; we have to shoot!") Nicholas hesitated: *"Vous voulez que je verse le sang de mes sujets le premier jour de mon règne?"* *"Pour sauver votre Empire."* ("You want me to spill the blood of my subjects on the first day of my reign?" "To save your Empire.") The emperor gave the order to the artillery: "Fire!"[1]

"Long live freedom!" was the mutineers' response to the first round. But they fled after the second and subsequent rounds. It was over in fifteen minutes. The number of losses is still in dispute: officially, there were fewer than one hundred; unofficially, more than a thousand. In any case, Nicholas won the battle, as his personal fate and the future of the Romanov dynasty had hung by a thread that day.

That evening the leading Decembrists were arrested and brought to the Winter Palace, hands tied behind their backs. The new tsar's quarters resembled a military camp. In full uniform with scarf and saber, Nicholas sat in on the interrogations until dawn, using his formidable range of acting skills: tall and impressive, with a profile from an antique cameo, he stared with his piercing gray eyes at the rebels and was alternately stern, gentle, angry, kind. Some Decembrists behaved cockily, even insolently; others fell to the tsar's feet and tearfully begged forgiveness.

Hiding his fear and shock, Nicholas tried to find out the roots and causes of this attempted revolution. In his memoirs he wrote, "[T]he statements by the prisoners were so varied, expansive and complex, that it required especial firmness of mind to keep from getting lost in that chaos."[2]

Despite the confused accounts, an important detail immediately caught the new emperor's attention: during the interrogations, the Decembrists kept quoting Pushkin's freedom-loving poetry to explain their ideology. This made Pushkin a marked man.

By that time, Pushkin had spent sixteen months in exile in the village of Mikhailovskoe, Pskov Province, in his family estate. He had been sent there, to be supervised by the local authorities, on Alexander's personal orders. In 1824, the emperor struck Pushkin from government service. The poet had desired that himself, but life in the sticks of the countryside did not suit him at all. Still, Alexander, angered by Pushkin's defiant behavior, kept the poet in Mikhailovskoe.

Alexander's sudden death brought hope to the nearly desperate Pushkin, prepared to do almost anything to escape the countryside. News of the rebellion of December 14 began reaching Mikhailovskoe. Learning of its failure, Pushkin panicked; he later explained to Prince Vyazemsky, "I've never liked rebellion and revolution, that is true; but I was in contact with almost all of the conspirators and in correspondence with many of them. All inciting manuscripts were attributed to me, the way all the lewd ones go by Barkov's name."

Pushkin hoped for help from his mentors, Karamzin and Zhukovsky, who had retained their privileged court positions under the new emperor. Zhukovsky knew that the Investigative Commission was trying to tie Pushkin to the Decembrists. He wrote from St. Petersburg to Pushkin at Mikhailovskoe: "You are not involved in anything—that is true. But each of the conspirators had your poetry in his papers. This is a poor way to make friends with the government."[3]

After the Investigative Commission, the Supreme Criminal Court took over the case. Pushkin wrote to a friend, "I impatiently await the decision on the fate of the wretches . . . I have firm hopes in the magnanimity of our young tsar."

But many in Nicholas's entourage urged him to punish the rebels severely. When Nicholas asked one of the hard-liners whether he thought that a death sentence would be too harsh, he replied, "On the contrary, Sire, we fear that you will be too merciful." Nicholas countered, "Neither one—there's a need to give a lesson: but I hope that no one will argue with me about the best right of Sovereigns—to forgive and soften punishment."[4]

Was Nicholas being hypocritical? Or did he sincerely believe himself to be a merciful person? When the court sentenced the five revolutionary leaders to being quartered, Nicholas changed that to hanging; some others were condemned to hard labor for life instead of hanging. More than 120 men were sent to Siberia. Pushkin and his friends shuddered.

Pushkin, who knew all the executed men personally, obsessively drew a scaffold with five hanged men while writing his novel in verse, *Eugene Onegin,* and added the caption, "And I could have been . . ."

Pushkin wrote to Zhukovsky, "Perhaps it would please His Majesty to change my fate. Whatever my thoughts may be, political and religious, I keep them to myself and do not intend to madly contradict the generally accepted order."

Meanwhile, Zhukovsky went abroad, Karamzin died. Pushkin was left without protection at the court. Now the young tsar would decide the poet's fate by himself. Paradoxically, this was better for Pushkin.

Thirty-year-old Nicholas, imperious and determined, hated being pressured. He apparently sincerely esteemed Karamzin and Zhukovsky, but for him they were still Alexander's people, and despite all his protestations of great love for his older brother, Nicholas was jealous of him.

In Russian history, a new strong ruler usually rejected the policies of his predecessor and selected a more distant model to emulate. That was the case with Peter I, Elizabeth I, and then Catherine II, Paul I, and Alexander I: each tried as quickly as possible to erase the memories of the previous monarch's achievements, starting their own reign on a clean page.

Nicholas I was no exception: he did not orient himself on Alexander I but on Peter the Great. Like his brother, Nicholas was an excellent actor, but unlike Alexander, he wore his mask (or masks) much more comfortably. He was not burdened by his power, he relished it.

Nicholas I read a lot—primarily books on military issues, geography, and history, but also fiction, mostly foreign. One of his favorite writers was Sir Walter Scott, whom he met in 1816, when he traveled to England as a duke. Curiously, Scott predicted to Nicholas that he would be the tsar (there was no hint of it at the time), which elicited an embarrassed response: "Fortunately, poets are not oracles."

When Nicholas became emperor, literature became another stage on which he decided to wrestle with his late brother: Alexander had banished the poet, so he, the new ruler, would allow Pushkin to rehabilitate himself.

In late August 1826, in Moscow for his coronation, he ordered "Pushkin to be sent here."[5] Nicholas knew little about Pushkin. But he intuited that there was an opportunity for an effective symbolic gesture. But, as people would say a century later, "it takes two to tango." The presumed paradigm required a ready partner. Would the stubborn, volatile, and insolent Pushkin take the part?

As it happened, Pushkin was ready for a dialogue with the tsar. The shift in his position was due to the political situation, the advice of friends, and age, but also to the completion of his tragedy *Boris Godunov*, ten months before Nicholas summoned him. Pushkin proudly informed a friend, "My tragedy is finished; I read it out loud, alone, and I clapped my hands and shouted, Bravo, Pushkin, Bravo, you son of a bitch!"

Its theme was a dramatic historical event in the early seventeenth century: the fall in 1605 of Boris Godunov, the clever boyar who had usurped the throne. The Time of Troubles followed, ending in 1613 with the coronation of Mikhail, the founder of the Romanov dynasty.

A powerful impulse for writing *Boris Godunov* came from reading volumes 10 and 11 of Karamzin's *History of the Russian State*, a monumental work that began publication in 1818 and was an instant sensation, literary and political. Pushkin called Karamzin "the first historian and the last chronicler" of Russia.

Tall, pale, and elegant, thirty-three years older than Pushkin, Karamzin was a father figure for him: gentle, attentive, kind, and pointedly calm. But Pushkin would not be Pushkin without complicating this almost idyllic relationship: he fell in love with Karamzin's wife, who was twenty years his senior. Some Pushkin scholars believe that she remained the great love of his life.

Pushkin devoured the first eight volumes of Karamzin's *History* (from Russia's origins to 1560). The following three volumes covered events until the start of the seventeenth century. (The final, twelfth volume, would have brought the narrative to the election of Mikhail Romanov; Karamzin's death before his sixtieth birthday interrupted the work.)

Pushkin wrote that Karamzin discovered ancient Russia as Columbus had America. He borrowed the plot and many details of his *Boris Godunov* from Karamzin, and did not conceal it: the tragedy is dedicated to Karamzin "with reverence and gratitude." But Pushkin did not fail to indicate the other sources of his inspiration: ancient Russian chronicles and Shakespeare.

As an experiment in "Shakespearean" tragedy, the work is not a complete success: it never became a repertory staple, and in the West is better known through Modest Mussorgsky's operatic interpretation. But as an essay on political power in Russia, *Boris Godunov* was a breakthrough unsurpassed to this day; many lines are still used as aphorisms: "Living authority is hated by the masses. They love only the dead"; and the succinct statement on the inhuman burden of power, symbolized by the tsar's crown, that has been quoted by Russians for almost two hundred years: "Oh, how heavy is the crown of Monomakh!"

Studying Karamzin's *History* and working on *Boris Godunov* confirmed Pushkin in his dream to become a "state" writer, whose opinions would be listened to by rulers. He learned in Karamzin's work that distant relatives in the Pushkin line had taken part in the 1613 election of the first Romanov tsar, Mikhail. Now Pushkin had yet another reason to be angry with Alexander I and all the Romanovs: "Ingrates! Six Pushkins signed the election paper! And two made a mark, unable to write! And I, their literate descendant, what am I? Where am I?"

Pushkin realized that after Nicholas quashed the Decembrist rebellion, the only way to implement his newly discovered mission as "state" writer was under the aegis of the monarchy: if not in union, then at least in dialogue.

So the scene of the meeting of Nicholas I and Pushkin on September 8, 1826, in Moscow, where the emperor had urgently summoned the poet six days after his coronation from his exile in Mikhailovskoe, went as if rehearsed, even though both participants had improvised. Its success was due in part to the actors' typecasting: the stern but just and merciful Tsar and the independent, impulsive, but honest genius Poet who sincerely wants to serve his country.

Nicholas set the tone for the scene: "My brother, the late emperor, exiled you to the countryside, while I free you of that punishment on the condition that you write nothing against the government." Pushkin's reply: "Your Majesty, I no longer write anything against the government."[6]

Then came the tsar's key question: "What would you have done if you were in St. Petersburg on 14 December?" Pushkin's honest admission—"I would have stood in the ranks of the rebels"—was arguably the watershed in this historic conversation: Nicholas hated weasels, but he respected forthrightness and honesty (even in his foes).

His reminiscences show how he reacted to Pushkin's openness: "When I later asked him: had his thinking changed and would he give me his word to think and act differently in the future if I set him free, he vacillated for a very long time and only after a long silence he offered me his hand with the promise to change."[7]

The audience in the emperor's Kremlin office lasted at least an hour (some sources put it at two hours), an incredible amount of time given the tsar's busy schedule. It was also long enough for the tsar and the poet to come up with a striking finale to this symbolic play. Pushkin walked out of the office together with Nicholas "with tears in his eyes, cheerful, energetic, happy." The tsar, tenderly indicating the poet, loudly said to the courtiers, "Gentlemen, now Pushkin is mine!"[8] That same evening, he told a courtier that Pushkin was "the wisest man in Russia."

The practical result of this brilliant performance was Pushkin's release from general censorship so that his "personal" censor would be the tsar himself. But even more important was the enormous public resonance of that meeting, as reflected in the memoirs of the great Polish poet Adam Mickiewicz: "It was an unheard-of event! It has never been seen that the tsar would speak with a man who in France would be considered a proletarian and who in Russia has much less significance than a proletarian in our country, for Pushkin, albeit of noble birth, had no rank in the administrative hierarchy."[9]

There were political and economic reasons why this meeting of the tsar and the poet became paradigmatic for Russian culture. Nicholas's reign was the zenith of Russian autocracy and in many ways the model of authoritarian rule in Russia. In particular, in the twentieth century Stalin learned a lot from Nicholas, although the Soviet dictator hid this carefully, insisting instead on parallels with other tsars, Ivan the Terrible and Peter the Great.[10]

Pushkin became a symbolic figure, too, not only as the father of new Russian literature and as its most popular and arguably greatest figure, but as its first professional. Two of Pushkin's maxims (he admitted they were a bit cynical) are still used as *professions de foi* by many Russian writers: "I write for myself, but I publish for money" and "Inspiration is not for sale, but a manuscript can be sold."

Pushkin was seriously concerned with questions of authors' rights, censorship, fees, and publishing, and he worked as a journalist and an editor. His attitude toward these issues was ambivalent. He wanted popularity with the mass readers, but on his own terms. His self-esteem and ideas of aristocratic honor and dignity (the poet, as we know, was very proud of his six-hundred-year-old ancestry) did not allow him to follow the capriciously changing tastes of readers as easily as some of his more clever and successful (and now forgotten) colleagues—Mikhail Zagoskin, Ivan Lazhechnikov, Osip Senkovsky, and Faddei Bulgarin. They were paid more and sold more than Pushkin in their lifetimes.

Of course, young Pushkin had enormous success. The exotic "Romantic" poems (imitating Byron) that he wrote after visiting the Caucasus and the Crimea in 1820—"Prisoner of the Caucasus," "The Fountain of Bakhchisarai," and, later, "The Gypsies"—were a hit. A bookseller paid Pushkin 3,000 rubles for the first edition of "The Fountain of Bakhchisarai," but upped it to 10,000 for the second edition.

The slim and elegant volume *Poems by Alexander Pushkin,* which appeared in St. Petersburg two weeks before the Decembrist uprising, was also met enthusiastically: costing 10 rubles (a mid-level bureaucrat's monthly salary was 60 rubles), twelve hundred copies were sold out quickly, bringing the author pure profit of 8,000 rubles.[11]

Eugene Onegin was a sensation; Pushkin started publishing it in installments in 1825. The public was intrigued by the new genre—"novel in verse"—and by the unusual free form of presenting the material and the charm of the poetry. ("Charm" was the operative word used by many contemporaries for *Onegin.*) The first chapter had two printings (2,400 copies, extraordinarily large for poetry).

The publisher declared *Eugene Onegin* a "gold mine" and told Pushkin, "Your imagination has never created, and probably never will, a work that with such simple means moved such an enormous mountain of money."[12]

The plot of *Onegin* is quite simple and known now to every Russian schoolchild: the St. Petersburg dandy Eugene Onegin moves to the country and rejects the meek love of the provincial young lady Tatiana, kills his best friend, the poet Lensky (suitor of Tatiana's sister, Olga) in a meaningless duel, and then, after a lengthy absence, returns to St. Petersburg, where he meets Tatiana again. Now she is a well-known society lady, married to a distinguished general. This time Onegin is at her feet, but she remains faithful to her husband.

The magic of Pushkin's novel was not in this simple story but in the innumerable digressions and author's asides—melancholy, philosophical, playful, mocking—creating the illusion of a heart-to-heart chat with the reader. Threading words in a playful chain of these inimitable digressions that contained a treasure chest of future popular aphorisms, Pushkin in fact was creating a new literary language.

The opening chapters were the subject of lively discussion. According to the magazine *Moscow Herald* (1828), young and old, society ladies, and young girls and their suitors all chattered on about: "What is Tatiana like, Olga like, Lensky like." But subsequent chapters pleased the mass audience less and less.

This notable shift in readers' perceptions was in great part due to the wild fad for Sir Walter Scott's historical novels, which had swept Russia. Pushkin himself, asking his brother to send new books to the country from the capital, admitted, "Walter Scott! It's food for the soul."

Pushkin began experimenting with historical fiction: his unfinished *The Blackamoor of Peter the Great* (about Pushkin's African ancestor), and then *Dubrovsky* (also unfinished, about a noble robber, with an obvious bow to the great Scotsman's *Bride of Lammermoor*) and "The Captain's Daughter," about the adventures of a young officer during the rebellion led by the Cossack Emelyan Pugachev during the reign of Catherine the Great, are clearly modeled on Scott's "Scottish" novels.

Pushkin hoped that his historical fiction would capture the readers' slipping attention, "for is not poetry always the pleasure of a small number of the select, while novellas and novels are read by all, everywhere?" But as it often happens, his competitors, incomparably less talented, knew better what the mass audience craved.

Bulgarin's *Ivan Vyzhigin* (the first "moral-satirical novel" on a Russian theme) sold like hot pirozhki: four thousand copies in three weeks. Zagoskin's *Yuri Miloslavsky, or Russians in 1612*, also sold well, even though it cost 20 rubles; it was read "in hotels and workshops, by simple folk and at the royal court,"[13] and Nicholas I gave the author a ring.

Pushkin wrote great prose that is now the pride of not only Russian but world fiction of the nineteenth century: his novellas *The Coffinmaker, The Station Master,* and *The Queen of Spades* paved the way for Gogol's "The Overcoat" and Dostoevsky's *Poor Folk.* But the contemporary press and readers gave Pushkin's prose a cold shoulder. Pushkin was sure that he wrote "simply, briefly, and clearly" (and entertainingly), while the readers demanded more melodrama, color, plot twists, horrible secrets, and secret horrors.

Pushkin had to face facts: he was no longer the readers' idol. This filled his heart with bitterness, which was confirmed by hard numbers. Even at the best of times he received a chervonets (10 rubles) per line of verse, while the truly popular Krylov was paid a thousand chervonets for each of his short fables.

Pushkin's attempts to guarantee himself a stable income (and independence) as a freelance writer failed, as did his later plan to get rich by publishing his own journal, *Contemporary.*

There was one last way, which suddenly became open thanks to Nicholas's benevolence: take up the vacant post of state poet (the Zhukovsky model) or state historian (the Karamzin model). Karamzin was dead, Zhukovsky ill and depressed, while Pushkin, inspired by his work on *Boris Godunov,* felt strong enough to replace both. He had every reason to assume that Karamzin and Zhukovsky saw him as an heir.

It would be wrong to presume that Pushkin's aspiration to be "counselor to the tsar" was based only on greed or vanity (although D. S. Mirsky in 1934 accused him of being a "lackey" and "vulgar conformist").[14] That "inspiration is not for sale" Pushkin believed to the end of his days. But the inexorable evolution of his professional and political outlook eventually made him a "liberal conservative," according to his friend Prince Vyazemsky.

Pushkin still demanded certain freedoms for himself and the elite and still thought the emancipation of the serfs necessary, but by now he firmly believed that these goals could be achieved not by revolutionary means, but through universal education, which could be inculcated in Russia only by the tsar: "Since the Romanov house came to the throne, our government has always been in the forefront of enlightenment. The people follow lazily and sometimes reluctantly."

The mature Pushkin, despite his French-based education and cosmopolitan orientation, could be called a patriot, even a nationalist, albeit a paradoxical one: "Even though personally I am heartily attached to the Sovereign, I am far from pleased by what I see around me; as a writer, I am irritated, as a man with honor, I am offended, but I swear that I would not want to change my homeland or have another history than the history of our ancestors just as God gave it to us."

That Pushkin, with that system of views, Nicholas had every reason to call "my Pushkin." Nevertheless, their differences would have inevitably grown: after all, the tsar was leader of a huge empire, while Pushkin was only one of his fifty million subjects, however much a genius ("the wisest man in Russia").

Later commentators on the relationship between Nicholas I and Pushkin seem to have forgotten this obvious gap in their respective hierarchical positions. Soviet scholars in particular seemed to think that the sole priority of Nicholas's reign was to provide ideal conditions for Pushkin's life and work.

But Nicholas I was not at all like King Ludwig II of Bavaria, for example, who tried to satisfy every whim of Richard Wagner. The Russian emperor was stern and valued subordination to law and order above all.

His exemplar in this was his great-grandfather, Peter the Great, the first ruler in Russia to make serving the state the main criterion for evaluating any person, from emperor to serf. For Nicholas I (as for Peter, too) the army was the model for society: "There we see order, strict unconditional abidance of the law, no know-it-alls or contradictions . . . I look at human life only as service, for everyone serves."

In this, Nicholas's ideological orientation on Peter the Great was obvious to many of his contemporaries, including Pushkin, who in late

1826 wrote an ode to the tsar called "Stanzas" ("In hopes of glory and goodness . . ."), in which he directly compared the emperor to his legendary ancestor and called on him to follow Peter's example: "to sow enlightenment" boldly, to be "like him, tireless and hard, / and like him, without rancor" (the latter a hint to Nicholas to show mercy to the Decembrists exiled in Siberia).

The poem, approved by Nicholas and published, cost Pushkin dearly: it finally destroyed his reputation as dissident poet. Many of his friends (but not Zhukovsky) shunned him; behind his back they called him "court toady" (as both Karamzin and Zhukovsky had been called). Nor were the Decembrists, languishing in Siberia, pleased by Pushkin's verse appeal on their behalf—on the contrary, they thought it "completely dishonorable."[15]

Pushkin's tragedy was that, having left the liberal camp, he never won the complete trust of conservative circles: the tsar and his court never considered him "one of them." Pushkin complained that the attitude toward him was "one minute rain, sun the next."

Nicholas would commission Pushkin to do a special memorandum on national education (a sign of high trust) and have him told that he was reading *Eugene Onegin* "with great pleasure," but then he would suggest that he rewrite *Boris Godunov* as "a historical novella or novel, like Walter Scott" and "clean up" "The Bronze Horseman," perhaps Pushkin's greatest work (the author, showing considerable willpower, declined both proposals); sometimes he treated Pushkin in a gentle and friendly manner, and sometimes he "gave me a dressing down," as the poet put it.

Some commentators tend to see this ambivalent behavior as evidence of Nicholas's congenital hypocrisy. They interpret the tsar's talk with Pushkin in the Kremlin on September 8, 1826, as a kind of "contract" that Nicholas violated, thereby "deceiving" the poet.

But Pushkin could never be the emperor's equal partner. Nicholas viewed his relationship with the poet in a completely different paradigm: the stern but just pedagogue and his talented but unruly student; or, perhaps, the strict parent and his headstrong child (which would later be the relationship between Lenin and Maxim Gorky).

In that paradigm, approval or punishment is determined by the pedagogue/father not within the framework of some nonexistent—and impossible, in that situation—contract, but in response to the behavior of the student/child.

From the point of view of Nicholas, Pushkin's behavior frequently left much to be desired: parties, cards, women, and blasphemous poems (the infamous "Gabrieliad," Pushkin's frivolous satire on the Bible story of the virgin birth).

One can be indignant about Nicholas's position, but could it have been any different? In decrying the emperor's treachery, did Pushkin scholars try to see the situation not from Pushkin's point of view (which they all do) but from Nicholas's?

Even the outstanding expert on the Pushkin era Yuri Lotman described Nicholas as "untalented, uneducated, and dull . . . tormented by uncertainty, suspicious, painfully aware of his mediocrity and terribly envious of bright, merry, and successful people."[16] Lotman seems to be describing his boss at a state university in Soviet times rather than the autocrat of all Russia, who, as Lotman correctly pointed out elsewhere, was absolutely certain of his divine right to rule.

While understanding that Pushkin was a genius and soberly assessing the political achievements and human qualities of Nicholas I, we must also remember that the main sticking points in these intertwined and uneven relations were their diametrically opposed ideas of what constituted "service."

This difference imbues "The Bronze Horseman," Pushkin's shortest (only 481 lines) but most complex narrative poem, written in 1833. The plot centers on the clash between the poor clerk Yevgeny (Pushkin originally planned him to be a poet) and the famous equestrian statue of Peter the Great by Falconet towering over Senate Square in St. Petersburg. This fantastic confrontation, perhaps a delirious dream, perhaps not, playing out during the terrible flood of 1824, remains the most potent Russian literary symbol of the conflict of the all-powerful state and the defenseless individual.

The flood kills Yevgeny's bride, and, maddened by grief, he blames her death on Peter, who insisted on erecting his new capital in a treacherous location. Yevgeny, "teeth clenched, fingers in a fist," threatens the statue: "All right, you miracle-working builder! You'll get it!"

Suddenly, the statue comes to life: a wrathful Peter on his steed pursues the poor madman through the empty, moonlit streets of St. Petersburg. Yevgeny dies, while the great city created by the emperor still stands, "as steadfast as Russia," with the Bronze Horseman reigning in its center.

Both Yevgeny and the emperor are in the right, according to Pushkin, and it is up to the reader to decide whose right prevails. This philosophical ambivalence confused and angered its first reader, Nicholas I. For him the answer was obvious—the monarch, the embodiment of the state, was right. He leads the country to greatness, paying no attention to human sacrifices, and the people must obey him—that is, "serve": that is God's will.

Nicholas read the manuscript closely and underlined and crossed out many passages. He was particularly outraged by Yevgeny's threat to Peter. Pushkin was ordered to change the poem in accordance with Nicholas's ideas, and the poet accepted some of them, but he refused to eliminate the challenge to the mighty ruler from his wretched subject: "All right, you miracle-working builder! You'll get it!"

For Pushkin, this passage was the poem's climax (which Nicholas seemed to intuit). Pushkin preferred to leave "The Bronze Horseman" in his desk drawer, where it lay until his death, first appearing in a mutilated form in April 1837. Ever since, the poem has remained at the center of Russia's continuing debate over which is more crucial: the power and majesty of the state, or the rights and happiness of the individual? And how to compare the achievements of the national leader and those of the national poet? Which is more important for history and the country's self-image?

. . .

Karamzin as author of the *History of the Russian State,* which Pushkin called "not only the creation of a great writer but the exploit of an honest man," was Pushkin's model of how a poet should serve the state.

The reference to "an honest man" underscores Pushkin's conditions for his collaboration with the state, in which his concept of honor must not be threatened. He liked Karamzin's aphorism "*Il ne faut pas qu'un honnête homme mérite d'être pendu*" ("An honest man does not deserve hanging"). In 1831 he wrote to Alexander Benckendorff, chief of the Third Department of the Imperial Chancellery (overseeing state security) and official intermediary between Pushkin and Nicholas, that he wanted to do "historical research in our state archives and libraries. I do not dare nor wish to take on the title of historian after the unforgettable Karamzin; but I can with time fulfill my long-held desire to write the History of Peter the Great and his heirs."

Nicholas approved the ambitious application from the poet still considered politically unreliable. Soon afterward, Pushkin was able to tell a friend, "The tsar (between us) has taken me into service, i.e., given me a salary and permission to dig in the archives to compile a History of Peter I. Long live the tsar!"

Suddenly setting aside the promised history of Peter the Great, Pushkin rather quickly wrote "The History of Pugachev," based on classified materials at the Ministry of Foreign Affairs. The topic was still too hot—it wasn't even sixty years since the bloody uprising of Cossacks and peasants led by Pugachev had been suppressed ruthlessly, shocking Russia in the reign of Catherine the Great, and some witnesses of the events were still around. Therefore Pushkin presented the completed manuscript for Nicholas's examination with trepidation.

Contrary to expectations, the emperor was satisfied and made only a few corrections (which Pushkin characterized as to the point)—for example, revising the manuscript's title, "The History of the Pugachev Rebellion."

Moreover, Nicholas ordered that the state printing press publish the book, thus giving the author a chance to earn some 30,000 rubles, Pushkin calculated, and "live the sweet life." (The book, however, was a flop.)

As for the history of Peter the Great, Pushkin continued working on it intermittently until his death, but he left nothing but two dozen notebooks with notes and extracts from numerous documents and books. Nicholas read that manuscript, too, after the poet's death, and at first did not recommend it for publication, but finally agreed with Zhukovsky's arguments that it should be printed. Still, no publisher for this project was found. Pushkin's manuscript was returned to the poet's widow, and the tsar hired a professional historian for a book about Peter I.

In 1831, Pushkin married a Moscow beauty from a once wealthy but now bankrupt family, the eighteen-year-old Natalie Goncharova. The tsar was pleased that "his" Pushkin was settling down. Pushkin seemed happy. They had children: between 1832 and 1836 two girls and two boys. There were no signs that this marriage would start a chain of events that would lead to the poet's tragic death.

There is no more famous mythos in Russian culture than the story of Pushkin's marriage, duel, and death. Many books and innumerable articles have appeared on the subject, presenting starkly different interpretations. The more we learn of the events, the more inexplicable they seem.

Here is a brief summary. The marriage sharply exacerbated Pushkin's chronic lack of funds; he always lived beyond his means and gambled at cards, as well. He had hoped to improve his financial affairs by publishing *Contemporary* magazine. He knew that a general-interest magazine could be profitable—the popular monthly *Library for Reading,* with its seven thousand subscribers paying 50 rubles annually, made the publisher Senkovsky a wealthy man.

Pushkin managed to put out four issues of *Contemporary.* It was a quality journal, but too serious for the audience Pushkin hoped to attract. Its rivals called it elitist and the circulation fell continually, destroying Pushkin's fantasy of a way out of his financial dead end.

Nicholas I became Pushkin's major benefactor: he gave the poet two loans (totaling 50,000 rubles).[17] All around, at the end of his life Pushkin owed a vast amount of money: around 140,000 rubles.[18]

This made his position very vulnerable in late 1833 when Nicholas granted him the court title of gentleman of the chamber, with required attendance at court ceremonies and balls. This was the lowest court title, formally in strict accordance with Pushkin's low civil rank. The vain poet was furious.

Zhukovsky barely restrained his impulsive friend (literally pouring cold water on him) from "speaking rudely" with Nicholas himself. The irony is that Pushkin brought upon himself the appointment that he felt was so incommensurate with his achievements and therefore so humiliating.

Once Natalie was taken to a court party without Pushkin's knowledge, and she pleased the empress very much. Angry, Pushkin declared, "I do not wish my wife to go where I do not go." A contemporary reported, "His words were passed along, and Pushkin was made a gentleman of the chamber."

Pushkin tried to retire, but his desire contradicted Nicholas's fundamental belief in service for everyone. Avoiding service made a man suspect. The emperor threatened to take away Pushkin's salary and end his access to the archives. This would have made further work as a state historian impossible and imperiled his livelihood. Pushkin had to give in.

There was one more point: Pushkin thought (or needed to think) that Natalie's beauty was so overwhelming that even the emperor could not resist her. The poet thought the court title was forced on him so that Nicholas could see Natalie at court balls.

In a letter dated October 11, 1833, he warned his wife, "Don't flirt with the tsar." And a few weeks later, "You're happy that dogs run after you like a bitch, their tails erect and sniffing your ass; a fine thing to be happy about! . . . Alas, that's the whole secret of coquetry: as long as there's a trough, pigs will come."

Pushkin bitterly complained to a friend that Nicholas "courted his wife like a lousy officer; having his carriage pass under her windows several times in the morning, and in the evening, at balls, asking why her blinds were always shut." Pushkin could learn this only from Natalie—was she trying to make him jealous? (In 1848, more than eleven years after Pushkin's death, the emperor recalled during a dinner conversation how Pushkin spoke with him three days before the fatal duel: "I confess sincerely, that I suspected even you of courting my wife.") The poet Anna Akhmatova, a great connoisseur of the Pushkin era and of human psychology, blamed Natalie for boasting about her conquests to Pushkin; Akhmatova felt this led to the catastrophe that ensued.

Pushkin was an insanely jealous man. Did he have any reason to suspect Nicholas of improper intentions? In the Soviet era, many historians said yes, stressing the emperor's supposed "vile lust," even though the most cynical contemporaries never presumed that the emperor's attention to Pushkin's wife was anything but innocent flirtation.

The final tragedy was not caused by Nicholas; however, without meaning to, he helped set the scene. Balls in St. Petersburg really were the place where numerous love affairs began, often ending in social scandals and sometimes in tragedy.

At a ball in 1835 or early 1836, Georges D'Anthès met Natalie Pushkin and apparently fell madly in love with her. He was a young cavalry officer, a French émigré and adopted son of Baron Jacob Burchard van Heeckeren, the Dutch ambassador. The tall, blond, and handsome D'Anthès cut a dashing social figure, and his attraction to Natalie soon was noticed. She was flattered, and enjoyed telling her husband about him.

This was a mistake. Pushkin was agitated, and only a spark was needed to set him off. That spark was an anonymous letter, which Pushkin and several of his friends received, bestowing a "diploma of cuckolds" upon him, implying that Natalie had succumbed to D'Anthès (which Pushkin considered a lie).

Pushkin challenged D'Anthès to a duel. Zhukovsky, terrified, managed to settle the affair: he told Nicholas, who then invited Pushkin to an audience, an extraordinary gesture. This conversation, unlike their meeting in the Kremlin in 1826, was not publicized; the topic was quite sensitive. The outcome was this: Nicholas made Pushkin give his word that he would not fight a duel (they were officially banned), and if new complications were to arise, he would promise to appeal to the tsar.

Pushkin was always proud of his noble ancestry and of being a man of honor, but he did not keep his word. On January 25, 1837, he sent an insulting letter to Baron Heeckeren in order to provoke a duel with his son.

The duel took place on January 27 at five in the evening outside St. Petersburg. Pushkin was mortally wounded and died two days later, after receiving the final rites, in terrible suffering, at the age of thirty-seven. His last words were "It's hard to breathe, I'm suffocating."

The night after the duel, Pushkin sent word to the tsar that he was sorry for not keeping his word. In response, the emperor sent a note: "If God does not allow us to meet in this world, I send you my forgiveness and last advice: die a Christian. Do not worry about your wife and children: I will take care of them."[21]

In fact, Nicholas paid all the late poet's debts, assigned a pension to the widow and daughters and a special stipend for the sons, and ordered the publication, at state expense, of a collection of Pushkin's works to benefit his family.

These were all signs of special attention (comparable to those given to Karamzin's family after the historian's death), and they stunned contemporaries: one courtier noted, "This is wonderful, but it's too much."[22]

Only insiders knew that Nicholas rejected Zhukovsky's request to accompany the financial generosity with a special imperial rescript. One was published upon Karamzin's death, reiterating the official recognition of his outstanding achievements for the state. The tsar told Zhukovsky, "Listen, brother, I've done everything I can for Pushkin, but I won't write the way I did for Karamzin; we barely forced Pushkin to die like a Christian, while Karamzin lived and died like an angel."

Unexpectedly, Pushkin's death incited a wave of nationalist emotions in St. Petersburg. Crowds gathered outside his apartment; according to Zhukovsky, some ten thousand people paid their respects to his body laid out in a coffin—a huge number for those days. Foreign ambassadors reported in their dispatches of a new "Russian Party," and calls for "hanging foreigners."

No less surprised than the ambassadors was Nicholas. On his orders, measures were taken to keep Pushkin's funeral from turning into an opposition political demonstration: he had not gotten over the shock of the Decembrist rebellion of 1825.

The planned funeral service in St. Isaac's Cathedral was moved to a small church, the coffin delivered at night, under police escort. From there, still under police guard, the body was hastily moved to the Svyatogorsk Monastery, not far from Pushkin's family estate in Pskov Province.

A St. Petersburg newspaper printed a small obituary: "The sun of poetry has set! Pushkin passed away, in his prime, in the midst of his great life work!" The next day the editor was called on the carpet by the chairman of the capital's censorship committee, who demanded, "Why this publication about Pushkin? Why such honor? Was Pushkin a military leader, a minister, a statesman? Writing little verses does not yet mean a great life work."

The editor was told that the criticism came from Sergei Uvarov, minister of education. But behind that strict reprimand loomed the regal figure of Nicholas I.

PART III

CHAPTER 7

Lermontov and Briullov

The Pushkin mythos began to form while he was still alive. In the fall of 1833 he wrote to his wife in St. Petersburg from his family estate, "Do you know what the neighbors say about me? Here's how they gossip about me working: How Pushkin writes poetry—he has a decanter of the finest liqueur before him—he downs a glass, another, a third—and starts writing! That's fame, dear."

The poet as drunkard and libertine: that was one of the most popular images of the creative figure then, harkening to the Barkov tradition and entrenched among the general public, as well as the elite. Baron Modest Korff, who had studied with Pushkin at the Lycée and knew him well, was a high official and confidant of Nicholas I, and he described the poet this way: "Always without a kopeck, always in debt, sometimes even without a decent tail coat, endlessly in trouble, frequently dueling, closely acquainted with all the inn keepers, whores and wenches, Pushkin represented a person of the filthiest depravity."[1]

Such a tirade about Karamzin or Zhukovsky was impossible: they were "angels." That was also a legend, of course, and like any legend it was created by people. One of the authors of the posthumous image of Karamzin was Zhukovsky himself.

With Pushkin dead, Zhukovsky attempted to create a new image for him, too. He wrote two "historic" letters about Pushkin with that in mind. One, dated February 15, 1837, was addressed to the poet's father, but actually intended for wide distribution; accordingly, it was printed in *Contemporary* soon after.

Zhukovsky's other letter, written at the same time, was also planned as a historical document. It was to chief of the gendarmes Benckendorff, who had supervised Pushkin on Nicholas's command.

These letters initiated a radical transformation of Pushkin's image. Any memory of the dissipated, hard-drinking, freethinking poet had to be erased. In its stead, Zhukovsky offered a new concept of Pushkin: the national genius, true Christian, and loyal subject of the tsar, who sent a message to Nicholas from his deathbed, "I hate to die; I would be all His."[2]

These letters belong to Zhukovsky's highest creative achievements. He accomplished his intricate mission of changing public opinion of Pushkin with great care, choosing precisely the right words—his Pushkin dies "with a calm expression" and "radiant thoughts," surrounded by a pious crowd of mourners, and is transfigured by death: "there was something striking in his immobility, amidst that movement, and something touching and mysterious in that prayer that could be heard amidst the noise."[3]

This new Christian image of Pushkin was not cut from whole cloth. In going through Pushkin's papers on the tsar's orders (and in the presence of a vigilant gendarme general), Zhukovsky discovered not only the unpublished "Bronze Horseman" and another masterpiece, his testament-like "The Monument" (after Horace), but also a cycle of poems on biblical themes, known to no one; Zhukovsky was particularly struck by the verse transposition of St. Efraim of Syria's prayer for Great Lent, "Lord and Master of my life . . ."

The poem, probably written a few months before Pushkin's death, was so sincere and powerful that Zhukovsky took it to Nicholas, who was also quite moved by it. The empress asked for a copy of Pushkin's prayer for herself.

This "new, improved" Pushkin—a firm Christian and faithful servant of the Sovereign, carefully presented by Zhukovsky—proved to be an extremely successful construct, surviving eighty years, until the revolution of 1917. In the Soviet era this image of Pushkin was, of course, rejected and replaced with just the opposite—Pushkin as flaming atheist and revolutionary. But the old image rose once again from the ashes, like the Phoenix, after the fall of the Soviet Union in 1991, by now lasting longer than some of Zhukovsky's best poems.

Nicholas found Zhukovsky's image of Pushkin as an Orthodox national poet and monarchist attractive also because it fit the new ideological formula "Orthodoxy, Autocracy, and Nationality," conceived by his minister of national education Sergei Uvarov and approved by the monarch in 1833 as the state doctrine.

Historians point out that Uvarov (a liberal in his youth, a friend of Pushkin's, who had reoriented himself and made a brilliant career under Nicholas) created the triad as a polemical response to the slogan of the French Revolution—"Liberté, Egalité, Fraternité"—using a Russian military battle cry during the war with Napoleon: "For Faith, Tsar, and Homeland!"[4]

Minister Uvarov was a smart and cynical man. In 1835 a subordinate recorded in his diary Uvarov's political and cultural credo: "We, that is, people of the nineteenth century, are in a difficult position: we live among political storms and turbulence. People are changing their way of life and themselves, agitating, moving forward. But Russia is still young, virginal, and must not taste, at least not yet, these bloody troubles. We must continue her youth and in the meantime educate her."[5]

Nicholas I's policies (as were those of almost every Russian ruler after him, to the present day) were intended to maintain the country's cultural "innocence" for as long as possible. At some point the emperor decided that Pushkin, much more suitable as the instrument of cultural manipulation now that he was dead, could be used for this purpose. That is why the tsar eventually approved the legend that Zhukovsky created. There was, however, a subversive element in the legend.

The oppositionist aspect of Pushkin's posthumous image was also formulated by the clever Zhukovsky, in the letter to Benckendorff: "Russia's first poet" fell "victim of a foreign libertine," who was outrageously shielded by the government and police.

Zhukovsky's description of the great poet as victim of the intrigues and hypocrisy of the upper circles was directly influenced by a poem that circulated throughout Russia right after Pushkin's death, written by an unknown twenty-two-year-old Hussar, Mikhail Lermontov.

The effect of his poem, "The Death of a Poet," was an illustration of the clichéd story of the young genius who wakes up famous one day. Brought up by a wealthy grandmother, Lermontov started writing at fourteen and at sixteen noted, "I am either God or no one!" He had written about three hundred poems before "The Death of a Poet"—that is, almost three-fourths of his lyric output—and also twenty-four epic poems and five dramas. But by 1837 only one poem and one epic poem had been published, both attracting little notice.

But "The Death of a Poet" stunned contemporaries, one of whom later recalled, "I doubt that a poem in Russia ever had such a huge and universal effect."[6] Lermontov spoke out against Pushkin's persecutors passionately and powerfully:

> You, greedily crowded around the throne,
> Executioners of Freedom, Genius, and Glory!
> You hide behind the law,
> The justice and truth must be silent!

There is so much bitterness and anger in the poem that we tend to forget that Lermontov began writing it the minute he heard of the duel and finished his verse obituary (the first fifty-six lines) while Pushkin was still alive—he was in such a hurry to express his emotions.

"The Death of a Poet" was Lermontov's "graveside homily and simultaneously his throne speech,"[7] with thousands of copies flooding St. Petersburg. Lermontov was immediately declared Pushkin's heir, and, inspired by the sudden fame, he wrote the last sixteen lines, ending with the famous words:

> And you will not be able to wash away with your black blood
> The Poet's righteous blood!

A copy of the poem, with someone's caption "Call to Revolution," was immediately brought to Nicholas. At the same time, the emperor received a denunciation from Count Benckendorff: "This poem is insolent and its ending is shameless free-thinking, more than criminal."[8]

Nicholas irritably minuted in response, "Fine poem, I must say . . . For now I have commanded the senior medic of the guards corps to visit this gentleman and determine if he is mad; and then we will deal with him in accordance with the law."[9]

As punishment for his "seditious" poem, Lermontov was sent to the army in the Caucasus, where a war continued between Russian troops and intransigent mountain tribes. (He was soon returned to St. Petersburg through the efforts of his influential grandmother.)

Lermontov's reputation as the reincarnation of Pushkin was thereby entrenched, which was a paradox, for his creative credo was rather anti-Pushkin in its radical Romanticism, darkened by ennui and wild passions.

Even more curious was the beneficent attention that some of his works—for example, his blasphemous narrative poem "The Demon" (about the fatal love of a fallen cherubim for a mortal woman and his battle with God over her soul), not published in his lifetime—received in the salon of Empress Alexandra Fedorovna, Nicholas's wife. (More understandable is why the deeply religious empress copied lines from Lermontov's touching "Prayer" into her diary when she mourned her father's death.)[10]

According to Lermontov, Nicholas learned that he wrote poetry when he was still at the military school (Grand Duke Mikhail, Nicholas's brother, was head of the school) and in all probability kept an eye on his work. This is what the emperor had to say about "The Demon": "The poem is undoubtedly good, but its subject matter is not particularly pleasant." (Later Anton Rubinstein based his 1871 opera, which is still hugely popular in Russia, on the poem.)

By far more notorious was Nicholas's reaction to *A Hero of Our Times,* Lermontov's prose masterpiece, published in St. Petersburg in 1840.

The novel is actually a chain of short stories united by a single hero: Pechorin, an officer and self-absorbed cynic who flaunts his immorality. Pechorin is the literary younger brother of Pushkin's Onegin and precursor of Russian literature's "superfluous man." For Lermontov, he is the hero of our times, but Nicholas was attracted to another character in the novel: Captain Maxim Maximych, a veteran of the war in the Caucasus, a simple soldier with a mustache of silver and a heart of gold.

Nicholas read *A Hero of Our Times* on board the ship that brought him from Germany to Russia in June 1840. On his travels, he wrote letters to his wife, who remained in Germany for treatment. In one letter (written in French), he said that he found the novel "well written," but from the ethical point of view deserving strong condemnation:

> Such novels ruin the mores and coarsen the character. And even though you read those feline sighs with revulsion, they still have a morbid effect, because you eventually get used to believing that the whole world consists only of such people, who even when they perform apparently good deeds act only out of vile and filthy considerations. What kind of a result can that yield? Scorn or hatred of humanity! But is that the goal of our existence on earth? People are too inclined as it is to become hypochondriacs or misanthropes, so why prompt or encourage such tendencies with this kind of writing?[11]

Nicholas finds Captain Maxim Maximych incomparably more worthy than the egocentric Pechorin: "The captain's character is sketched successfully. As I began the novella, I hoped and was heartened to think that he would be the hero of our days ... However the captain appears in this work only as a hope that is finally unrealized, and M. Lermontov did not manage to follow that noble and simple character."[12]

Paradoxically, Nicholas's point of view triumphed in Stalin's day, when it was declared that Lermontov, by then firmly established in the national pantheon, "condemns Pechorin's egotistical character, his narrow individualism, which is juxtaposed in the novel to the humanity and simple-heartedness of Maxim Maximych."[13] Thus, Nicholas I extended his hand across a century to Soviet Lermontov specialists.

At the same time, those specialists accused the emperor of allegedly personally organizing the poet's death. Although many mysteries remain in Lermontov's brief life (he died at twenty-six), the known facts do not support this conspiracy theory.

Lermontov was ugly—short, bowlegged, with a large head and small (but expressive) eyes. He was morbidly vain and incredibly volatile. (Pushkin was a saint compared to Lermontov.) That mix was a surefire recipe for catastrophe.

The military habit of solving all sorts of conflicts with a duel must have been in Lermontov's blood. He was always living dangerously: it suited his character and his idea of a Romantic poet. For his duel with the son of the French ambassador over a woman, Nicholas had Lermontov exiled to the Caucasus again, where he argued with an old school friend, also an officer, and was killed in a duel in 1841.

The death of the young poet, who had written for only thirteen years and had accomplished so much in such a short time (and promised so much more), stunned Russian readers. Against the background of universal mourning, Nicholas's crude epitaph, recorded by several memoirists, stood out: "A dog's death for a dog!" (Or, in a milder version that was still outrageous: "Serves him right.")[14]

This ugly remark was explained by the historian Peter Bartenev in

1911. According to Bartenev, Nicholas said it at tea, in a family setting, right after receiving word of the fatal duel, and elicited a "bitter rebuke" from his elder sister, Maria. After that reaction from his family, the emperor went out to meet his courtiers with a completely different statement: "Gentlemen, I have received word that the one who could have replaced Pushkin has been killed."[15]

In the family circle, Nicholas, who considered Lermontov, like Pushkin, a good poet but a bad person (and an even worse servant), could have barked out a remark with soldierly directness. But outside that room, he spoke as politician, head of state, and father of the nation.

As a man, Nicholas could have been outraged by Lermontov's inglorious death (as he saw it), especially since dueling had been banned by the emperor and was punished severely. But Nicholas also understood that Lermontov's death, like Pushkin's four years earlier, would not add any glory to his reign. His final words were damage control.

Much more humane was the simple and sincere response from the empress, who wrote to a friend, "A sigh for Lermontov and his broken lyre that had promised Russian literature to become its leading star."[16]

Before his final departure for the Caucasus, Lermontov and a friend dropped in on the German fortune-teller who lived in St. Petersburg and was famous for having told Pushkin that he would be killed over a woman at the age of thirty-seven by a tall, blond man.

Knowing that her prediction had come to pass, Lermontov asked her about his fate: would the tsar allow him to retire? Would he return to St. Petersburg? People said that "the answer was that he would never be in St. Petersburg again, nor be retired from service, but that another retirement awaited him, 'after which you will not ask anyone for anything.'"

Were these predictions legends or fact? At the very least they were characteristic of the atmosphere around the great poets. In their lifetime, but especially after their deaths, both Pushkin and Lermontov were turned into Romantic figures, surrounded by rumors, gossip, and posthumous legends.

Tsar Mikhail (1596–1645), the first in the Romanov dynasty

Ivan Susanin, the peasant who saved Tsar Mikhail, as portrayed by the bass Ossip Petrov, in a photograph

The composer Mikhail Glinka (1804–1857), whose opera *A Life for the Tsar* (1836) glorified Mikhail's accession to the throne in 1613

The second Romanov on the throne, Tsar Alexei (1629–1676)

Peter the Great (1672–1725), Tsar Alexei's famous and controversial son

The poet and diplomat
Antioch Kantemir (1709–1744),
Tsar Peter's apologist

The multitalented
Mikhail Lomonosov (1711–1765)

Ivan Barkov (c. 1732–1768),
the Russian François Villon

Catherine the Great (1729–1796)
who was vilified in Soviet times as a
"depraved and criminal woman"

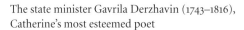
The state minister Gavrila Derzhavin (1743–1816),
Catherine's most esteemed poet

Alexander I (1777–1825), Napoleon's nemesis

Nikolai Karamzin (1766–1826), Alexander's court historian

Alexander Pushkin (1799–1837), Russia's greatest poet

The poet Vassily Zhukovsky (1783–1852),
Pushkin's mentor and protector

The popular fabulist Ivan Krylov (1769–1844)

Nicholas I (1796–1855), who called Pushkin
"the wisest man in Russia"

The poet Mikhail Lermontov (1814–1841), Pushkin's heir

Nikolai Gogol (1809–1852), in a
drawing by his friend Alexander
Ivanov

The painter Alexander Ivanov (1806–1858),
Gogol's protégé

The painter Karl Briullov (1799–1852),
Nicholas I's favored artist

The progressive critic Vissarion
Belinsky (1811–1848), Gogol's
early advocate and later foe

The poet Fedor Tyutchev (1803–1873), Nicholas I's
unofficial spokesman

Alexander Herzen (1812–1870), the rebel and
literary innovator

A young Leo Tolstoy (1828–1910), whom Turgenev called a troglodyte for his directness and coarseness

Ivan Turgenev (1818–1883), Russia's most Westernized writer

Alexander II (1818–1881) who was educated by the poet Zhukovsky

Fedor Dostoevsky (1821–1881), the last great Russian pro-monarchist writer, in a wood engraving (1929) by Vladimir Favorsky

Grand Duke Konstantin (1858–1915), the future poet K.R. and Dostoevsky's ardent admirer

Modest Mussorgsky (1839–1881) in a drawing (1881) by Ilya Repin. Alexander III personally banned a production of his opera *Boris Godunov.*

Peter Tchaikovsky (1840–1893), the Romanovs' most admired composer

Nikolai Chernyshevsky (1829–1889), a radical writer who influenced Lenin

Alexander III (1845–1894), who clamped down on revolutionaries

Painting (1885) by Ilya Repin depicting a revolutionary refusing final confession and communion

Nicholas II (1868–1918), the last Romanov to rule

Ballerina Mathilde Kschessinska (1872–1971), notorious for her affair with Nicholas when he was heir to the throne

Vladimir Lenin (1870–1924), who displaced Nicholas II as Russia's autocratic ruler. He disliked opera and ballet. A sketch (1920) from life by Natan Altman

A young Anton Chekhov (1860–1904), a favorite writer of both Nicholas II and Lenin

top: The Bronze Horseman by Etienne Falconet—a dynamic Peter the Great on a rearing steed, erected by Catherine II in 1782

right: The official unveiling of the statue of Alexander III by Paolo Trubetskoy in 1909

The "private" portrait of Nicholas II (1900) by Valentin Serov. It depicts the last tsar sympathetically, but underscores his lack of leadership.

A Romantic hero had to have a commensurate appearance. Lermontov's eyes, like those of an unattractive woman, became the feature most mentioned; allegedly they were mesmerizing, with pupils that started moving quickly, "like an animal's," in moments of agitation. It was said that only the famous painter Karl Briullov could depict Lermontov properly, "since he painted not portraits, but gazes, putting fire in the eye."

Briullov was the most celebrated Russian painter of the era, the only one to have achieved real success even in Europe, where his 1833 masterpiece *The Last Day of Pompeii* was a hit. He was, like Lermontov, not tall, with a big head and broad shoulders, but he had the face of Apollo, framed by luxuriant hair.

Like Lermontov, Briullov was a man out of Romantic legend, the personification of the idea expressed by the mad poet Konstantin Batyushkov: "Live as you write, and write as you live."[17] When he was seducing women, Briullov would tell them, "Don't you know that every person is a novel, and what a novel! But God spare you from looking into my novel!—There are such black pages in it that they would soil your pretty little fingers."[18]

When Briullov exhibited *The Last Day of Pompeii* at the St. Petersburg Academy of Arts, the enormous canvas that depicted with operatic melodrama a terrifying moment of natural cataclysm, a volcano spilling its lava on the ancient Roman city, captured the imagination of the northern capital, from ordinary folk to the emperor.

Anatole Demidov, a wealthy Russian who lived in Europe, had commissioned the painting and paid 40,000 francs for it; he presented it to Nicholas I, who "graced this gift with his magnanimous acceptance" and awarded Briullov the Order of St. Anna, Third Degree. The tsar summoned Briullov from Europe and appointed him as a professor at the academy. That moment began the unprecedented relationship between Nicholas and the painter.

The Imperial Academy of Arts was closely supervised by Nicholas I. He not only appointed and fired directors and teachers, he controlled the curricula, student competitions, and all commissions, observing their execution and giving "advice" (read: commands) on what to improve in a painting, sculpture, or architectural project. He considered himself a particular expert in battle and historical painting (he wasn't bad at drawing).

Founded in 1757 by Empress Elizabeth I, in 1850 the academy was moved to Nicholas's Ministry of the Imperial Court, and he turned it into a bureaucratic institution that functioned in strict accordance with the official Table of Ranks. Artists were given ranks equal to civil servants, with quasimilitary discipline and a detailed system of rewards and punishments.

At first this concept had a rational element: it helped turn Russian artists into respected members of society by putting order into their rise up the state ladder. But naturally, there was a danger that soon manifested itself: dressed in impressive uniforms with gold braid and medals and orders, artists began to feel like officials, with diminishing creative results. Among these obedient and cautious bureaucrats with palettes and brushes, Briullov was like a "lawless comet" in the gray St. Petersburg sky.

Yes, Nicholas valued talent, but he valued order, discipline, and zeal even more. The emperor hated indolence, drunkenness, and negligence in Russian artists, according to reminiscences of contemporaries. To everyone's horror, Briullov worked only when the mood struck him and periodically went on legendary drunken benders; even though he was a professor at the academy he somehow managed to never wear the uniform—not even on formal occasions—and his behavior should have outraged the emperor. But no. Something about the "great Karl" fascinated Nicholas, who forgave Briullov's romantic peccadilloes that would have been unthinkable for anyone else.

Everyone in Russia tried to be in the tsar's good graces, but not Briullov. In that sense, the artist was even more independent than Pushkin, who had also showed the tsar his lion's claws from time to time.

Examples of Briullov's affronts are numerous, each more colorful than the last. Nicholas visited his studio unexpectedly, and the artist refused to come out: he was not well, he claimed. Nicholas ordered a series of paintings depicting his Guards regiments on parade, but the artist replied that he did not know how to paint parades and would not do it. Briullov also rejected the tsar's pet idea for a historical painting— Ivan the Terrible praying with his wife in a peasant hut during the taking of Kazan.

It got worse. Briullov did everything he could to avoid the most desirable commission possible—portraits of Nicholas and his family. In the summer of 1837, Nicholas invited the artist to his summer residence in Peterhof, where Briullov began a double portrait on horseback of the empress and her daughter. He painted sitting by the window in a garden pavilion, while the royal riders posed outside.

A downpour began. The court physician, worried about the empress's frail health, tried to stop the session, but she refused: "Don't bother him while he is working!" The empress and her daughter were soaked to the skin. On that occasion, Briullov played the role of enraptured genius to the hilt, but he never did complete the portrait.

Once, Briullov was summoned to the Winter Palace to paint another daughter of the tsar. Nicholas came in during the session and as usual made suggestions. The painter put down his brush. "I can't continue, my hand is trembling with fear." The contemporary who noted Briullov's reply added, "Artists will understand the mockery, but I don't know whether or not the emperor did."[19]

Of course Nicholas did, but he pretended not to be offended. He wanted a portrait by Briullov as a necessary attribute of imperial majesty. But even his own portrait created a problem. The tsar informed Briullov that he would come to his studio to pose, and then was twenty minutes late. When he arrived, Nicholas was told by Briullov's terrified apprentice that the artist "expected Your Majesty, but knowing that you are never late, thought that you had canceled the session."

The perplexed Nicholas left Briullov's studio, murmuring, "What an impatient man!"[20] Work on the portrait ended before it began.

Briullov positioned himself as a Romantic and, therefore, free figure. "It was easier for him to anger the Sovereign and bear his wrath than to paint his portrait," a contemporary noted. But there was an area where the tastes and preferences of the artist and tsar coincided: erotic art.

Nicholas liked pictures of buxom, voluptuous women. Briullov was a specialist of that genre. His early work *Italian Morning,* depicting a beauty with bared breasts, ended up in the imperial family's private collection. Nicholas was so pleased with it that he commissioned a painting in pendant, in the same spirit. So *Italian Noon,* slightly less erotic but no less tempting, came to be.

Nicholas thought himself a moral person. His treatment of his wife was markedly courtly. (She was his first woman.) But that did not keep him from enjoying his enormous collection of erotic drawings, which experts acquired for him all over Europe; he also had a good collection of medieval chastity belts.[21]

Briullov's painting *Bacchanalia,* which had belonged to Nicholas, has survived. It was kept in a special frame with a lock and covered by a lithograph. When it was unlocked, Briullov's painting appeared: a depiction of the Bacchae in a love scene with satyrs and an ass, a traditional erotic motif.

This may be one of the reasons for Nicholas's indulgent attitude toward Briullov. His education, etiquette, and Christian morality demanded strict behavior of the emperor. Art and artists opened a window into another beckoning world.

All of St. Petersburg gossiped about the love affairs of fashionable artists. Orest Kiprensky, author of perhaps the best portrait of Pushkin (1827) and drawing teacher of Grand Duke Mikhail, was rumored to have murdered his Roman mistress and model. A long trail of colorful stories followed another prominent artist of the period, the Pole Alexander Orlovsky, a favorite of Grand Duke Konstantin: as a youth he had participated in the Polish uprising against Catherine II, then traveled around Europe with an Italian circus, and supposedly lived a life of drunkenness and revelry.

Settled in St. Petersburg with his French wife, who owned the capital's zoo, Orlovsky became a master of lithography (taking pride in having introduced the technique to Russia). One of Orlovsky's friends was

Pushkin, who mentioned the artist in a frivolous fairy-tale poem, *Ruslan and Lyudmila* (1820): "Take up your quick pencil, / Orlovsky, draw the night and battle." But what "nocturnal battle" did Pushkin have in mind?

Orlovsky's album of erotic drawings, dating to 1810–1821, was reproduced for the first time in Russia in 1991: a penis taking a walk, observed by a lovely lady; a caricature of an official with a phallus for a face; and so on. This made previously secret aspects of Orlovsky's scandalous popularity more obvious.[22]

Briullov's love affairs were also the subject of much talk (a young Frenchwoman drowned herself in the Tiber over him). But most of the gossip was over his family drama. At the age of thirty-nine he married the eighteen-year-old beauty Emilia Timm, daughter of Riga's burgomaster, and on the eve of the wedding learned from her that she was in an incestuous relationship with her father. Nevertheless, Briullov and Emilia wed, but according to the artist, her affair with her father continued.

Briullov applied for a divorce. Learning that Nicholas had taken a personal interest in the case, Briullov wrote an explanatory letter to Count Benckendorff: "The girl's parents and their friends have slandered me in public, giving as the reason for the divorce a completely different circumstance, an alleged argument, which never happened, between me and her father while drinking champagne, as if I were a drunkard."[23] (Briullov's love of wine was no secret. Even Gogol, his devoted admirer, called the artist a "well-known drunk" in a letter to a friend.)

It was very hard to astonish St. Petersburg with excessive drinking: it was the natural attribute of the creative personality, since the legendary times of Lomonosov and Barkov. But incest was another matter, adding spice to the divorce case, and transforming it into a "story."

Lermontov explained what that meant in his unfinished novel about high-society life, *Princess Ligovskaya*: "O! A story is a terrible thing; whether you behaved nobly or vilely, are right or not, could have avoided it or not, but if your name is mixed up in a story, you lose everything: the approval of society, career, respect of friends . . . Being caught up in a story! There can be nothing worse, no matter how the story ends!"

After Nicholas's intervention, Briullov was granted his divorce almost immediately: it was decided that "relations between spouses were extremely sad" and "neither trying church repentance nor living apart for several months can bring about reconciliation." But disapproving glances from high society followed Briullov for a long time.

An interesting phenomenon in Nicholas's strict era was the allure of erotic poetry. Like nineteenth-century Russian erotic drawings, it had its roots in French erotic verse and lithographs.

Ivan Barkov, the scandalous poet of Catherine's day who wrote obscene odes, ballads, and epigrams that circulated in innumerable copies, intrigued Pushkin. Pushkin as a great master of erotic poetry was a topic that in Russia was practically banned for a long time, and even now they try to tiptoe around it: the authorities still believe that writing about it would demean the image of the country's greatest poet.

Yet the erotic line was always important for Pushkin. People sometimes forget that Pushkin's *Ruslan and Lyudmila,* which is now studied in schools, was considered indecent in its day.

The seriously obscene ballad "Barkov's Shadow," which specialists today almost unanimously ascribe to Pushkin, was not published in Russia until 1991—that is, after the collapse of the Soviet regime. In it, the defrocked priest Ebakov ("Fuckov") is visited by the ghost of Barkov, who gives him fantastic sexual powers in exchange for the promise to praise Barkov everywhere.

"Barkov's Shadow," a dirty joke delivered with a non-Barkovian light touch, was a literary lampoon attacking Pushkin's poetic opponents, who are thwarted by the towering figure of the legendary Barkov,

> With lowered pants,
> With fat prick in hand,
> With sagging balls . . .

In this dangerous genre, which requires considerable panache and at the same time self-control to succeed, Pushkin had also a good teacher in the family: his uncle Vassily Pushkin (1766–1830), author of the frivolous poetic masterpiece "Dangerous Neighbor," a hilarious tale of debauchery in a Moscow bordello.

Vassily Pushkin has two buxom whores whiling away the time between clients by reading the works of the author's literary foe: "A real talent will find admirers everywhere!" This sarcastic line became popular. ("Dangerous Neighbor" fared better in Soviet times than "Barkov's Shadow"—it was published several times, perhaps because Lenin once approvingly quoted a line from Vassily Pushkin.)

Young Pushkin's erotic masterpiece was the narrative poem "The Gabrieliad," written in 1821, when he wasn't yet twenty-two. It does not contain a single vulgarity, which makes it all the more alluring. Its offense comes from the blasphemous plot, a parody of the Annunciation: the holy Mary gives herself "in the same day to Satan, archangel, and God."

The poem, like many of its ilk, was circulated widely in anonymous handwritten, samizdat copies. It was forbidden fruit twice over, being both erotic and profane. The thunder struck in 1828 when the serfs of a retired officer reported to the metropolitan of St. Petersburg that their master read them a "blasphemous poem," which turned out to be "The Gabrieliad."

The case reached Nicholas, who inquired whether Pushkin was the author of those sacrilegious verses. Pushkin denied it at first, maintaining that "not in one of my works, even those of which I most repent, is there a trace of sacrilege." But in the end, the poet tried repeating the gambit that he had played two years earlier in his historic conversation with Nicholas at the Kremlin: in a personal letter to the tsar he admitted his authorship. After that Nicholas stopped further investigation: "The case is known to me in detail and completely closed."

As the French ambassador perceptively wrote of Nicholas, "He is appreciative of those who trust him and is hurt when he is not trusted ... Inspiring fear and respect in those around him, he is at the same time a reliable friend and in his heartfelt tenderness often resembles a romantic young woman, although sometimes along with that feeling he displays incredible severity and implacability at the slightest mistake on someone's part."24

It was this somewhat mystifying duality that made Nicholas I so terrifyingly unpredictable (like Stalin later). Just a little more than a month after the audience he granted Pushkin in Moscow on September 8, 1826, which was so favorable for the dissident poet, Nicholas subjected another poet in Moscow to a harsh interrogation with tragic results.

The night of July 28 the young Alexander Polezhaev, a recent graduate of Moscow University and author of the poem "Sashka," a satirical and very licentious imitation of the recently published first chapter of *Eugene Onegin,* was brought to the palace. That nocturnal summons (in fact, an arrest) was the result of an informant's report to Nicholas that students at Moscow University were lewd drunkards, full of dangerous ideas. As an illustration, a manuscript copy of "Sashka" was appended.

Polezhaev's poem, still printed only with cuts in Russia, is a bizarre example of Russian Romanticism, combining openly dissident statements ("Oppressing minds with chains, my stupid Homeland!") with outright obscenity: "Flee, sadness and sorrows, into your fucking mother's cunt! We haven't fucked for such a long time / in such divine company!"

It has been said that Russians take every romantic idea to its extreme by trying to realize it in real life. This certainly holds true for Polezhaev's strange fate. His life was changed irreversibly in 1826 by his encounter with Nicholas. The emperor commanded the poet to read his poem aloud. "I will show you what young men are studying at the university," the tsar said to the minister of education, standing there, white with fear.

When the reading was over, Nicholas addressed the minister again: "What do you have to say? I will put an end to this libertinism, I will root it out!" He turned to Polezhaev: "You need to be punished as an example to others."

Polezhaev was drafted as a soldier and sent with the infantry to the Caucasus, where he spent almost four years fighting in Chechnya and Dagestan, while continuing to write poetry.

In the fall of 1837, eleven years after that meeting with the emperor, Polezhaev died in a military hospital in Moscow, exhausted by tuberculosis and alcoholism. Alexander Herzen described what happened to the poet's body in his book of memoirs, *My Past and Thoughts:* "When a friend came to claim the body for burial, no one knew where it was; the soldier's hospital trades in corpses: it sells them to the university, to the medical academy, it boils down skeletons, and so on. Finally, he found the body of poor Polezhaev in the cellar—it lay beneath others, and rats had gnawed off a foot."

"Sashka" and other unprintable poems by Polezhaev became widely known, especially in military schools. This was an important subculture, since military service was central in the value system of the Russian elite: it was considered the only worthy occupation.

Drinking, debauchery, gambling, coarse and dangerous practical jokes, and hazing were typical military rituals. Dirty poems were an important component, and they were copied down in special underground notebooks. Lermontov had such a notebook with Polezhaev's "Sashka" and other obscene works.

It is not surprising that Lermontov tried his hand at this genre. His so-called "Hussar" poems ("Peterhof Holiday" and "Ulan Woman," among others) were popular at the military school where Lermontov was enrolled and later in the Guards, which were headed by Grand Duke Mikhail.

"Ulan Woman," which graphically depicts group rape, was "the cadets favorite poem; probably even today the old notebook is secretly passed from hand to hand," wrote a friend of Lermontov's in 1856. Surely Grand Duke Mikhail knew the poem. The poet assumed that Mikhail gave it to his brother, Nicholas. But in this case, no punishment followed.

This was because, unlike Polezhaev's works, Lermontov's indecent poetry had no political underpinnings and as such became an accepted part of the Guards' rituals. Lermontov's obscenities were seen as mischief among one's peers, while Polezhaev was an outsider: *quod licet Jovi, non licet bovi.*

But naturally, Lermontov's licentious poems (like similar works by Barkov and Pushkin) could never become part of the official culture. For the Romanovs, these "illegal" works by great poets (which could be read with a grin for relaxation—let's not forget the tsar's collection of erotica) made their creators somewhat unsavory.

Grand Duke Mikhail had Lermontov's "Ulan Woman" in mind when he commented on Lermontov's "The Demon": "We had the Italian Beelzebub, the English Lucifer, the German Mephistopheles, and now there is the Russian Demon. That means there is more deviltry around. I just don't understand who created whom: did Lermontov create the spirit of evil or did the spirit of evil create Lermontov?"[25]

CHAPTER 8

Gogol, Ivanov, Tyutchev, and the End of the Nicholas I Era

The literary sensation of the spring of 1835 was an essay by Vissarion Belinsky, a rising star of Russian criticism, which appeared in issues 7 and 8 of *Telescope,* a Moscow magazine. It was called "On the Russian Novella and the Novellas of Mr. Gogol," and ecstatically praised two recently published collections by the twenty-six-year-old writer, which included his "Notes of a Madman," "Nevsky Prospect," and "Taras Bulba."

Belinsky ended on an extremely high note: "What is Mr. Gogol in our literature? What is his place? . . . At the present time he is the head of literature, head of the poets; he is taking the place left by Pushkin."

This provocative statement (later the critic would be dubbed "furious Vissarion") hit two targets, pulling Pushkin from the literary throne and crowning young Gogol.

In his lifetime, Pushkin was buried more than once as a writer, but Belinsky was a particularly persistent gravedigger, writing that even in 1830 "the Pushkin period ended, since Pushkin himself ended, and with him his influence." And this, even more painful (about the still-living Pushkin): "He died or maybe he's just in a coma for a time."

This was a hatchet job. What could Pushkin have felt reading these vicious attacks, while writing "The Bronze Horseman" and other poetic masterpieces?

Tellingly, Pushkin did not explode and merely rebuked Belinsky ironically in an anonymous note in his magazine, *Contemporary:* "If he combined his independence of thought and wit with more scholarship, more reading, more respect for tradition, more circumspection—in a word, more maturity, we would have a marvelous critic in him."

The extremely ambitious Gogol was naturally very flattered by Belinsky's praise. But it also put him in a corner: Gogol had positioned himself from the start as Pushkin's most loyal student. He could not publicly agree with burying his idol alive.

(The prospect of literally being buried alive had always terrified Gogol. He began his famous "Testament" of 1845 with the following spooky directions: "I will that my body not be buried until clear signs of decomposition appear." Like everything written by Gogol, this strange request can be interpreted not only literally but also symbolically. Gogol explained that he had "witnessed many sad occurrences resulting from our irrational haste in all matters" and expressed the hope that his posthumous voice would remind people of "circumspection," the same word Pushkin used in chiding Belinsky in 1836.)

Russia's Millennium, a monument designed by Mikhail Mikeshin and erected in 1862 in Novgorod, depicts the main figures of Russian history (a list approved by Emperor Alexander II), and the sculptor shows a sorrowful Gogol leaning on a radiant and angelic Pushkin.

Readers are generally aware that Ivan Turgenev, Fedor Dostoevsky, and Leo Tolstoy did not get along. But a legend persists about the incredible closeness of Pushkin and Gogol: after all, Pushkin hailed the young genius from Ukraine, laughing till he dropped at his satirical works and sighing over the elegiac ones, and he gave him the plot ideas for the comedy *The Inspector-General* and the epic *Dead Souls.* But were relations between Pushkin and Gogol truly so idyllic?

Gogol was the sole manufacturer of the legend, and it remains one of his greatest creations. Making his acquaintance in St. Petersburg in May 1831, Gogol sat down to write an article about Pushkin, proclaiming him the chief national poet and adding that "Pushkin is an extraordinary phenomenon and perhaps the unique manifestation of the Russian spirit: this is Russian man in his evolution, the way he might appear two hundred years hence."

This was shameless flattery, of course, but so inspired that it became very popular in Russia and is quoted to this day, when it should be clear that Gogol's prediction was unlikely to ever come true.

There is no doubt that the thirty-two-year-old Pushkin came to like Gogol, ten years younger, an oddly dressed, short provincial with lanky blond hair, pointy nose, and sly gaze. He liked his works, full of attractive Ukrainian exotica, and his raconteur's gift of telling funny stories. (Gogol could tell scabrous jokes just as easily; a friend marveled, "it was Ukrainian *salo* [lard] sprinkled with Aristophanes salt.")[1]

Pushkin immediately hired Gogol to work at his magazine; *Contemporary* needed "golden pens." But this brought about their first serious conflict: Pushkin commissioned a manifesto from Gogol for the first issue, but its cocky tone offended many readers. Consequently, Pushkin had to disassociate himself from the article, deeply wounding Gogol's vanity.

Presumably, it had been Pushkin's little revenge on Gogol for stealing a plot Pushkin had intended to use himself—about a petty crook who arrives in a provincial town where he is taken for an important official from the capital traveling incognito. Laughing, Pushkin told his wife, "You have to be careful around this Ukrainian: he steals from you, and you can't even complain."[2]

Gogol wrote the comedy on Pushkin's theme, *The Inspector-General,* in record time, and immediately started reading it in influential salons in the capital, hoping to get it onstage faster this way. Gogol was a master manipulator, having learned early in his youth the secrets of "reading minds, influencing hearts, and flattering with tenderness" and developing a virtuoso ability "to subordinate other people's wills," according to a memoirist.

Through Zhukovsky's good offices, Gogol managed to interest Nicholas I in *The Inspector-General*—the tsar liked it "very much."[3] That was the green light for the play: it sailed past all the dangerous censorship reeds and was quickly accepted by the Imperial Alexandrinsky Theater. From its completion (on December 4, 1835) to its premiere on the country's main stage (on April 19, 1836) took only four and a half months, and a month after that the play was presented in Moscow, too.

At the very same time that *The Inspector-General* was being rehearsed onstage at the Alexandrinsky Theater with Gogol present, the composer Glinka was in the building lobby, working with the soloists and chorus on his new opera *A Life for the Tsar*, while the opera theater was being renovated.

The patriotic grand opera about the rise of the Romanov dynasty and a biting satire attacking the Russian bureaucracy were both supported by Nicholas I, who brought them to the stages of his theaters—evidence of how broadly the tsar interpreted the ideology of "Orthodoxy, Autocracy, and Nationality." (Nicholas also liked two other great Russian comedies that scared his censors: Alexander Griboedov's *Woe from Wit* and Alexander Ostrovsky's *Don't Get into Someone Else's Sleigh*.)

At the premiere, Nicholas and his heir, the future Alexander II, sat in the royal box, laughing wholeheartedly and applauding demonstratively, prompting the applause of the aristocrats who had filled the hall, knowing that the tsar would attend.

Some ministers hissed angrily, "Why did we bother to come for this stupid farce? As if there is a city like this in Russia! Couldn't Gogol portray one decent, honest man?" But because the monarch liked the play, they could not express themselves openly. Still, it was a mystery to many courtiers why Nicholas had approved a play that mocked the authorities so blatantly.

When the performance was over, the actors heard the emperor's loud voice as he came onstage from his box: "Everyone got what he deserved in this play, and I more than the others!"[4] The leading actors were given a raise and valuable presents. Gogol, who had been paid 2,500 rubles for the play, also received a gift from the tsar.

This was the first of the financial handouts from the imperial treasury that Gogol would request and receive until the end of his life. Pushkin asked for money with great reluctance, considering it extremely humiliating. Gogol, much more practical, was a great fund-raiser and usually got what he wanted (mostly with the help of Zhukovsky).

Pushkin did not show up at the premiere of *The Inspector-General:* was he demonstrating his unhappiness over the stolen plot? The fact is that Pushkin suddenly became alienated from Gogol, and at the very moment when the young writer was hysterical. After the premiere, Gogol fell into a panicked state: "Everyone is against me. Esteemed officials scream that nothing is sacred to me. The police are against me, the merchants are against me, the writers are against me. If not for the high protection of the Sovereign, my play would never have been staged. Now I see what it means to be a comedy writer. The slightest hint of truth—and everyone rises up against you, not just one person, but entire strata."

So Gogol took Pushkin's coolness—perhaps overreacting—as betrayal. Six weeks after the premiere, in June 1836, Gogol fled Russia for Europe, whining to a friend, "A contemporary writer, a comedy writer, an observer of morals must be far away. No man is a prophet in his own land." From Hamburg, Gogol complained in a letter to Zhukovsky, "I did not have time and could not say good-bye even to Pushkin; of course, that is his fault." On that bitter note, Gogol's personal relationship with Pushkin ended.

In Europe, Gogol learned of Pushkin's death. From that moment, Gogol seemed to forget how Pushkin had injured his feelings. He began integrating Pushkin into his own mythos, sending letters from Rome to various Russian friends, all with much the same message: "My loss is greater than anyone else's . . . My life, my highest pleasure died with him . . . I never undertook anything, I never wrote anything without his advice. Anything that is good in me I owe to him."

Although settling in Rome, Gogol did not become a dissident. On the contrary, he quickly distanced himself from the satiric extremes of his play and embraced the Nicholas I–Uvarov ideological triad, "Orthodoxy, Autocracy, and Nationality." In fact, he was the first great Russian writer to accept this doctrine fully and unconditionally. (The second was Dosto-evsky.)

Gogol's evolution was apparently sincere. While the path had been cleared somewhat for him by the late Pushkin, Gogol went much further.

This is Gogol on Orthodoxy: "Reason does not give man full ability to strive forward. There is a higher ability; its name is wisdom, and only Christ can give it to us." Gogol explains that the poet "better than others hears God's hand in everything that happens in Russia, and feels the proximity of another Kingdom. That is why our poets' sound turns biblical."

On autocracy, Gogol cites what he allegedly heard from Pushkin: "The state without a plenipotentiary monarch is an automaton: at best it could achieve what the United States has achieved. And what is the United States? Carrion; a man there is so worn down that he's not worth a shelled egg. A state without a plenipotentiary monarch is like an orchestra without a Kapellmeister."

Gogol hailed the patriotic peasant Ivan Susanin, the hero of Glinka's opera *A Life for the Tsar:* "No royal house began as unusually as the house of Romanov. Its beginning was already an exploit of love. The last and lowliest subject in the state laid his life down in order to give us the Tsar, and with this pure sacrifice he tied inseparably the Tsar with his subjects. Love entered our blood, and it bound all of us to the Tsar."

The trickiest part for Gogol was to preach about nationality and the Russian national idea, precisely because he was living in the West. Gogol found wiggle room in an explanation (with Solzhenitsyn-like overtones): "I knew that I was not traveling in order to enjoy foreign places but rather to suffer—as if I had a premonition that I would learn Russia's value only outside Russia and would add to my love for her from afar."

For Russian liberals and Westernizers, all this sounded like hypocritical drivel. They reacted with fury to Gogol's book *Selected Passages from Correspondence with Friends,* published in early 1847 in St. Petersburg, and the source of almost all the citations above. The harshest criticism came from the influential progressive critic Belinsky.

Dying of consumption, the thirty-six-year-old Belinsky was being treated in Europe. He wrote Gogol a long scathing letter, which turned into his *profession de foi.* The dissident Herzen printed the text for the first time in 1855 in his antigovernment almanac, *Polar Star,* which he published in London. In Russia, the letter was considered revolutionary propaganda and banned.

Pavel Annenkov, who was a friend of both Gogol and Belinsky, recalled how the critic, emaciated and resembling an old man with his deathly pale face, said in his muffled voice as he sat down to write his letter (which, in Annenkov's words, "sounded throughout intellectual Russia like a trumpet call"), "What can I do? We must use every method to save people from a madman, even if it's Homer himself who went mad."[5]

Imagine Gogol's reaction to his former apologist addressing him this way: "Preacher of the knout, apostle of ignorance, proponent of obscurantism, panegyrist of Tatar mores—what are you doing! Look down at your feet—you are standing at the abyss . . . That you align yourself with the Orthodox Church, I can understand: it always supported the knout and despotism; but why did you drag in Christ here?"

In publishing his *Correspondence with Friends,* Gogol wanted to "endow dissolute Russian life at last with a code of great rules and unshakable axioms that would help organize its inner world as a model for all other nations," said Annenkov. The book consisted of his real letters (naturally, expanded and edited) and essays especially written for the book.

Gogol turned out to be a powerful preacher. The letters have the best qualities of Gogol's prose, making it so difficult to translate: they are vivid, musical, with their own rhythm and imbued with passion for Russia, whose salvation Gogol saw in Christian self-betterment.

Belinsky, for whom purely literary qualities were always less important than ideology, disagreed with Gogol. "Russia sees its salvation not in mysticism, not in asceticism, not in pietism, but in the successes of civilization, enlightenment, humanism. It does not need preaching (it has heard plenty), or prayers (it has repeated enough of them), but the awakening in the people of human dignity, lost for so many centuries in mud and manure."

The dying but still fiery Belinsky tore apart the ideological triad of Nicholas-Uvarov-Gogol, in passim taking a swipe angrily (and unfairly) at Pushkin; he declared to Gogol that in Russia "the popularity drops quickly of great talents that give themselves sincerely or insincerely to the service of 'Orthodoxy, Autocracy, and Nationality.' A striking example is Pushkin, who needed only to write two or three sucking-up poems and don the court uniform to lose the people's love!"

Of course, Pushkin had never lost the people's love, whatever that may be; his reputation suffered only in a small albeit influential circle of progressive intelligentsia, whose spokesman was Belinsky.

For that radical group, Gogol's evolution, which began with the colorful, quasifolkloric "Evenings on a Farm Near Dikanka," then moved through his mystical and tragic "St. Petersburg Stories" ("Nevsky Prospect," "Notes of a Madman," "The Nose," "The Overcoat") to the powerful, bitter satire of *The Inspector-General* and volume 1 of *Dead Souls,* came crashing down in the Christian sermonizing of *Selected Passages from Correspondence with Friends.*

Progressives, like their leader Belinsky, saw Gogol's ideological shift as either a bizarre psychological digression or the desire to suck up to Nicholas, whose financial aid to the writer was widely known (Gogol proudly told his friends about it). But in fact, Gogol's transformation was organic, if ultimately tragic.

Gogol always felt what he called "a passion for painting." He took drawing classes at the Academy of Arts and loved making "architectural landscapes": churches, temples, ruins. He wrote two important pieces about contemporary Russian artists: the essay "The Last Day of Pompeii," written in 1834 in response to the notorious painting by Briullov on exhibition in St. Petersburg, and "Historical Painter Ivanov," written in 1846 about Gogol's friend Alexander Ivanov and his enormous canvas *Christ Appearing to the People,* created in 1837–1858 and now regarded as one of the greatest nineteenth-century Russian paintings.

The Romantic Briullov attracted the twenty-five-year-old art lover Gogol as an exotic figure and as a master celebrated in Europe, whose style—striking composition, vivid contrasts, bold chiaroscuro, and hot colors—were close to Gogol's early writings.

In his essay, Gogol compared *The Last Day of Pompeii* to opera. But even then Gogol was expressing some doubts on the value of "operatic effects" in art: "In the hands of a real talent they are true and can turn man into a giant; but used by a pretender, they are disgusting to connoisseurs."

Reaching for a higher spiritual plane, while rejecting everything "false," brought Gogol to a friendship in 1838 with Ivanov, thirty-two and living, like Gogol, in Rome.

Like his new friend, Ivanov was strange and rather mysterious ("helpless and weak, one of those who think with their heart,"[6] as the poet Rainer-Maria Rilke later described him). He was the complete opposite of the flashy, confident epicurean Briullov.

In his St. Petersburg period, Gogol envied Briullov's unprecedented access to the emperor and high society, so tempting—and unattainable—to the provincial Gogol. Briullov liked Gogol, but regarded him a bit down his nose. The innocent and naive Ivanov was another matter completely; when Gogol arrived in Rome, already a maître, he became the painter's guru and patron.

In Rome both Gogol and Ivanov were toiling on their magnum opuses: the writer was wrestling with *Dead Souls,* the artist with *Christ Appearing to the People.* Both came to regard their work as a spiritual exploit, a religious service to the Russian national idea. Both unmarried (and not attracted by women), Gogol and Ivanov labored far from Russia, in the colorful world of Rome that had enchanted them and was such a contrast to their previous life in the severe Russian capital. In Rome, Gogol and Ivanov were the central figures in the small colony of Russian artists studying in Italy on stipends from the Imperial Academy of Arts.

Short Ivanov in those years was "rather portly, with a little beard, sad brown eyes and a typical Slavic face."[7] Gogol still enjoyed eating well and drinking in good company, preferring pasta with grated cheese and red wine. He liked crostata with cherries. He learned to add rum to warmed goat's milk, calling the drink "gogol-mogol." (He liked to joke, "Gogol loves gogol-mogol.")

But gradually his mood and health deteriorated: he complained of migraines, pains in his stomach, nervous fits, and faints, growing gloomy and cranky. He became unbearable at his favorite taverna, sending a dish back two or three times in a row, until the waiters refused to serve him: "Signor Niccolò, there is no pleasing you, and the owner charges us for the dishes you send back."

Strangely, Ivanov's health declined in parallel with Gogol's: he too lost weight, turned pale, and became paranoid. Turgenev suggested that in Rome Ivanov "went a bit crazy: the twenty-five years of solitude took their toll." In a confidential letter to his friend Annenkov, the writer described how Ivanov began to assure him, "turning white and laughing nervously that he was being poisoned with a special potion, therefore he often did not eat."[8] Ivanov was afraid to drink water in taverns and preferred to fill bottles from fountains.

In his essay on Ivanov, Gogol praised him as the Russian Raphael. He described him as a man who "was dead to everything in the world except his work." That was now the model of a truly artistic life for Gogol, not the glamorous existence of his former idol, Briullov.

In the end, Gogol did not finish writing *Dead Souls* and Ivanov did not complete *Christ Appearing to the People.* Even unfinished, these monumental works occupy a central place in the panorama of Russian nineteenth-century culture.

A painterly approach colors *Dead Souls,* and Ivanov's canvas is dominated by a religious idea. Rilke, with his subtle feeling for Russian culture, described this idea as "profound Russian piety that demanded its embodiment in painting."

Both Gogol and Ivanov became outsiders for the Russian establishment, and yet Tsar Nicholas I supported both. In 1845, in Rome on state business, the tsar visited Ivanov's studio; he had been warned that the painter was a "crazy mystic," but he found his magnum opus "wonderful" (the heir, Alexander, liked it very much too).⁹ Aid from the imperial treasury eased Ivanov's lot in Rome.

Now the final act of Gogol's tragedy was starting. Gogol had worked on *Dead Souls* since 1835. The writer always said that the plot (like that of *The Inspector-General*) had been "a gift" from Pushkin. By making Pushkin the godfather of *Dead Souls*, Gogol positioned his novel as the poet's "sacred will" and thus raised its status.

The plot is extremely simple: the crook Chichikov travels around the Russian provinces, visiting local landowners to buy up their serfs—not living serfs, but dead ones. These serfs, referred to in legal documents as "souls," had not yet been removed from the tax rolls and therefore could be used fraudulently as collateral for loans from the state treasury, which Chichikov planned to do.

Nothing much happens in the book: Chichikov travels from one place to another, encountering various bizarre landowners. But Gogol turns those owners of "dead souls" into unforgettable characters whose names have become symbols in Russia. (As, of course, did the book's title.)

Gogol's concept of the book kept changing, and eventually he came to see it as something like Dante's *Divine Comedy* or even Homer's *Odyssey*. (He was often compared with Homer later by his fervent admirers in Russia.) Gogol decided that his work was not a mere novel, but a "poem." This again connected him with Pushkin: "This work of mine is his creation. He made me swear to write it."

In 1842, with the help of court circles, Gogol managed to get around the censors and published the first volume of *Dead Souls* in Russia. "Writers, journalists, book sellers, lay people—all say that there hasn't been so much hullabaloo in the literary world in a long time, with some reviling your work and others praising it,"[10] a friend wrote to Gogol from Moscow.

Dostoevsky later confirmed this: "This was the way young people were then; two or three would get together: 'Why don't we read Gogol, gentlemen!' and they would sit and read aloud to one another, perhaps the whole night through." But such literary acclaim was no longer enough for Gogol. He perceived himself as a prophet exiled from his homeland, whose writing could miraculously transform all of life in Russia: "Like a silent monk, he lives in the world without belonging to it, his pure, unsullied soul conversing only with God."

When this ideal author (in fact, Gogol's self-portrait) appeals to Russia, "The sermon will pierce the soul and will not fall on barren soil. Like an angel's grief, our poetry will flare up and strike all the strings that there may be in the Russian person, bringing holiness into the most coarsened (read: 'dead') souls."

In the summer of 1851, Gogol informed friends that he had finished the second volume of *Dead Souls* and began reading chapters to them. He planned a trilogy, something like the "Inferno," "Purgatory," and "Paradise" of *The Divine Comedy.* The friends were impressed, but Gogol, hurt by the failure of *Correspondence with Friends,* was dubious.

He had always suffered bouts of profound melancholy. The condition was exacerbated by his return to Russia in 1848, where everything—climate, landscape, food, authorities—depressed him: "You feel that Russia is not a brotherly warm place, but a cold blizzardy post station, where the station master, totally indifferent to everything, has only one curt reply, 'No horses!'"

Gogol stayed at the house of his Moscow friend Count Alexander Tolstoy. He stopped writing, read only religious books, went to church assiduously, spent his nights in prayer, and imposed a debilitating fast upon himself: he ate once a day, and then just a few spoons of oatmeal soup made with water or cabbage broth. He refused any other food, explaining that it made his "intestines twist."

On Sunday, February 10, 1852, Gogol asked Count Tolstoy to keep the manuscript of the second volume, explaining, "I have moments when I want to burn all of it. But I would regret it. I think there is something good in there."[11] The count refused: he did not want to feed Gogol's depression.

Two days later, on Tuesday morning, the count entered Gogol's room and found him weeping by the stove, where the last manuscript pages were burning: "Look what I did! I wanted to destroy a few things, which I set aside, but I burned everything! How powerful the devil is—look what he made me do! . . . Now it's all lost."

Tolstoy, realizing in horror that Gogol had burned the second volume of *Dead Souls,* tried to calm him down: "But you can remember it, can't you?" Gogol stopped weeping. "Yes, I can, I can; it's all in my head." (He used to read entire chapters from the manuscript to his friends by heart, like poetry.)

But Gogol had no strength or desire to work or even to live. He never left his room again, lying on the couch with eyes shut and worry beads in his hands, no longer eating or interacting with people.

A week passed this way. The count called in the best doctors in Moscow. A concilium gathered: six doctors examined and palpated the suffering patient (his stomach was so soft and empty that they could feel the vertebrae of his spine through it) and decided that he needed to be bled. They attached six large leeches to his nose, overcoming his resistance.

Gogol groaned and screamed, "Don't touch me! Leave me alone!" But they held his hands so that he would not tear off the leeches. They put a mustard plaster on his feet and ice on his head, and poured medicine into his mouth. After a few days of this torture, Gogol breathed his last, with the words "How sweet to die."

.   .   .

Gogol's death at age forty-two stunned the Russian intellectual elite. Turgenev, then thirty-three, proclaimed in the obituary published by the *Moscow Gazette,* "Yes, he died, that man whom we now have the bitter right given by death to call great; a man whose name marked an era in the history of our literature."

It was soon discovered that Gogol had kept rough drafts of five chapters from the second volume of *Dead Souls,* which were published three and a half years later (to mixed reviews). In the meantime, the authorities reacted with bewilderment: how should they respond to Gogol's demise? Fifteen years earlier, Nicholas I made sure that Pushkin's end was presented as the death of a Christian. Why did he not want to use the death of the greatest advocate of "Orthodoxy, Autocracy, and Nationality" for the same propaganda purposes? Many felt that Gogol died "a Christian, saint, and monk." (A posthumous inventory of his estate showed that all his possessions were worth a miserable 43 rubles, 88 kopecks.)

Paradoxically, Gogol's evolution to fanatical Christianity and boundless loyalty to the tsar was too extreme and off-putting to the authorities in Russia. While demanding fealty to the state, they never trusted real fanatics and feared them. The administration needed dutiful servants, not idealistic knights on white chargers.

The authorities banned all obituaries for Gogol, and the tsar had Turgenev arrested for a month and then sent into exile to his country estate in Orlov Province for publishing one. (During his confinement, Turgenev wrote his powerful antiserfdom story "Mumu," the drama of a deaf-mute servant of a cruel owner, who forced him to drown his beloved dog.)

This fear of uncontrollable, "freelance" ideological activity explained why Nicholas and his ministers so disliked the Slavophiles, an influential group of Moscow intellectuals who propagated a romantic theory that Russia should not emulate the West, but instead pursue its unique and independent cultural and political path.

The Slavophiles also believed in "Orthodoxy, Autocracy, and Nationality," but for them it was not a bureaucratic formula but a broad philosophical foundation for a national culture. They therefore criticized what they saw as ossified aspects of the contemporary Russian state. Calling for a free, nationally oriented Russian culture, the Slavophiles challenged the official line, but also the ideas of such radical antimonarchist Westernizers as Belinsky and Herzen.

The great Slavophile poet Alexei Khomyakov proclaimed that Gogol, Ivanov, and Glinka were the Holy Trinity of truly Slavophile artists. But the supreme power was just as uncomfortable with Alexander Ivanov as it was with Gogol. When the artist returned to St. Petersburg in 1858, after thirty years in Italy, the authorities did not know what to do with this mad mystic who babbled about the messianic destiny of the "Slavic tribe."

Ivanov did not want to accept official commissions, which made him clearly unfit for service. Feeling injured and snubbed, he died two months after returning to his homeland, just two weeks short of his fifty-second birthday.

In the summer of 1844, Nicholas read an anonymous brochure in French, just published in Munich. It expressed bold ideas about Russia's modern geopolitical role in Europe. The author wrote that as a result of Russia's victory over Napoleon, Western Europe ("The Europe of Charles the Great") was at last face-to-face with Eastern Europe ("The Europe of Peter the Great"). This Eastern Europe, with Russia as its heart and soul, was the legitimate heir of Byzantium and must make one more decisive breakthrough, vanquishing Turkey and establishing hegemony in the Middle East.

Nicholas I told Count Benckendorff, chief of the gendarmes and his closest adviser, that he "found all my thoughts"[12] in that brochure and commanded him to find out the author. The omniscient Benckendorff already had: it was written and printed by someone he knew well, Fedor Tyutchev, forty years old, a former Russian diplomat in Munich and Turin, an amateur poet who had been living abroad for twenty-two years.

Tyutchev, Yevgeny Baratynsky, and Afanasy Fet are the three great Russian poets of the nineteenth century, unheralded in the West but revered by educated Russians. Leo Tolstoy rated Tyutchev higher than

Pushkin. (Joseph Brodsky sometimes held Baratynsky at that level, while being more skeptical about Tyutchev's standing.)

When Tolstoy read Tyutchev's poetry aloud to his guests, he invariably wept: in his sophisticated proto-Symbolist philosophical miniatures, Tyutchev captured the most subtle emotional nuances, not unlike Tolstoy's prose. Tyutchev began writing poetry at the age of ten, and when he was thirty-three, in 1836, Pushkin printed twenty-four of his poems in *Contemporary.*

Tyutchev called his poems "scribbles," writing them hurriedly on scraps of paper that his wife then gathered up. His output was not large—around four hundred little poems over sixty-nine years of life, including *pièces d'occasion,* epigrams, and such.

He published his first book of verse when he was in his fifties, yielding to the urging of his friend Turgenev, who edited the publication. Tyutchev considered his true calling to be politics and political writing, and that is how Nicholas I noticed him.

Nicholas appreciated political poetry when it suited his propaganda goals. When he suppressed the 1831 Polish rebellion against Russian occupiers and Pushkin and Zhukovsky celebrated the victory with ultrapatriotic poems, the emperor issued the poems instantly in a special edition published by the military printing press.

At the time, the West supported the Poles. Western parliamentarians and journalists were especially vociferous. Pushkin's poems, defending Russia's position, was addressed to them. He intended to publish his anti-Western poems in the Paris press, but failed: Pushkin did not have the necessary contacts.

Tyutchev, on the other hand, was a professional diplomat with a vast network of influential European intellectuals (he was friends with the philosopher Friedrich Schelling and the poet Heinrich Heine) and a good understanding of their psychology. Nicholas decided it would be a terrible waste not to use such a person for pro-Russian propaganda in the West, especially since that was Tyutchev's ardent wish.

·   ·   ·

On the emperor's orders, Tyutchev was quickly reinstated to service in the Ministry of Foreign Affairs. He made a strange official. Of medium height, frail, with a pale, clean-shaven face and unruly, prematurely gray hair, carelessly dressed, seemingly clumsy and distracted, Tyutchev spent all his time in St. Petersburg's high-society salons.

He spoke French better than Russian and, eagerly turning the conversation to foreign policy, would instantly become the center of attention at every gathering, so witty and to the point were his opinions.

Seemingly casual improvisations, his political aphorisms and *bon mots* spread throughout the capital and regularly appeared in dispatches of foreign ambassadors in St. Petersburg. Tyutchev's commentaries were all the more effective because they so little resembled the dull official statements of the authorities. One perceptive observer noted that these "spontaneous" chats in society were Tyutchev's "real job."[13]

Tyutchev effectively executed delicate special assignments for the tsar. Nicholas was terribly upset by the French revolution of 1848. The emperor was prepared to play his assumed role of gendarme of Europe and defender of European monarchy. Tyutchev wrote a large article in French, *"La Russie et la révolution,"* stating that the only obstacle to a European revolutionary explosion was the Russian "Christian Empire."

Nicholas read it in manuscript and had it printed in Paris as "Mémoire présenté à l'empereur Nicolas depuis la révolution de février, par un russe, employé supérieur aux affaires étrangères," in an extremely limited edition of twelve copies. Tyutchev's brochure was sent by special channels to the political leaders of France, including Louis Napoleon Bonaparte, president of the republic. The French correctly regarded this as a "quasi-official document," and it was widely quoted in the European press.

The international situation was unfavorable for Russia then. France, with Napoleon's defeat in the War of 1812 a distant memory, wanted to limit Russia's role as arbiter in European affairs; so did England. Both countries were worried by Russia's pressure on Turkey, which Nicholas I called "the sick man of Europe." England feared that if Russia affirmed itself in the Balkans, home to millions of Orthodox Slavs, it would be a major threat. Anti-Russian rhetoric ran high in the European press.

On the Russian side, the Slavophiles tried to fire up Nicholas's hidden pan-Slavic ambitions, which Tyutchev supported. In 1849 he wrote "The Dawn":

> Arise, Rus! The hour is nigh!
> Arise for the sake of Christ's service!
> Isn't it time to make the sign of the cross
> And toll the bell of Tsargrad?

Tyutchev and his fellow thinkers did not limit their goals to the taking of Tsargrad (as Russians called Constantinople). This is how he defined the borders of the "Russian Kingdom" in another poem of that year, "Russian Geography": "From the Nile to the Neva, from Elba to China, from the Volga to the Euphrates, from the Ganges to the Danube."

Such voracious geographical appetites struck even Nicholas as excessive, so this poem remained in manuscript. Later, when the emperor read Tyutchev's poem "Prophecy" in *Contemporary,* in which the poet predicted that Nicholas would triumphantly enter St. Sophia in Constantinople as "All-Slavic Tsar," the monarch crossed out the lines and wrote, "Such phrases must not be allowed."[14] Nicholas's decision was handed down to the minister of foreign affairs.

But despite Tyutchev's political extremes, Nicholas valued him highly as an agent of influence. In 1853, on the eve of armed conflict with Turkey, Tyutchev was sent to Paris on a special assignment to work on French journalists, who were almost all in favor of Turkey in the conflict with Russia. The French ambassador in St. Petersburg warned his government about this, advising that Tyutchev "must be kept under observation," which the French police did.

The British ambassador also informed his department about Tyutchev's assignment in Europe, adding, "One gets the impression that at the present moment the Russian government is making great efforts to influence the public press in foreign nations and, as is known, has spent significant sums on this."[15]

Equipped with royal subsidies, Tyutchev did what he could in Paris. It was too little, too late: no propaganda moves on the part of the Russian government could prevent England and France from siding with Turkey in the coming war.

In September 1854, the sixty-thousand-strong Anglo-French expeditionary corps landed in the Crimea and with the Turks besieged Sevastopol, an important naval base on the Black Sea. From the start, the war did not go the way Nicholas wanted. He had overestimated Russian military might. Nicholas was certain that in his thirty years on the throne, he had turned Russia into an undefeatable colossus. Suddenly, he discovered that the colossus had feet of clay.

Nicholas had almost a million armed men. But the Russian soldiers used obsolete rifles and artillery, the provisioning was terrible (there wasn't a single railroad connecting continental Russia with Sevastopol), and the Russian sailing fleet could not compete with European steamships.

The war turned into a competition of technology and, more broadly, of economies; serf-holding, backward Russia could not beat the advanced West. The bravery of the Russian soldiers was of little help.

The bad news from Sevastopol plunged the proud and severe Nicholas into a deep depression. That magnificent giant, fifty-eight years old, with a rich commanding voice that sometimes made even experienced officers faint, now wept like a child when he received dispatches about defeats in the Crimea, and at night he prayed fervently, bowing low before the icons in the Winter Palace chapel.[16] The once ironclad health of the emperor collapsed along with his faith in Russia's military power.

Nicholas I burned up in a few days, dying February 18, 1855; the official cause of death was pneumonia. It came so unexpectedly that there was talk in St. Petersburg that he had committed suicide by poison.

That conspiratorial theory, so typical for Russian history, with its secrets and mysterious deaths of national leaders, is still kept alive by several suspicious circumstances: the suddenness of Nicholas's death, its coincidence with bad news from the Crimean front, and the contradictions in the official reports on the emperor's final illness.

Dying in the Winter Palace, where he lay on a simple iron bed under a soldier's overcoat rather than a blanket, Nicholas I spoke haltingly with a rasp to his heir, Grand Duke Alexander: "I hand over command, unfortunately not in the good order I would have liked, leaving you many worries and concerns."

Those bitter words concerned the military and diplomatic situation, the only one that worried Nicholas. The failure in the war in the Crimea revealed the great vulnerability of his empire.

Nicholas had no idea that he was leaving yet another legacy to his son—a group of young men, his subjects, who would constitute the glory and pride of nineteenth-century Russian culture. They were Ivan Turgenev, thirty-six, Afanasy Fet, thirty-four, Fedor Dostoevsky and Nikolai Nekrasov, both thirty-three, Alexander Ostrovsky, thirty-one, and Leo Tolstoy, twenty-six.

All these young lions formed in Nicholas's reign, when, according to yet another great contemporary of Nicholas I, the dissident Alexander Herzen, "educated Russia, with a ball and chain, eked out a pathetic existence in profound, humiliating, insulting silence."

This polemical evaluation of cultural life under Nicholas as an intellectual desert was taken up by Soviet propaganda and survived for three-quarters of a century, turning into dogma. The real situation was not quite so black-and-white.

Let us recall such cultural titans as Pushkin, Gogol, and the composer Glinka, who all interacted with Nicholas. It is true that Catherine II was in close contact with the poet Derzhavin, and Alexander I with Karamzin and Zhukovsky. But in those days the Russian cultural elite was a compact group and its members naturally were part of the court circle as well.

The situation under Nicholas I was different: Glinka and Gogol had no entrée into royal circles. Their promonarchist views were not the result of special status in the court, but rather were formed at least in part thanks to the emperor's skillful attitude and personal attention.

It should be no surprise that his contemporaries often had diametrically opposed views of Nicholas, influenced by their political convictions. In the opinion of conservative writer and critic Konstantin Leontiev, Nicholas I was the "ideal autocrat the likes of which history has not produced in a long time."[17]

The radical liberal Herzen, on the contrary, saw in Nicholas misfortune for Russia and considered him one of the "military leaders who have lost everything civilian, everything human, and have only one passion left—to rule; narrow mind, no heart at all."

Nicholas I's historical standing was hopelessly damaged by the humiliating failure in the Crimean War. Even the monarchist and nationalist Tyutchev was disillusioned in his former idol.

Since Nicholas's own main criterion for a nation's grandeur was its military might, the severity of this judgment was warranted. The army created by Nicholas, his beloved child, did not stand the test. However, the ideological triad "Orthodoxy, Autocracy, and Nationality," developed under his aegis, proved to be much stronger. While sometimes vanishing from the cultural horizon, it has survived in its basic form to this day. It was used, with modifications to suit changing political realities, under Alexander II, Alexander III, and Nicholas II, and later even by Joseph Stalin, Leonid Brezhnev, and Vladimir Putin. For the Soviet leaders, orthodoxy was the Communist ideology, autocracy—the rule of the Party—and nationality remained. Under Putin, the triad morphed again: Russian Orthodoxy was returned, autocracy became paternalistic rule, and nationality persisted as nationalism.

PART IV

CHAPTER 9

Alexander II, Tolstoy, Turgenev, and Dostoevsky

Alexander II, the son of Nicholas I, who took the throne on February 19, 1855, had been prepared for the role of monarch—thanks to the poet Zhukovsky—as none of his predecessors or descendants were or would be.

Zhukovsky oversaw the heir's education for twelve years, from 1826 until 1838. All the classes throughout the period were guided by his detailed plan, approved by Nicholas. Zhukovsky concentrated on Russian literature and Russian history, and other experienced instructors taught the many other subjects.

Zhukovsky, with the tsar's support, declared an active, energetic monarch the goal of his training, and developed a rather tight schedule for Alexander: reveille at six a.m., lights out at ten p.m. After prayers and breakfast, there were five hours of classes (with an hour break), two hours for lunch (with a walk and rest before and after), more classes from five to seven, then gymnastics and dinner. Before bed, there was time for reflection and diary writing, which Zhukovsky considered mandatory.

Nicholas believed that as a Romanov, the heir "must be military to the bone, otherwise he will be lost in our age."[1] Zhukovsky disagreed: "The passion for military craft will cramp his soul: he will become accustomed to see the people as his regiment and his Homeland as a barracks."[2]

Following Zhukovsky's curriculum, Alexander read *The Iliad, Don Quixote,* and *Gulliver's Travels* and, in Russian literature, works by Karamzin and Pushkin; once, Pushkin read aloud his ultrapatriotic poem "To the Slanderers of Russia" in the heir's presence. Zhukovsky and the fabulist Krylov read and explained their own writings to him.

The young heir learned to shoot and fence, and he rode well and danced gracefully. Like his father, he liked to draw (especially sketches of new military uniforms) and loved opera (especially Rossini and Glinka, for his *A Life for the Tsar*). Alexander and his two classmates published a children's magazine called "The Ant Hill," which was supervised by Nicholas I personally.

Alexander was brought up to be rather broad-minded with a European worldview (he knew English, French, German, and Polish), and he grew up to be much milder and more compassionate than his severe father. Zhukovsky enjoyed a good cry (a tribute to Romantic ideals) and taught his pupil not to be ashamed of tears. The poet wanted to form a clement sovereign. Zhukovsky had released his serfs, a rare gesture that even Pushkin had not attempted. He taught Alexander that serfdom was evil.

Tellingly, Nicholas did not oppose this. He had long contemplated emancipation of the serfs but never took the step: he was afraid it would shatter the empire. Nicholas refused to pardon the Decembrists he had exiled to Siberia, despite the requests from Zhukovsky and others. But he listened to his son. When Alexander and Zhukovsky and their retinue traveled through Russia in 1837 (part of the heir's education), Alexander met the Decembrists in distant Siberia and was horrified by their ordeal. He asked his father to at least ameliorate their living conditions, which was done. (Later, when he became tsar, his first act was to pardon the Decembrists.)

Zhukovsky considered bringing up Alexander to the Russian throne as the most important work of his life—his best poem. In 1841 he retired from his post as tutor and moved to Germany, having married a Romantic maiden almost a third his age. After bearing two children, his wife fell into a deep depression (it was hereditary), spending weeks at a time in bed. Zhukovsky lived in despair: "My poor wife is like a skeleton, and I can't alleviate her suffering: there is nothing to relieve her of her black thoughts!"

Zhukovsky went blind, but continued to record his poems with a machine he invented. He died in Baden-Baden at the age of sixty-nine. His body was shipped to St. Petersburg, where he was buried at the Alexander Nevsky Monastery, next to the grave of Karamzin. The proximity was symbolic. If not for Pushkin, Zhukovsky and Karamzin would be considered the fathers of the new Russian literature: Karamzin of prose, and Zhukovsky of poetry. The rare combination of talent, grace, and kindness that these two men embodied was probably not seen again in Russian culture until Anton Chekhov.

On February 6, 1856, the writer Dmitry Grigorovich went to a dinner given by *Contemporary* (arguably the best Russian magazine of the time). The monthly dinners celebrating the latest issue were a tradition started by the editor, the great poet Nikolai Nekrasov, at the helm from 1847.

Grigorovich was bringing another of the magazine's authors with him—the clumsy, ugly, and passive-aggressive Count Leo Tolstoy. The twenty-seven-year-old count had already published several prose pieces in *Contemporary*, including the novellas *Childhood* and *Adolescence* and sketches from his experiences in the Crimean War, but he still did not feel like an insider.

On the way, the gentlemanly Grigorovich gave the grumpy Tolstoy advice on how to behave at the dinner—not in the sense of social etiquette (the magazine's crowd did not care about that) but in terms of political correctness. Grigorovich worried that the young count, the only of the magazine's authors to sport a military uniform, had an embarrassing inclination to shoot from the hip, making provocative pronouncements—for example, that Shakespeare was nothing more than an empty phrasemonger.

Grigorovich particularly asked Tolstoy not to berate George Sand, for he had often heard the count attack the celebrated French novelist and feminist. They "fanatically adored" her at *Contemporary*, Nekrasov and his closest associate, the radical critic Nikolai Chernyshevsky, and the magazine's constant contributor, liberal writer Ivan Turgenev.

Later Grigorovich recalled, "At first, the dinner went well; Tolstoy was rather taciturn, but toward the end he gave in. Hearing praise for Sand's latest novel, he abruptly declared that he hated her, adding that the heroines of her novels, if they existed in real life, should be put in stocks and driven around the streets of St. Petersburg as a lesson."[3]

Nekrasov was offended and wrote to a friend about Tolstoy's outburst: "What nonsense he babbled at my dinner yesterday! The devil knows what's in his head! He says such stupid and even nasty things. It would be a shame if these traits of landowning and military influence do not change in him. An excellent talent will be lost!"[4]

Turgenev was also outraged: "I almost quarreled with Tolstoy—really, it's impossible for ignorance not to show in one way or another. The other day, at Nekrasov's dinner, he said so many trite and crude things about G. Sand that I can't even convey it all."[5]

In our day, very few people read the novels of George Sand (she wrote almost sixty) with the same interest as progressive intellectuals all over Europe did at the time; people look at her books today primarily because they have heard about her notorious affairs with Chopin, Alfred de Musset, and Prosper Mérimée. But in the mid-nineteenth century, Sand's works were perceived as more than romans à clef or entertaining superromantic narratives; they were textbooks of life.

Dostoevsky recalled that he considered Sand then as the head of a movement for a radical social renewal of humanity. The adoration of Sand in Russia was particularly fervent, and Dostoevsky explained why: "Only this was permitted, that is, novels, the rest, practically every thought, especially from France, was strictly banned." (According to Dostoevsky, the Russian censors made a huge error in allowing the works of George Sand.)

Turgenev was a "georgesandista," and the most ardent Westernizer among them. He had read Shakespeare, Byron, and Schiller in their original languages as a child. Later, in St. Petersburg, he argued with Nekrasov and his other friends from *Contemporary* that even Pushkin and Lermontov, "if you look closely," were only imitating European geniuses like Shakespeare and Byron.[6]

Early on as a writer, Turgenev focused on the West, measuring himself against Western literary criteria, and declaring, according to friends, "No, I'm a European at heart, my demands of life are also European! . . . At the very first chance, I'll flee without looking back, and you won't see hide or hair of me!"[7]

In order to realize his European ambitions, which were rather unusual even for his elite cosmopolitan circle, he needed a starting point in the West. The fulfillment of Turgenev's dream, strangely enough, came via George Sand.

In early 1842 the Paris glitterati were excited: the new left-radical magazine *La Revue indépendante* started serializing George Sand's sensational novel *Consuelo,* a story about the adventures of a fictional great singer in eighteenth-century Venice. The novel's immediate success was due in part to it being a roman à clef: the readers easily recognized the heroine as contralto Pauline Garcia-Viardot, a close friend of the author.

Viardot's life did resemble a novel, or a fairy tale. Born to a family of singers from Spain (her older sister was the famous mezzo-soprano Maria Malibran), she debuted in Paris in 1838 at the age of seventeen, stunning the public with her phenomenal vocal gifts (she had a range of two and a half octaves) and her exceptional musicality.

Pauline was not pretty, she was tiny with an enormous nose and mouth, bulging eyes, and wide hips, but the Romantic poet Alfred de Musset, enchanted by her talent and intellect, proposed to her. She rejected him and, taking George Sand's advice, married the theater impresario and liberal journalist and translator (Dostoevsky read *Don Quixote* in his French rendering) Louis Viardot, who was more than twenty years her senior. *Le tout Paris* gathered in their salon, and the brilliant Pauline, who also played piano and composed, was its main star.

La Revue indépendante was an influential promoter of socialist ideas in France and Europe. Amazingly, by hook or crook, the journal reached St. Petersburg, where it was devoured by progressives. Given the Russians' adoration of George Sand, the adventures of Consuelo/Pauline Viardot were a hot topics in the Russian capital.

By this time, Turgenev was a rather well known poet—tall, broad-shouldered, handsome, and a dandy (multicolored vests, lorgnette). However, his domineering mother thought he was too flighty.

His personal life was confused: he was having an affair with a sister of Mikhail Bakunin, later a notorious anarchist (Bakunin had more than brotherly feelings for her as well), but had a child with a serf laundress of his mother. He did not renounce his daughter, Pelagia, which would have been unseemly, given her strong resemblance to him.

Turgenev's life changed in an instant when Pauline Viardot came to perform in St. Petersburg in the fall of 1843. She came to the capital because Nicholas I wanted a court Italian opera—he sang and played flute and trombone and loved Italian music. On his orders, the best singers were brought to Russia for huge fees. It was a cultural revolution for St. Petersburg, and the public went wild with heated arguments and endless gossip.

Viardot, who came with her husband, immediately conquered St. Petersburg; audiences "groaned with delight." Turgenev, who had not been a major music lover before, began an adroit campaign on the famous singer. First he arranged to be in a hunting party outside the capital with Louis Viardot, who was as passionate about hunting as Turgenev; then he attended a performance of Rossini's *Il Barbiere di Siviglia* with Viardot singing; and at last he was presented to the star—all in the course of a few days.

Many years later, Pauline Viardot recalled her first meeting with Turgenev with a laugh: "He was introduced as a young Russian landowner, a good hunter, splendid raconteur, and bad poet."[8] Turgenev was enchanted by her, but no one could have predicted that their relationship would last for forty years.

Avdotya Panaeva (Nekrasov's outspoken common-law wife) disapproved: "He shouted about his love for Viardot everywhere, and among friends he talked of nothing but Viardot." Even the critic Belinsky, who liked the writer, once reprimanded Turgenev: "Really, how can one believe in a love as voluble as yours?"[9]

Gradually, everyone believed in it, and most importantly, so did Pauline and her husband. A strange ménage à trois formed. Many assumed that it was purely platonic on Turgenev's side, and that Louis Viardot had homoerotic feelings for the writer. The union turned out to be exceptionally stable, and wags hinted that it was fueled by Turgenev's wealth (his mother died in 1850, leaving a large fortune) and fame.

Turgenev's popularity increased rapidly. His *A Sportsman's Sketches,* which attracted a lot of attention when published in 1852, was rumored to have hastened the abolition of serfdom in Russia. *Rudin, Asya, First Love, Nest of Gentlefolk, On the Eve,* and *Fathers and Sons* followed, each sparking a lively debate, and soon Turgenev was the recognized leader of Russian prose. But his life was forever tied to the Viardot family—he went wherever they did: France, then Baden-Baden, and then Paris, where Turgenev died in the Viardots' summer villa in 1883, having outlived Louis Viardot briefly.

This union existed under the aegis of George Sand, who felt sincere amity for Turgenev, valuing him as a writer and human being: she thought him cheerful, simple, and modest ("He was extremely surprised when I told him he was a great artist and great poet").

Leo Tolstoy's opinion was rather different, as recorded in his diary in 1856: "His whole life is pretended simplicity." Many other Russian observers described Turgenev as capricious, irresponsible, and vain. Foreigners, on the contrary, were all charmed by him: for them the gray-haired Russian giant was a fairy-tale character.

.   .   .

Turgenev wanted to live a life that was free, elegant, comfortable, and situated in the center of European culture. Before him, no Russian writer lived that way—nor has any since. Turgenev managed to achieve all this in no small part thanks to his relationship with the Viardots, whose salon was a magnet for French celebrities. One starstruck Russian woman described an evening she spent at the Viardots', when the other guests included Gustave Flaubert, the violinist Pablo Sarasate, and the composers Charles Gounod and Camille Saint-Saëns: "White lacquered furniture upholstered in pale silk left the center of the room open. To the left of the grand piano two steps led to the picture gallery, illuminated from above. There was an organ in there and a few, but very valuable, paintings . . . Mme Viardot came to the middle of the room . . . After the aria from Verdi's opera, came Schubert's 'Erlkönig,' accompanied by Saint-Saëns."[10]

Turgenev took great pleasure in the monthly "Flaubert dinners," held in a private room of a Parisian restaurant for five famous writers: two close friends, Flaubert and Turgenev, and Zola, Alfonse Daudet, and Edmond Goncourt. Daudet recalled that they spoke of their own works and those of others (each time at least one of the participants brought along a just-published book), about women, and also about their ills, "the body that is becoming a burden like a ball and chain on a convict's leg. Those were sad confessions of men who had turned forty!"[11] Turgenev concentrated on the caviar, nevertheless.

The writers began their evenings at seven, and the feast would still be going strong at two a.m. The loud-spoken Flaubert would remove his jacket, the others following his lead; Turgenev, who suffered from gout, would lie down on the couch.

At those moments Turgenev undoubtedly imagined himself on the literary Olympus, one of the masters of the cultural universe. I saw similar emotions on the face of the poet Joseph Brodsky when he appeared in New York in the company of Czeslaw Milosz, Octavio Paz, and Derek Walcott (four Nobel laureates!).

Everything Turgenev wrote was instantly translated into several languages. For good reason—and like Brodsky a century later—Turgenev considered himself an arbiter and connoisseur of what contemporary Russian literature would please foreigners and what would not. He was a bit condescending about Tolstoy: "Foreigners don't appreciate him. *Childhood and Adolescence* was translated into English and did not do well: it was taken for an imitation of Dickens. I wanted to translate *War and Peace* into French, but skipping all the philosophizing, for I know the French: they won't see the good beyond the boring and silly."

When Tolstoy rejected the radical editing, Turgenev was hurt, telling a friend, "Someone else translated it, and probably the French won't read it." Turgenev considered himself an excellent editor. He was particularly proud of his editing work on the books by two great Russian poets who were not so lucky with publications in their lifetime: Tyutchev and Afanasy Fet.

At a dinner in his honor in 1856 when he came to visit St. Petersburg, after many toasts, Turgenev responded with an allegedly impromptu gem:

> All this praise is undeserved
> But one thing you must admit:
> I forced Tyutchev to unzip
> And I cleaned Fet's pants.

This auto-epigram was greeted with howls of laughter from the bibulous writers, who understood the references: Turgenev had persuaded Tyutchev, engrossed in political and social intrigues, to agree to issue his verse, to which he was rather indifferent. It was edited by Turgenev and Nekrasov.

As for Fet, he had also given Turgenev a free hand, but when the book appeared in 1855, Fet found it "as cleaned up as it was disfigured."[12] Tyutchev too felt that Turgenev's editing was heavy-handed, and that "many of his corrections ruined things."[13]

Turgenev was friendly with everyone, but he also quarreled with everyone at some point—Nekrasov, Fet, Ivan Goncharov, author of *Oblo-*

mov, Dostoevsky, and Tolstoy. Essentially, it was a conflict between a Westerner to the marrow of his bones and nationalists, whatever they may have called themselves. The suspicious Fet thought that Turgenev had become a Westernizer "under the influence of Mme Viardot." Turgenev readily agreed: "I do not undertake anything important in my life without the advice of Mme Viardot."

Turgenev's Russian friends nagged him to return to his homeland to live, instead of just visiting. He assured them that he missed Russia very much, but he always found an excuse why he couldn't move just then. He did admit once that he felt "family" was not Russians but the Viardots: "If they were to move tomorrow to the most impossible city, say, Copenhagen, I would follow."[14]

The main magnet was Pauline Viardot, and not only for her vocal genius. She drew well, read five languages, knew Russian well, and had a sophisticated taste in art and literature. Viardot once confided in a Russian friend, "Not a single line of Turgenev's gets into print without his showing it to me first. You Russians do not know how much you owe me that Turgenev continues to write and work."

Turgenev entrusted the upbringing of his daughter (whose name he changed from Pelagia to Paulina) to the Viardots. When visiting France, the poet Fet listened in amazement as Paulina "quite sweetly declaimed Molière's poetry; but because she looked just like Turgenev in a skirt, she could make no claim on prettiness."[15] The girl had forgotten how to speak Russian.

The girl's upbringing led to a furious row with Leo Tolstoy that almost ended in a duel with rifles. Turgenev was boasting in company that included Tolstoy how Paulina did charity work: she mended the clothing of the poor. Tolstoy (whom Turgenev dubbed a troglodyte for his directness and coarseness) sarcastically countered that "a dressed up girl, with filthy and stinking rags on her lap, is playing an insincere, theatrical scene."

The argument suddenly flew out of control, and although bloodshed was avoided it left a break in relations between the two writers that lasted twenty years. The true cause of the altercation was still the same:

the Christian anarchist Tolstoy hated Turgenev's liberal posturing, and the animosity was returned. The role of women in society was part of the conflict.

Turgenev's ideal woman was a mix of the real Pauline Viardot, her depiction in the novels of George Sand, and a big dose of Pushkin's Tatiana from *Eugene Onegin*. All of "Turgenev's maidens" are like that— pure, idealistic, and strong. The men in Turgenev's works were mostly weak and indecisive. A pervasive melancholy envelops Turgenev's prose, but there is always an acute sense of the bigger social issues important for Russia. That's what made Turgenev's writing so topical, and his eye for a telling detail and fine craftsmanship ensured lasting success with Western readers. But his moderation was ultimately his undoing.

In June 1880, Turgenev appeared as guest of honor at the unveiling of the first monument to Pushkin in Moscow. As a natural centrist, he found himself at the crossroads of clashing political forces. Alexander II wanted on this occasion to send an encouraging signal to the Russian intelligentsia. The unveiling of the Pushkin monument was taken under royal patronage.

The progressive intellectuals also wanted to be heard. For the liberal elite, the event was an opportunity to stress the independence of culture. In this situation, Turgenev appeared to be the spokesman of choice for all parties concerned, since he was looked upon as Pushkin's successor.

But in Russia, being a moderate liberal and Westernizer is the most precarious position, especially in tense moments. This is where Turgenev lost. At the solemn convocation in the auditorium of the Nobility Assembly, with *le tout Moscou* present, Turgenev gave a mellow speech in which he took neither the side of the government (which Alexander II had expected of him) nor the side of the opposition (as the students present had hoped).

For all his admiration of Pushkin, Turgenev praised him cautiously, since he knew that Pushkin was not particularly famous in the West. The disappointed audience reacted with little enthusiasm. Turgenev was perceived as one of his own indecisive characters. But the true blow came from Dostoevsky, who delivered his Pushkin oration the next day in the same hall.

In his fiery speech, Dostoevsky declared Pushkin a world genius who was greater than Shakespeare or Cervantes because of his special, somehow purely Russian quality of "universal receptivity." That was exactly what the whole audience—conservatives and progressives alike—desperately wanted to hear.

Turgenev's careful equivocations were rejected, while Dostoevsky's emotionally charged exaggerations carried the day. The stark contrast between the big, handsome Turgenev and the small, emaciated, hunched, and ugly Dostoevsky, whose coat drooped as if on a hanger, worked in the latter's favor: Dostoevsky was one of their own, a Russian sufferer, while Turgenev looked like a wealthy tourist from Paris.

The audience was spellbound by the extraordinary nervous energy of Dostoevsky's delivery. When he concluded with the words that Pushkin "carried away with him to the grave a certain great mystery. And now we must uncover it without him," a hysterical cry came from the crowd—"You have uncovered it!"—which was picked up by other loud voices: "You have! You have!"

People in the audience shouted and wept and embraced one another. Dostoevsky wrote to his wife, "I hurried to save myself backstage, but they forced their way in, especially the women. They kissed my hands, tormented me. Students ran in. One of them, in tears, fell before me in hysteria and then passed out. It was a total, complete victory!"[16]

While he was speaking, someone managed to sneak out and get an enormous laurel wreath for him; as he reported triumphantly in the same letter, "a multitude of ladies (more than a hundred) rushed up on the stage and crowned me in front of the entire audience with the wreath." (A telling detail: when the volunteers were bringing in the laurel wreath, they bumped into Turgenev, and one of the women pushed him aside, muttering scornfully, "It's not for you!")

Turgenev reacted angrily to his defeat. When he returned to Paris, he told friends how much he "hated all the lies and falsehoods of Dostoevsky's sermon" and how everyone "seemed to lose their minds, awed by the incongruous nonsense from Dostoevsky, how all of them, as if drunk or on drugs, practically climbed the walls . . . and cried, and wept, and embraced as if it were Easter."[17]

Some seven months later, Dostoevsky died in St. Petersburg at the age of fifty-nine of hemorrhage in his throat, and two and a half years after that, in Bougival outside Paris, in terrible suffering from spinal cancer alleviated only with massive doses of morphine, Turgenev died at the age of sixty-four.

A few years before his death, Turgenev wrote in his diary, "Midnight. I am at my desk again; below, my poor friend is singing something in her completely broken voice; and my soul is darker than the darkest night . . . The grave seems in a hurry to swallow me up: like an instant, the day flies by, empty, meaningless, colorless . . . I have no right to live, nor any desire to do so; there is nothing more to do, nothing to expect, nothing even to want."[18]

CHAPTER 10

Herzen, Tolstoy, and the Women's Issue

After the death of Nicholas I in 1855, the moral climate changed: the poet Tyutchev called it a thaw. A contemporary marveled, "Everyone senses that a huge stone has been lifted from each of us, and that it is easier to breathe."[1] The new monarch, Alexander II, sent clear liberal signals.

Expectation of reforms was in the air, clearly needed after the disastrous Crimean War. From the abolition of serfs to fashions and hairdos, everything was subject to debate. Suddenly, there was talk of the "new man."

While Russia was backward, the Russian elite was in the avant-garde when it came to navel gazing and sophisticated emotions. While millions of Russian serfs lived under medieval laws, a handful of refined minds experimented with new relations between the sexes and the "emancipation of the flesh."

Russia had no real bourgeoisie, but the radical intellectuals were already rejecting bourgeois views of morality. The American cultural historian Marshall Berman dubbed this "the modernism of underdevelopment," when culturally innovative models were debated in a bubble, based on social fantasies and dreams.[2]

One of those isolated dreamers was the great Russian dissident and social philosopher Alexander Herzen, born in the fateful year of confrontation with Napoleon, 1812 (he was saved from a burning house as an infant during the fire of Moscow), to the family of Moscow millionaire Ivan Yakovlev, who named his illegitimate but beloved son (his mother was a poor German woman) Herzen, from the German *das Herz,* the heart.

Brilliantly educated, Herzen grew up a rebel; reading Pushkin, Schiller, and Rousseau (he knew German and French fluently from childhood and then added Italian and English) awakened in him, as he later recalled, "an insuperable hatred of all slavery and all tyranny." Inevitably, Herzen was sent by Nicholas I into exile in the provinces. In 1847, Herzen and his family fled to Europe: "I was beckoned by distant vistas, open struggle and free speech."

Herzen was a short, plump gentleman, clean shaven, with long hair combed straight back in the Moscow manner, very mobile, and his constant inner agitation made him speak standing, quickly, in a loud voice. When he settled in Paris, Herzen transformed himself: he grew a stylish beard, cut his hair, and traded the clumsy Moscow long frock coat for a fashionable Parisian jacket.

Cosmopolitan at heart, Herzen quickly plunged headlong into the turbulent life in Paris—political, cultural, and social—that was in such sharp contrast with his Moscow existence, swallowing up all the latest books and splashing happily in the "sparkling sea," as he called it, of the European press. He entered Parisian democratic and socialist circles, and leftists of every rank, stripe, and nationality delighted in Herzen's heartfelt speeches denouncing serfdom and other horrors of the autocratic Russia they all hated.

It was difficult to make such an impression on this brilliant group of ambitious and confident activists who lived in a dizzying world of bold ideas and pitiless polemics, and Herzen would not have been able to do it, had he not arrived in Paris a very wealthy man.

In Moscow, Herzen inherited a lot of money from his father, but that just alienated him from his old friends there. Herzen recalled that "the appearance of some silver tray and candelabra in his new household stunned his friends into silence: sincerity and fun vanished as soon as they encountered ready comfort."[3]

On the contrary, in the West Herzen's money not only made him accepted even in the democratic milieu, but it also allowed him to launch his revolutionary activity: he founded the Free Russian Press in London, which printed antigovernment leaflets, brochures, and books, and subsequently the dissident almanac *Polar Star* and then the first Russian revolutionary newspaper, *The Bell* (1857–1867).

The Bell's circulation was 2,500, some of which reached Russia, where the paper was read with trepidation and acute attention, even in the tsar's court. They said that Alexander II sometimes asked close friends, "Have you read the eighth issue? How about the tenth?"[4] Everyone knew he meant *The Bell*. It was a historic breakthrough for Russian dissident literature.

The tumultuous cosmopolitan life in the West transformed Herzen's wife, Natalie, too, and it led to a family drama. In an ordinary family it would probably have remained a private affair, but it prompted Herzen to write a masterpiece of the Russian memoir genre, his magnum opus, *My Past and Thoughts*.

Natalie was his cousin. Like Herzen, she was illegitimate, and she was brought up by a wealthy aunt, which created psychological issues. Beautiful and intelligent, she imagined that everyone was mocking her, humiliating her, keeping her illiterate, while her calling was to astonish the world: "My cheeks burned, I was hurrying somewhere, I could see my paintings, my students—but they wouldn't give me a piece of paper or a pencil . . . My desire to get out into a different world grew stronger and stronger and along with it grew my scorn for my prison and its cruel sentry."[5]

When she married Herzen, he and his friends put her on a romantic pedestal: they all tried "to prove to her that she was immaculate in every action." One friend kept telling Herzen, "You are a pig before your wife."[6]

Belonging to the "fasting girl" type, fashionable in mid-nineteenth-century Europe—thin, small, and introverted creatures, whom many found to be incredibly spiritual—Natalie Herzen made it a habit to lecture her female friends in a smooth, quiet voice on the lofty purpose of women, annoying them no end.

It was his wife who pushed Herzen out into Europe once he got his inheritance. In Paris, Natalie Herzen, according to friends, changed from a "quiet, thoughtful romantic lady" into a "brilliant tourist."[7]

Among the new admirers of the Herzen family were the German émigré poet Georg Herwegh and his wife. Herwegh was famous for his passionate political poems and pamphlets, which received the approval of Karl Marx himself. The great Heinrich Heine called Herwegh the "iron lark" of the revolution. He was very attractive, with a dusky face and fiery eyes, soft, long hair, and a silky beard.

At first relations between the Herzens and the Herweghs were idyllic: the men called each other "my double," "my twin," and the women discussed the possibility of communal living, both families with their children. The inspiring works of Rousseau and George Sand were reread and discussed. It ended with Herwegh and Natalie becoming lovers, although she did not want to leave Herzen.

Feeling a "revulsion for bourgeois virtues," as an observer put it, Natalie Herzen imagined that this situation would work out well and that they would create a great new model of family relations (as some now assume, on a bisexual basis) before which "one day people will prostrate themselves, blinded by our love, as if by the Resurrection of Jesus Christ."[8]

But the progressive Herzen, who readily recognized the right of every woman to enjoy free love in theory, somehow recoiled from this prospect. The duality of his position was later described ironically by Dostoevsky: "He rejected the foundations of the previous society, denied family, and still was, I believe, a good father and husband. He denied private property, and while waiting for its abolition managed to arrange his affairs and enjoyed his prosperity abroad. He fomented revolutions and incited others but at the same time loved comfort and family peace."

Dostoevsky was unduly sarcastic. It is easy to accuse Herzen of inconsistency or even hypocrisy, but the letters and diaries of the couple show how sincerely and strongly they believed in new, elevated forms of family life and how terribly they suffered when their fantasies were shattered.

At first Herzen and Herwegh planned to solve the conflict with a duel. But instead Herzen imprudently decided to make the affair public, wanting Jules Michelet and Pierre Proudhon, whom he called the "generals of democracy," and the great George Sand, for Herzen and his circle "the highest authority on everything to do with women," to rule on the situation.

Nothing but a Europe-wide scandal came of it. The "generals" refused the invitation to be on the jury *d'honneur,* and the composer Richard Wagner, to whom Herzen also wrote about the affair, supported Herwegh. Karl Marx, who disliked Herzen politically and personally, gloated, "Herwegh not only made Herzen a cuckold, but he milked him for 80,000 francs."

The unfortunate Natalie Herzen died in 1852 of tuberculosis, leaving her husband inconsolable to the end of his days. But Herzen, in his youth convinced of the "unlimited value of the personality" (particularly his own), immediately placed his personal catastrophe into the broader context of the crisis of contemporary European culture. "Everything has collapsed—public and private, European revolution and home and hearth, freedom of the world and personal happiness." That big idea fueled Herzen's innovative memoirs *My Past and Thoughts,* which he began right after his wife's death as a confessional about his family's tragedy. Over the course of fifteen years of work it became a "biography of humanity," as he put it. "Jealousy . . . Fidelity . . . Betrayal . . . Purity . . . Dark forces, threatening words, which caused rivers of tears, rivers of blood—words that make us shudder, like memories of inquisition, torture, plague . . . and yet words beneath which, as if beneath the sword of Damocles, lived and lives the family."

My Past and Thoughts makes for difficult, occasionally irritating, but ultimately rewarding reading: an odd mix of sharp observations colored by the author's inimitable irony; vivid descriptions of historical events; subtle landscapes; and witty philosophical and political digressions. The author is in continual dialogue with the reader, who delights in Herzen's speech—voluble, sarcastic, tragic.

Herzen inserted fragments from letters and diaries into the text, not in their original form but edited to suit the needs of the narrative. Herzen was just as free with historical facts; he admitted that his memoirs "are not historical monograph, but the reflection of history in a man who accidentally ended up in its path."

Herzen used the word "accidentally" coquettishly: he expended superhuman efforts to put himself "into" history—not just political history, but artistic as well—and *My Past and Thoughts* provides a series of sharp vignettes: Nicholas I, loathed by Herzen, looks like a "shorn and slimy jellyfish with a mustache"; his son, the future Alexander II, is more kindly drawn—"His features expressed kindness and weakness . . . The few words he spoke to me were gentle . . . without the father's habit of frightening the listener into a faint."

In *My Past and Thoughts,* Herzen predicted that if democracy prevailed in America, "people there would not become happier, but they would be more sated. Their satisfaction will be flatter, poorer and drier than the one borne in the ideals of romantic Europe, but with it there will be no tsars, no centralization, and perhaps, no hunger."

The emotional center of *My Past and Thoughts* is the passionate and frank description of the love drama of Herzen and Natalie ("The poor sufferer—how much I participated in her murder, loving her limitlessly!"), a drama presented as the result not just of mere personal rivalry but, more grandiosely, of the clash of reactionary and progressive forces: "And my hearth was extinguished by the crush of two wheels of world history . . . Life deceived me, history deceived me."

·   ·   ·

Herzen died in Paris in 1870, politically marginalized, just two and a half months short of his fifty-eighth birthday. In his lifetime, the full text of *My Past and Thoughts* did not appear in print: Herzen considered the portrayal of his intimate life a tad too frank. Turgenev, who read the manuscript, given to him by Herzen's daughter six years after the writer's death, was disturbed: "It is written in fire, tears, and blood."[9] But "I am definitely against publication, even though as a reader, I regret it."[10] The complete text was not published until fifty years after Herzen's death, in 1919–1920. In the postrevolutionary flames, Herzen's lyrical outpouring had little impact. Many considered them old-fashioned.

Leo Tolstoy, a great admirer of Herzen, often expressed regret about the unfortunate fate of his prose in Russia. In his own works, Tolstoy always strived for topicality.

When Tolstoy's novel *Anna Karenina* began serialization in 1875 in the conservative journal the *Russian Herald* (he had ended his collaboration with the liberal *Contemporary*), it met a squall of negative reviews. Turgenev was outraged: "With his talent, to wander into the high society swamp and lose his way there, treating all that piffle not with humor but seriously—what nonsense!"[11]

The liberal Nekrasov nailed *Anna Karenina* with an epigram:

Tolstoy, you proved with patience, talent, and great delay
That if she is a wife and mother, a woman should not stray.

One influential critic wrote that Tolstoy's new novel "arouses disgust in everyone," because instead of genuine love he depicts "naked and purely animal sensuality"; the critic saw nothing but "unfettered lust" in the relations between Anna and her lover, Vronsky.

The most scathing (unprinted but popular) remark came from the idol of the progressives, the satirical writer Mikhail Saltykov-Shchedrin, who called it "a novel about improving the life of genitalia." He added in a letter to a friend, "I find it vile and immoral. And the conservative party is using it and gloating. Can you imagine turning Tolstoy's bovine novel into some kind of political banner?"[12]

These angry words about Tolstoy's novel being used as a political banner for the conservatives explain the liberal outrage over *Anna Karenina*. As contemporaries recalled, Alexander II "hated learned women," seeing them as both potential and actual revolutionaries.[13] His high officials were in complete agreement on this. The liberal press and public opinion pushed for women's access to higher education. The wary government did not give in.

In 1873 a special commission, which included the minister of public education, the minister of internal affairs, and also the chief of gendarmes, sent Alexander II a report on women's education and the "women's issue," which the commission felt was being used by enemies of autocracy to push through demands of "a utopian, almost revolutionary character: to make a woman's rights equal to that of men, to allow her to participate in politics, and even give the right to free love, which destroys the family and turns extreme licentiousness into a principle."[14]

For the authors of the report and Alexander II, who approved it, women's radicalism in both sex and politics was equally frightening and repulsive. A noted conservative journalist, Prince Vladimir Meshchersky (a known homosexual in St. Petersburg) maintained that female students were "the most fanatical, and one must truthfully say, the ugliest maidens, shorn, in blue spectacles and men's jackets,"[15] for whom education was just a smokescreen for sexual and political anarchy.

That is why the conservative camp hailed *Anna Karenina*, a love story in high circles, in which the heroine, seeking sexual independence, is punished by society and consequently throws herself under a train.

Reading *Anna Karenina*, explained a right-wing critic, "you are freed from mediocrity and filth, you stop breathing the fetid air of taverns, hospitals, and prisons, where most of contemporary belles-lettres are gasping." At last one could enjoy fine descriptions of the life of aristocratic salons, ladies' boudoirs, fashionable restaurants, and the races.

The left fumed over why Tolstoy did not write about the simple folk or, for example, students: "What a shame that Tolstoy has no ideals! . . . He cares more about a she-buffalo than an advanced woman." The ultra-conservative poet Fet reported those liberal opinions to Tolstoy in a letter and added a response to them: "Because a she-buffalo is perfection in its species, while your advanced woman is God knows what."[16]

Tolstoy chose the epigraph to *Anna Karenina* from the Bible: "Vengeance is mine, and I will repay." The full quote is this: "Dearly beloved, avenge not yourselves, but rather give place unto wrath: for it is written, Vengeance is mine; I will repay, saith The Lord." A lively polemic over the epigraph began immediately, and it continues to this day. Is the unfaithful Anna a criminal and God punishes her justly? Or is she innocent, and it is not the business of people to judge her?

In other words, does Tolstoy have sympathy for Anna, or did the "rubbishy old man" (as protofeminist Anna Akhmatova angrily called him) truly believe, as Akhmatova maintained, that "if a woman leaves her rightful husband and joins another man, she inevitably becomes a prostitute"?[17]

Tolstoy avoided a straightforward comment on the novel. "If I wanted to summarize what I wanted to express in the novel, then I would have to write exactly the same novel that I have written, from the beginning."

We can assume that the epigraph from St. Paul's Epistle to the Romans was chosen by Tolstoy after reading Schopenhauer's philosophical treatise *The World as Will and Representation,* where this passage is interpreted. At the same time, Tolstoy was responding to the misogynistic pamphlet by Alexandre Dumas fils, "L'homme—femme," which posed the question: What should be done with an unfaithful woman—forgive her, throw her out, kill her?

The highly moral Dumas strongly suggested killing unfaithful wives, but Tolstoy, generally very sympathetic to antifeminist ideas ("Women's only purpose is to give birth and bring up children"), in this case was arguably mercifully inclined to leave the act of punishment to God.

.   .   .

Tolstoy's views obviously evolved over time: in his most sensational work on relations between the sexes, *The Kreutzer Sonata* (1889), the hero kills his wife, whom he suspects of having an affair with the violinist with whom she plays Beethoven's *Kreutzer* Sonata, "a terrible thing," and the court finds him not guilty.

In his feverish monologue, the protagonist explains his crime by the fact that women have acquired "a terrible power over people" in modern society: "Women, like empresses, hold 90 percent of the human race in slavery and hard labor. And all because they have been humiliated, deprived of equal rights with men. And so they get their revenge by acting on our sensuality, ensnaring us in their nets."

According to Tolstoy, that shameful and immoral "slavery of sensuality" can be avoided only by total abstinence. Akhmatova commented on the late Tolstoy's idée fixe skeptically: the old writer, settled in his famous estate, Yasnaya Polyana, stopped lusting after the village girls and therefore decided to forbid the rest of the world to have sex too.[18]

In this case Akhmatova was wrong, if only because Tolstoy was still in his fifties when he wrote *The Kreutzer Sonata* and he had no problems with his sexual drive, judging by his diaries. The philosophy of the story is, of course, more complex, expressing the quasi-Buddhist idea that "if passions are destroyed including the last, most powerful one—physical love, then the prophecy will come to pass, people will be united into one, the goal of humanity will be reached, and there will be no reason for it to live."

The diaries also suggest that while one of the impulses for writing the story was, in fact, autobiographical, it was rather opposite to the reason Akhmatova attributed to Tolstoy.

Tolstoy had been waging a fierce psychological war with his wife, Sophia, a strong woman who tried to hold on to her position in the family vis-à-vis the dictator and tyrant her husband was.

When they married in 1862, he was thirty-four and she was eighteen, and in the subsequent thirty years of marriage, she bore him thirteen children; as one of their sons calculated, she was pregnant for almost ten years and breast-fed children for more than thirteen years, and also "managed to run the complex household of a large family and copied *War and Peace* and *Anna Karenina* and other works by hand eight, ten, and sometimes twenty times each."[19]

Sophia resisted her husband's intentions to turn her into a mere machine for producing and feeding children (with additional functions as housekeeper, secretary, clerk, and literary agent). There were endless arguments and quarrels, accompanied by Sophia's hysterics and nervous collapses. Time and again, Tolstoy would angrily write in his diary that the break with his wife was "complete." Things never reached divorce, even though each threatened to leave, and Sophia often mentioned suicide, a terrible sin for a Christian.

Tolstoy, the more powerful figure, always won. But there was one sphere—sex—where Sophia could get her revenge. In his youth, Tolstoy caroused and debauched, as did everyone in his milieu. Toward the end of his life, he admitted to Maxim Gorky, "I was an insatiable . . . '—' using a salty word at the end."[20]

Gorky insisted (and he knew!) that even with Tolstoy's "passionate nature," his wife "was his only woman for almost a half century."[21] It should be added that Sophia, according to contemporaries, was not only energetic and light on her feet, but amazingly youthful. When Tolstoy was writing *The Kreutzer Sonata,* she was in her early forties, but "there wasn't a single wrinkle on her smooth, rosy white face,"[22] as one of her daughters wrote.

Sophia did not use powder or any makeup and bore her imposing, full figure with grace and quiet confidence. In conversations, she liked to stress her youthfulness—and Tolstoy's age. She continued to arouse her husband and, well aware of it, turned sex into a weapon (both wrote about this in their diaries).

In one typical entry, Tolstoy described bitterly that he had asked his wife to join him that night but she "with cold anger and the desire to hurt me, refused." Tolstoy was infuriated that Sophia was turning conjugal sex "into a lure and a toy." *The Kreutzer Sonata* (like other works of the period on the humiliating power of lust and sex—*The Devil* and *Father Sergius*) was his revenge and exorcism.

The story became a major public event: in Russia (as in the West) questions of sex were discussed avidly and turned into a battlefield between conservatives and liberals.

The Kreutzer Sonata was translated into the main European languages and became perhaps the most popular work by Tolstoy in the West. In Russia, where it was blocked by the censors, the novella was distributed in thousands of handwritten copies, and it was read aloud and debated passionately. "It sometimes seemed that the public, forgetting its personal cares, lived only for the literature of Count Tolstoy . . . The most important political events rarely captured everyone with such force."

The "Tolstoyans" (followers of Tolstoy who lived in quasi-socialist communes, working the land, practicing nonviolent resistance to evil and moral self-perfection) discussed *The Kreutzer Sonata* with particular fervor. The young women in these communes swore, after a collective reading, that they would never marry, and if they were forced, they would rather drown themselves. There were instances of young Tolstoyans castrating themselves to escape the temptation of marriage.

Tolstoy's wife was deeply wounded by the popularity of *The Kreutzer Sonata:* she thought—not without reason—that the whole world interpreted it as a direct reflection of their family situation. Sophia was told that even Emperor Alexander II said, "I feel sorry for his poor wife"[23] upon reading the work.

So Sophia had a brilliant idea: she would go to St. Petersburg to get permission for publication of *The Kreutzer Sonata* from the tsar. If she succeeded, everyone would realize she was no victim.

Her plan worked. Alexander received her in the palace and after a friendly chat gave his consent to the publication of the novella in the next volume of Tolstoy's collected works. Sophia was triumphant: "I, a woman, got what no one else could achieve."

She was especially pleased that Alexander found her "young and beautiful" at forty-seven. Naturally, that provoked displeasure in Tolstoy, who was pathologically jealous. Hearing his wife's joyous account of her meeting with the emperor, Tolstoy grumbled angrily that "before he and Sovereign had ignored each other and now this new turn of events could create problems."

Tolstoy's jealousy finally brought his family to the brink of disaster, in a classic example of life imitating art. Like the protagonist in his novella, Tolstoy grew jealous of a musician, the composer and pianist Sergei Taneyev.

The Neoclassicist Taneyev was often called the Russian Brahms (even though he abhorred Brahms's music), and after the death in 1893 of his teacher and idol Tchaikovsky, Taneyev became the guru of musical Moscow. As a composer, Taneyev always stood apart: he had a special knowledge of the polyphonic technique of the old masters (Palestrina, Orlando di Lasso), and he used it in his own work.

Short, heavyset, bearded, nearsighted, and dumpy, Taneyev was a freethinker. During the census of 1897 he intended to fill in the religion question with "heretic not believing in God." He also openly despised the Romanovs. He liked to tell the story of how in 1881, during the celebrations of the coronation of Alexander III, he was asked to conduct a concert in Moscow in the presence of the emperor, and he "intentionally put on a boot with a hole specially for the tsar." "Alexander III gave me a gold ruble," Taneyev recalled with a laugh, "and I immediately gave it to the doorman as a tip."[24]

One of his favorite writers was Tolstoy, whom he had met in the early 1890s. Tolstoy was a fair amateur pianist and even composed a sweet little waltz, written down by Taneyev, who was a guest at Yasnaya Polyana in the summers of 1895 and 1896.

Neither man liked the late Beethoven, Wagner, or the "modernists" Richard Strauss and Claude Debussy. But Tolstoy found Palestrina, adored by Taneyev, boring, and he was rather skeptical about Taneyev's music, unabashed at telling him so to his face.

.   .   .

Soon, Taneyev became "disgusting" to Tolstoy, and in his diary Tolstoy compared the clumsy, shy, and kindly composer to a rooster: his wife had invented an "affair" for herself with Taneyev, and Tolstoy could not stand it.

Tolstoy ignored the fact that Taneyev was a completely asexual virgin. Sophia's tenderness toward the eccentric composer was more maternal than anything else. Taneyev had a calming effect on Sophia, and lofty music, which he embodied, gave her the illusion of an emotional harbor, a respite from the stormy atmosphere created by her tyrannical husband.

A controlling person, Tolstoy found the situation intolerable: he could not sleep, he wept, he kept arguing with Sophia, trying to separate her from that "fat musician." Sophia fought back aggressively, "I will love people who are good and kind, and not you. You're a beast." It went on for years, while the unsuspecting Taneyev calmly continued visiting the Tolstoy house and Sophia attended his concerts in Moscow.

What must have infuriated Tolstoy most was that Taneyev was a silent rebuke, the ideal Tolstoyan, a follower of his moral teachings: he lived simply, did not care about money, and did not chase after fame and glory; nor did he smoke or drink, and he was a vegetarian, like Tolstoy.

But while Tolstoy proclaimed in *The Kreutzer Sonata* that the key to the moral revival of humanity was celibacy, the writer himself remained a prisoner of sexual passions. And here was some musician ("All musicians are stupid," Tolstoy said, "and the more talented the musician, the stupider"),[25] almost thirty years younger, for whom the problem simply did not exist.

Looking at Taneyev, the world-famed prophet and stern judge of tsars saw himself as pathetic and ridiculous. His bedroom was his gallows: although only he and his wife knew it, he feared that everyone knew (or guessed). His dilemma was an irresolvable contradiction between his writing and his lifestyle, a fundamental problem that eventually drove Tolstoy to flee his house in 1910 and contributed to his death that same year at the age of eighty-two.

CHAPTER II

Tchaikovsky and Homosexuality in Imperial Russia

A paradox mentioned frequently by contemporaries of Leo Tolstoy: that stern brute would burst into tears at the least provocation. He was particularly moved by sophisticated classical music, whose right to exist he always stubbornly denied: Mozart, Beethoven, Chopin.

The sole contemporary composer who could wring tears from the great writer was Peter Ilych Tchaikovsky. In December 1876 a private performance of Tchaikovsky's music was arranged for Tolstoy at the Moscow Conservatory. The writer, listening to the soulful Andante from the First String Quartet, "began sobbing"[1] (according to Tchaikovsky), thereby pleasing the composer enormously.

Fired up by the idea of "gabbing" about music with Tchaikovsky, Tolstoy visited him several times, which made the composer (who considered Tolstoy a "semigod") "terribly flattered and proud."[2] But Tchaikovsky was a nervous and fragile person, and these contacts with Tolstoy ultimately brought "nothing but difficulty and torment, like any acquaintance,"[3] as he confessed in a letter to his patroness Nadezhda von Meck.

Tolstoy's drive and Tchaikovsky's neurotic reticence clashed. Right off the bat, Tolstoy ranted about Beethoven, putting Tchaikovsky off : "To lower an acknowledged genius to the level of their lack of understanding is a quality of intellectually limited people."[4]

Paradoxically, Tolstoy, justly celebrated for the psychological insights in his work, did not do so well in person with Tchaikovsky. He did not notice—or simply ignored—the extreme nervousness of that small, delicate, and seemingly acquiescent man with his neat gray beard. That is obvious from Tolstoy's later description of his meetings with the composer: "I think there was a bond between us." (If there was anything, it was lingering irritation on the part of Tchaikovsky.)

Tolstoy pursued his uninvited expansion into Tchaikovsky's realm, sending him an old edition of Russian folk songs, which he himself loved (he even figured out the piano accompaniment to one of them), with a suggestion that the composer write arrangements of them and with precise instructions how to do it: "In the Mozart-Haydn mode, not in the Beethoven-Schumann-Berlioz mode, so artificial and pretentious."[5]

Bearing in mind Tchaikovsky's shyness and his admiration for Tolstoy the writer, the response from the usually polite composer was uncharacteristically direct. Tchaikovsky wrote Tolstoy that the folk songs he had sent him ("an amazing treasure," Tolstoy had called it) were recorded "by an untutored hand and so bear only the traces of their original beauty."[6] He flatly refused to execute Tolstoy's idea about arranging the songs.

Still, Tchaikovsky buffered his refusal in some pleasantries and a request for a photograph as a memento of their meetings. But the angered Tolstoy did not oblige with his photograph, even though he routinely sent out hundreds to fans, and began denigrating the composer's works as an "artistic lie." In 1894, after Tchaikovsky's death, Tolstoy summed up his opinion of the composer this way: "So-so, one of the average ones."[7]

In October 1878, Tolstoy wrote to Turgenev in Paris, complaining that he had been suffering a "mental breakdown" of late, overcome by "a complex feeling in which the main part is shame and fear that people are laughing at me . . . it seems to me that you are laughing at me, too." At the end, Tolstoy asked an unexpected question: "What is Tchaikovsky's *Eugene Onegin*? I haven't heard it yet, but I am very interested."[8]

Everything about this letter is curious—Tolstoy's admission of his psychological vulnerability as well as his inexplicable interest in the latest work by a composer he so disliked (the piano score of the opera had just appeared).

In response, Turgenev, somewhat smugly, explained that although "some of your writing pleased me greatly, and others I did not like at all," he had never laughed at them and expressed the rather ironic hope that Tolstoy's "mental illness" had passed.

As for Tchaikovsky's *Onegin,* he had already gotten the piano score and heard it performed by the singer Pauline Viardot:

> It is without a doubt marvelous music; the lyrical, melodic parts are especially fine. But what a libretto! Just imagine, Pushkin's descriptions of the protagonists are put into their mouths. For example, Pushkin says of Lensky: He sang of life's end / At barely the age of 18, etc.
>
> And in the opera, Lensky sings: I sing of life's end, etc.
>
> And it's like that throughout.[9]

We know Tolstoy's reaction to Turgenev's letter from his own to his friend the poet Afanasy Fet: "Yesterday I received a letter from Turgenev, and decided to keep my distance from him. He's such an unpleasant bully." After that summary, the letter from the unpleasant bully should have sunk into oblivion. But no. Mysteriously, Turgenev's review of the opera—and, interestingly, only the negative part, with the criticism of the libretto—instantly circulated throughout Moscow's cultural circles.

The only person who could have given such publicity to Turgenev's letter was Tolstoy himself. He was a master of manipulating public opinion. His wife once compared him to a spider catching wretched buzzing flies in his web. Tolstoy must have really enjoyed humiliating Tchaikovsky using Turgenev's words.

The phenomenal speed with which the acidulous response traveled is explained by special circumstances. Music in Russia then (and now) played a marginal role compared to literature. But here was the opinion of one great writer in a letter to another about a new musical work based on Pushkin's *Eugene Onegin,* one of the cornerstones of Russian culture. The opera was being rehearsed just then at the Moscow Conservatory under Nikolai Rubinstein. It was a readymade bit of gossip in a highbrow cultural wrapping, the best candy to relish in salons.

No one cared that the particular example Turgenev used to prove Tchaikovsky's unforgivable distortion of Pushkin did not actually exist in the libretto. It was Turgenev's error, made worse by his assertion that the whole libretto was like that. His accidental mistake, disseminated by Tolstoy, and thereby supported by his powerful authority, was about to undermine the reputation of the as yet unperformed opera (which was probably what Tolstoy intended) among the literature-centric Moscow public.

It had that effect, according to Modest Tchaikovsky, the composer's brother, who was present at the premiere of *Eugene Onegin* on March 17, 1879. Modest recalled the "cold reception" from the public and tied it directly to the careless and unfair letter which "set the public against the composition" at the premiere. "The word 'blasphemy' raced around the audience. I remember hearing it several times that day."[10]

The impression Turgenev's letter made on newsmakers was so strong that even six years later, after the opera's premiere at the Imperial Maryinsky Theater in St. Petersburg in 1884, an influential journalist, Alexei Suvorin, quoted Turgenev in his review in the popular newspaper *New Times.*

Tchaikovsky was in a panic. He tried inviting Tolstoy to a Moscow performance of his opera, for him to see that there was no "blasphemy," but Tolstoy ignored the invitation and later recalled, after the composer's death, "I think he was hurt that I did not attend his *Eugene Onegin.*"

Trying to control the damage, Tchaikovsky literally dictated an article to a friendly music critic, which proclaimed that it was too easy "to dismiss the new opera with a few loud phrases about the profanation of Pushkin."[11] Following Tchaikovsky's prompting, the critic tried to explain both the innovative character of the work (not a traditional opera but "lyrical scenes," as Tchaikovsky called it) and the unusual degree of the composer's psychological identification with Pushkin's characters.

The article could only hint at what is now well known. In the spring of 1877, Tchaikovsky received several letters from one Antonina Milyukova, twenty-eight, a former student of the Moscow Conservatory who had fallen in love with him. The letters made a profound impression on the thirty-eight-year-old composer who consequently wrote the opera based on *Eugene Onegin,* where the plot revolves around the letter written by the infatuated provincial girl Tatiana to the social dandy Onegin.

Pushkin has the cold Onegin reject the letter of the naive, emotional Tatiana. He, and therefore his readers, interpreted the rational Onegin's attitude as a fatal mistake. Apparently, Tchaikovsky decided not to repeat Onegin's error, and he responded to Milyukova's letter and feelings. He married her.

It happened very quickly. Three months passed between her first letter and their wedding, and it ended in total disaster: right after the wedding, Tchaikovsky felt deep revulsion for his wife and eventually ran away.

No one doubts today that Tchaikovsky's marriage influenced his composing *Eugene Onegin.* But why did the homosexual Tchaikovsky marry in the first place?

What exactly do we know about Tchaikovsky's sexual orientation? As a young musician in the Soviet Union, I heard two oft-repeated rumors: one, that Tchaikovsky was homosexual, and two, that because he was, Alexander III (or his entourage) forced him to commit suicide.

The second rumor appears to have no solid documentary proof, while the number of accounts confirming the first rumor keeps growing. Tchaikovsky's homosexuality can be now considered a proven fact, despite the continuing attempts in Russia to deny it.[12]

Certainly, Tchaikovsky's sex life, like everyone's, influenced his worldview and his work (and vice versa). However, it was kept in the closet and thus artificially separated from his artistic output. Now it has become clearer how his creative strategies were dictated by his sexual orientation. In the West, where scholars started writing about the sex life of geniuses and about Tchaikovsky's homosexuality in particular long ago, there are two theories.

The first, which prevailed from the early twentieth century to the 1990s, depicted Tchaikovsky's homosexual life in tsarist Russia in an exclusively tragic light. Allegedly, Tchaikovsky lived in constant fear of exposure, which would have destroyed his career and life (as happened, for example, in 1895 to Oscar Wilde in England). The composer, according to this theory, unsuccessfully attempted to rid himself of his "perversion," suffered terribly, and therefore wrote tormented and "pathological" music.

This theory, accepted by music critics and many biographers, reflected the views of the mainstream majority that homosexuality was a "disease." It suited Western music scholars, too, for it helped to explain what they interpreted as overheated "camp" emotiveness and "incorrectness" (as compared to the classical Austro-German symphonic tradition) of Tchaikovsky's music.

But starting in the late 1990s, as a result of shifts in public opinion toward sexual minorities, the West (and particularly American academic circles) attempted a revisionist view of Tchaikovsky's image as a homosexual.

According to this new interpretation, Tchaikovsky's homosexual sex life, which began at the St. Petersburg School of Jurisprudence (where his classmates included such subsequently notorious homosexuals as Prince Vladimir Meshchersky and the poet Alexei Apukhtin), gradually settled down, and he was satisfied with it and even happy. It was an easy leap now to maintain that generally Tchaikovsky was "a reasonably happy man."[13]

This version, which also forcefully refuted charges of hysteria and pathology in Tchaikovsky's music, rested largely on two main considerations. First, its proponents claimed that Russia in the second half of the nineteenth century was, contrary to popular opinion, quite tolerant of homosexuality, having more in common with San Francisco a hundred years later than with contemporary Victorian London.

As proof, these American musicologists referred to the very kindly attitude of Alexander II, and then of Nicholas II, to Prince Meshchersky, a prominent conservative journalist of the era whose homosexuality was no secret in the highest circles of St. Petersburg.

The love of the Romanovs for Tchaikovsky goes without saying. Both Alexander III and his wife melted from his music. Alexander called *Eugene Onegin* his favorite opera. In 1888, the emperor awarded Tchaikovsky a lifetime pension of 3,000 rubles in silver annually.

Basically, the Romanovs perceived Tchaikovsky as their composer laureate, creating music for various ceremonial occasions (including a special cantata for the coronation of Alexander III) as well as church music at the emperor's personal request. The familial love of Tchaikovsky's music was passed on to Alexander III's son, Nicholas II.

Another source for this new theory of Tchaikovsky as a happy person, especially in his later years, are the memoirs of people who knew him in that period and often saw him "animated and full of life." Modest Tchaikovsky's evidence has great weight in this regard; the composer's younger brother wrote a fundamental biography, *The Life of Peter Ilych Tchaikovsky,* published in the early twentieth century. Modest stressed how "cheerful and lively" the composer was in his final days.

But Modest, author of the libretti for his brother's operas *Queen of Spades* and *Iolanthe*—and, like his brother, a homosexual, as evinced in his frank unfinished autobiography—had an agenda. He wanted to refute, without saying so outright, the rumors of Tchaikovsky's suicide, at that time already circulating in Russian musical circles; they were elicited in part by the fact that the composer's last work was his tragic Sixth ("Pathétique") Symphony, which many contemporaries considered a requiem for himself.

Modest, however, spoke of Tchaikovsky's "hysteria" in the biography and noted his "out-of-the-ordinary nervousness," adding, "according to some contemporary scientists, genius is a kind of psychosis."[14] (Modest was referring to the influential French psychiatrist of the period, Théodule Ribeaux, fashionable in Russia, too, who wrote in one of his popular works, "The character of hysterical patients can change like the pictures in a kaleidoscope . . . the most constant thing about them is their inconsistency. Yesterday they were cheerful, sweet, and polite; today they are gloomy, irritable, and inaccessible.")[15]

Tchaikovsky's doctor, Vassily Bertenson, also stressed the composer's "extreme nervousness," which forced him to lie awake at night "with the sense of overwhelming horror."[16] Lacking Prozac in those days, Tchaikovsky smoked "insatiably" (he had begun smoking at the age of fourteen), adding powerful doses of alcohol. According to Dr. Bertenson, the composer "abused cognac and there were periods, his brothers said, when he was on the verge of real alcoholism."[17]

Alina Briullova, who was close to Tchaikovsky for many years, confirmed that "he truly was a man with sick nerves," and had "a definite neurosis, that sometimes grew acute to the point of inexpressible suffering: a burning, causeless ennui, which he could not shake, an inability to control his jangling nerves, a fear of people . . . it tormented him terribly and poisoned his life."[18]

The psychiatrist Ribeaux described this type as having "sudden flares of anger and indignation, uncontrolled delights, fits of despair, explosions of crazy merriment, impulses of strong attachment, unexpected moments of tenderness or fits of temper, during which they, like spoiled children, stamp their feet and break furniture."

The best illustration for that page from a psychiatrist's treatise is this excerpt from Tchaikovsky's December 1877 letter to his brother Anatoly (first published by Valery Sokolov), describing the scene the composer made at his faithful servant, Alexei Safronov. "I suspected that there was something wrong with his genital member. I kept pestering him about how things were. He resisted. I suddenly grew furious, tore at my tie and shirt, broke a chair and so on. When I was indulging in these strange gymnastic exercises, my eyes suddenly met his. He was so terrified, he was looking at me so piteously, completely pale, he kept saying 'What's the matter with you, calm down,' and so on, that I instantly did."[19]

A nervous wreck (a modern diagnosis might be "borderline personality disorder") certainly can enjoy moments and even long periods of happiness, but it would be quite a stretch to call him happy. A similar stretch is calling the attitude toward homosexuality in Tchaikovsky's Russia tolerant.

Let's look at the case of Prince Meshchersky, the favorite example of the modern-day Tchaikovsky "revisionists." Yes, the Romanovs tolerated the openly homosexual Meshchersky (who, according to Alexander Poznansky, was Tchaikovsky's "intimate friend")[20] and supported his ultra-conservative publication, *The Citizen*, with generous government grants. But the Russian political elite seethed and kept looking for ways to open the eyes of Alexander III and then Nicholas II about Meshchersky.

Yevgeny Feoktistov, chief of the department overseeing press and publishing under Alexander III, recorded in his diary that Prince Meshchersky made "a very depressing impression on all decent people; his newspaper is considered the tsar's; they said that it should serve as the mouthpiece of the Sovereign himself, and just as if on purpose, the disgusting story with some flutist or drummer came to light . . . How could I not mourn that the Sovereign, distinguished by an instinctive disgust for everything base and perverted, has given a man shamed in public opinion the chance to abuse his name?"[21]

Such diary entries, made by some of the most influential figures of the period, were quite common.[22] Their hostile or mocking tone makes it clear: in a situation when sodomy was considered a crime (the Criminal Code read: "Anyone guilty of the unnatural act of sodomy is subject to being stripped of all rights and exiled to Siberia"), accusing someone of homosexuality was a potent weapon and was routinely used to discredit political enemies and for blackmail.

Homosexuals were under tight police surveillance in this period, as evidenced by an official memorandum of 1894 found in the archives of

the minister of state property, Mikhail Ostrovsky (brother of the drama-
tist Alexander Ostrovsky, who was a friend of Tchaikovsky's), which lists
and describes the most notorious homosexuals in St. Petersburg (approximately seventy men), based on agent reports.[23] It says about Prince
Meshchersky, "He uses young men, actors, and cadets and becomes their
patron for it . . . To determine the qualities of the rear ends of his victims,
he uses a billiards table."[24]

The author of the memorandum insisted that the government
increase its war on homosexuality: "The consequences of this evil, which
has apparently set deep roots in the capital, are varied and harmful to a
high degree. Besides perverting public morality and public health, it is a
particularly harmful influence on the family situation of young men, students of almost all educational institutions, and the discipline of the
troops."[25]

The idea that society and law in Russia were easy on homosexuals is a
myth. We also have to bear in mind the specific nature of laws in Russia—
in every period. Public life there is based not on laws but on "understandings." That means that formally existing laws are applied or ignored
depending on the position and wishes of the authorities. An unknown
peasant "sodomist" could be herded to Siberia in leg irons, but a member
of the elite, like Prince Meshchersky, under the patronage of the emperor,
could slip out of any dangerous situation.

No one could feel confident of the future in those conditions (which
is one of the goals of a society built on "understandings"). That life—and
not just for homosexuals—could not be called "happy." That is why
Herzen, Turgenev, Tolstoy, Dostoevsky, and Mussorgsky (and many other
contemporaries of Tchaikovsky from the artistic world) could hardly be
described as "happy" people.

Tchaikovsky's sense of a troubled existence, shared with the Russian
intelligentsia as a class, was exacerbated by his mental instability and, of
course, belonging to an ostracized sexual minority. In other words,
Tchaikovsky was unhappy not because he was homosexual but because
he was a neurasthenic Russian intellectual at a critical juncture in history,
and a homosexual to boot.

This is clear from Tchaikovsky's letter of January 1878 to Nikolai Rubinstein, in which he declines a flattering invitation to travel to the World's Fair in Paris as a representative of Russia. "In Paris, I would start to suspect every new acquaintance, and I would have many there, of *knowing* about me what I have been trying to hide so hard for so long. All right, I'm sick, I'm crazy, but now I can't live anywhere where I have to appear, be prominent, or call attention to myself."[26]

Tchaikovsky's hasty marriage to Milyukova represented, in fact, a way out and a cover—as it has been before and since for countless gay men who were forced to adjust to a hostile society. What complicated the situation for Tchaikovsky was that, even though he had a mind "with a large dose of humor and not without sarcasm," he was still first and foremost a hyperexcitable composer of genius.

He could not just conveniently take a wealthy wife, as did one of his gay friends, Vladimir Shilovsky. (Yet even the bon vivant Shilovsky had difficulties with the marriage, as Tchaikovsky informed his brother Modest: "Shilovsky's wedding has taken place. He boozed with no sleep, bawling and fainting all the time. Now he is completely happy and satisfied. He penetrated his wife [that is the complete truth] and he spends his days calling on aristocrats.")[27]

Tchaikovsky sublimated his emotions in music. It was his curse and his blessing, as it usually is with every creative personality, regardless of sexual orientation. Unable "to penetrate" Milyukova (from another letter to Modest: "The deflowering did not take place . . . But I have set myself up in such a way that there is no need to worry about that")[28], the composer wrote *Eugene Onegin*.

The autobiographical nature of the opera in view of Tchaikovsky's circumstances seems obvious. But it manifests itself not where earlier scholars had sought it, naively assuming that Tatiana was inspired by Milyukova, who had written love letters to Tchaikovsky. In fact, Tatiana is Tchaikovsky himself.

Freud believed that the hysterical personality is constantly playing out a role of the other—woman as male and man as female. The border-line personality is always breaking out of the framework of its gender. In Tchaikovsky's case, this was heightened by his creative impulse and also his homosexuality.

Expanding the gender field for his self-expression, Tchaikovsky appropriated Milyukova's behavior and letters. (Sokolov points out that even after he left Milyukova, Tchaikovsky continued using her letters as material for his work: the lyrics of at least one song in his vocal cycle op. 60 are a paraphrase of her words.) It was no accident that he began working on the opera with the episode in which Tatiana writes to Onegin. That scene is one of the opera's emotional and musical peaks. Tatiana's "gasp" as she anxiously awaits Onegin's response—"O my God! How miserable, how pathetic am I!"—is Tchaikovsky's emotion.

Tchaikovsky's strategy in *Eugene Onegin* is complex: his autobiographical "I" is divided into the shy but strong Tatiana and the fiery but elegiac young poet Lensky.[29] Turgenev was the first to note that Lensky in the opera is a much more formidable presence than in the work by Pushkin, who treated Lensky sympathetically but with irony. Tchaikovsky, contrary to widespread presumption, could be ironic in his music. But there isn't a trace of irony in his attitude toward Lensky. He admires him. Where Pushkin saw reason for mockery, Tchaikovsky elevates Lensky to a tragic pedestal.

The best example of this is Lensky's aria before his duel with Onegin. Pushkin makes Lensky's poem before his death a parody of the Romantic clichés of the time, but there is no parody in the music. The aria is the most popular number in the opera and the most famous tenor aria in Russian music. (I doubt Pushkin could have imagined such a rendering of his parody.)

Tchaikovsky accomplished this radical emotional transformation of Pushkin's text because of his identification with Lensky. For Tchaikovsky, Lensky is the victim par excellence, which was how he saw himself.

The choreographer George Balanchine, who came from the old St. Petersburg and had known people who had been Tchaikovsky's friends, often told me that the composer considered himself a martyr, the victim of society that rejected and persecuted his sexual orientation, this essential component of his ego.[30] This was also the posthumous perception of Tchaikovsky's image in Russian intellectual circles, succinctly summarized by Boris Asafyev, the best authority on the composer's works: "Tchaikovsky, finally, was a martyr."[31]

Describing Lensky, Pushkin tosses away a line that for Tchaikovsky could have been the key to his identification with Lensky; the poet mentions Lensky's "fear of vice and shame." The composer wrote about Lensky to Nadezhda von Meck: "Isn't the death of an enormously talented young man over a fatal confrontation with society's view of honor profoundly dramatic and touching?"

In Tchaikovsky's opera the real "couple" is not Onegin and Tatiana, whose love is the center of Pushkin's narrative, but Tatiana and Lensky.

According to Tchaikovsky, Lensky's death is the consequence and result of his "otherness," and Tatiana survives only because she submits to the dictates of high society and "*bon ton*," even though that brings her to a spiritual breakdown.

This is a George Sandian interpretation of Pushkin's work, coming via Herzen and Turgenev, whom the composer admired and read avidly. That is why Turgenev had reacted so sensitively to Tchaikovsky's innovative promotion of Lensky to major protagonist (less perceptive contemporaries did not notice this radical shift).

Transforming Pushkin's work into a Turgenevian novel with a hidden agenda, Tchaikovsky feared that his *Onegin* was doomed to remain a work "for a few" (although, like every author, he hoped for a miracle). The miracle took place: this was the opera that made Tchaikovsky the most popular Russian composer.

It happened gradually. First the Russian public bought the piano scores of *Onegin*. The demand for the sheet music grew steadily as more amateur singers began to study excerpts from the opera—primarily, Tatiana's letter scene and Lensky's aria before the duel. A typical reaction is in von Meck's letter of September 24, 1883, to Tchaikovsky: "When I hear the duel scene on the piano, I cannot express in words what I feel. I come to a state where I can only say, 'Ah, I can't take it anymore!' whereas when I read the same scene in Pushkin, I merely say, 'Poor little Lensky!'"

Eugene Onegin started to sell out every performance. The box office success increased the number of new productions. The opera became the absolute champion on every index: popular love of Russian audiences, number of performances, and, subsequently, critical esteem. By now it could be said that Tchaikovsky's interpretation is more entrenched than Pushkin's original approach. Thus, Tolstoy's attempt to nip the success of this opera in the bud failed, adding to the eternal quandary: how is the cultural canon formed, and who plays the more important role in the process—the experts or the consumers?

PART V

CHAPTER 12

Dostoevsky and the Romanovs

On Monday, April 4, 1866, Emperor Alexander II took his custom-ary stroll in St. Petersburg's Summer Garden. He liked his daily constitutional, perhaps imitating his father, Nicholas I. Besides the obvious health benefits, it gave the forty-seven-year-old ruler, tall and stately, with mustache and lush sideburns and slightly bulging eyes with a gentle gaze, a sense of unity with his people. He was not accompanied by retinue or bodyguards.

After his walk, Alexander headed toward his waiting carriage at the Summer Garden entrance. A pistol shot rang out from the crowd of gawkers. The assailant was a young student, Dmitri Karakozov, who belonged to a secret revolutionary society. He missed (he had an ancient double-barreled pistol), but the bullet whizzed by so close that it burned the emperor's military cap.

The terrorist was instantly captured. Alexander came up to him and asked, "Who are you?" The student replied, "I am a Russian." Then, turning to the stunned people around him, he shouted, "Folks, I shot for you!"

Alexander immediately went to the Kazan Cathedral, where a service of thanksgiving for his miraculous salvation was held. Then he returned to the Winter Palace. The investigative machine was set in motion, to dig up the roots of this unprecedented act of terrorism in Russia.

It seemed incredible that a Russian could lift his hand against the monarch, anointed by God. The authorities and the public at first assumed that the conspiracy was headed by Poles, who were constantly rebelling and demanding separation from Russia. (The most recent uprising had been cruelly suppressed by Alexander II in 1863.) Hence Alexander's question to the assailant.

The masses rejoiced that the tsar was unharmed and cursed the foreign Poles. At the Bolshoi Theater in Moscow, the scheduled ballet, *The Pharaoh's Daughter*, was replaced by a special performance of Glinka's 1836 classic opera, *A Life for the Tsar*, in which the peasant Ivan Susanin heroically saved the founder of the Romanov dynasty, Tsar Mikhail, from the villainous Poles in 1613.

Tchaikovsky was at the Bolshoi that night and he wrote to his family,

> I think the Moscow audience went beyond the bounds of sense in their outburst of enthusiasm. The opera was not really performed, for as soon as the Poles appeared onstage, the whole theater shouted, "Down with the Poles!" and so on. In the last scene of Act 4, when the Poles are supposed to kill Susanin, the actor playing him started fighting the chorus members who played Poles, and being very strong, knocked down several of them, while the rest of the extras, seeing that the audience approved this mockery of art, truth, and decency, fell down, and the triumphant Susanin left unharmed, brandishing his arms, to the deafening applause of the Muscovites.[1]

In an attempt to maximize the propaganda windfall, the authorities decided to create a "new Susanin," so as to promote loyalty to the tsar. They picked a young peasant, Osip Komissarov, who happened to have been near the terrorist attacking Alexander II. The police announced that

Komissarov had pushed Karakozov's elbow just when he pulled the trigger, thereby saving the tsar. The new myth benefited from the fact that Komissarov, like the legendary Susanin, came from Kostroma Province, thus creating a direct line between the two heroic promonarchist exploits, separated by two and a half centuries.

Komissarov was presented to Alexander II at the Winter Palace, and to the cries of "Hurrah!" from the staff he was embraced by the emperor and elevated to the nobility, becoming Komissarov-Kostromskoy. General Petr Cherevin, in charge of the Karakozov investigation, cynically noted in his diary, which was published posthumously, "I find it quite politic to invent such an exploit; it is a forgivable fabrication and one that influences the masses beneficially."[2]

It is difficult to imagine the psychological shock Alexander II experienced after this totally unexpected attempt on his life. The emperor sincerely believed himself to be the people's benefactor, and for good reason: five years earlier, on February 19, 1861, he signed the greatest progressive act in Russian history, the Manifesto of Emancipation of the serfs.

This historic decision, in a stroke of a pen moving Russia from a feudal state to the new era, was one toward which Alexander (later often accused of indecisiveness) had moved stubbornly from his accession to the throne in 1855, sweeping aside doubts, arguments, and even direct resistance from both the right and the left. His severe father, Nicholas I, never did take such a bold step.

The people hailed the manifesto at first. (The authorities feared that the tsar's ukase would lead to drunkenness and then disorder in the villages, but that did not happen.) In gratitude, they called Alexander the Tsar Liberator. He considered the day of emancipation the best of his life: "I have the sense that I fulfilled a great duty."

Even the intellectual elite (a stratum traditionally given to skepticism) felt that an event of extraordinary significance had occurred. Alexander Nikitenko, a professor at St. Petersburg University, read that "precious" manifesto aloud to his wife and children in his study beneath a portrait of Alexander II, "which we regarded with profound reverence and gratitude"[3] (as he recorded in his diary).

The great poet and editor of the leftist journal *Contemporary* Nikolai Nekrasov, in his poem "Freedom," addressed an imagined peasant infant, "God is merciful! You will not know tears!" He called upon his fellow writers, "O Muse! Greet freedom with hope!" Even the implacable opponent of autocracy, the revolutionary émigré Herzen, doffed his metaphorical cap to Alexander II: "You have won, Galilean."

But the honeymoon soon ended for the Tsar Liberator. It seemed that this reform and the important ones that followed (administrative, judicial, military) ultimately satisfied no one. The nobles worried about the erosion of their position as the leading political class. The peasants were unhappy with the small land allotments for which they had to pay high prices. The intelligentsia demanded a European-style constitution. The radicals among students, the so-called nihilists, dreamed of overthrowing autocracy altogether and establishing a "peasant" socialism in Russia.

Nikitenko wrote in horror in his diary, "To speak badly of the government and accuse it of all wrongdoing has become the fashion . . . Will the government have the strength to restrain this disorderly movement that threatens Russia with innumerable catastrophes? The main thing is a lack of national, patriotic feeling. Society is handicapped by the absence of lofty beliefs."[4]

Karakozov's attempt on Alexander II's life was used by the authorities as an opportunity to instill "lofty beliefs" from above. As usual in such cases, cultural figures were quickly brought into play. Poetry in honor of the "savior of the emperor" Komissarov-Kostromskoy was hastily written by Prince Petr Vyazemsky, seventy-four, once Pushkin's liberal friend and now a major official, and by Apollon Maikov, who had previously praised Nicholas I in his verse.

They were major poets, but not trendsetters. The ultrademocratic Nekrasov was one, and the authorities forced him—on pain of banning his progressive journal, *Contemporary*—to write an ode in honor of the "new Susanin."

Son of the People! I sing of thee!
You will be glorified a lot!
You are great—like the weapon of God
Who directed your hand!

All three odes—by Vyazemsky, Maikov, and Nekrasov—were included in a deluxe presentation book, *Osip Komissarov-Kostromskoy, Savior of the Emperor,* published in Moscow and ornamented by a portrait of Komissarov and his wife. Some think that bad verse looks better on good paper, but it didn't help here: even Nekrasov's work looked pitiful.

Was that all the government could squeeze out of Russian culture for its large-scale propaganda campaign? (Further poetry dedicated to Komissarov, and there was a lot of it, was even worse.) They did not manage to create a "new Susanin." That required authentic and not simulated "lofty beliefs" (both from the government and the cultural leaders), the absence of which was bemoaned by Professor Nikitenko. Glinka and Nicholas I had them: that is why their "cultural contract" brought about the great opera *A Life for the Tsar,* which still elicits "national, patriotic feeling" (as Nikitenko termed it). In Alexander II's Russia, there was an apparent shortage of "lofty beliefs" and "patriotic feelings."

The failure of this ambitious promonarchist cultural action in 1866 was symbolic of the ever-increasing alienation between the Romanovs and educated society. Autocracy was losing—slowly but inexorably—its former authority and its power over culture. The fear of the tsar's wrath was gradually replaced with the fear of losing one's audience. This was a historic transitional period.

The last great Russian monarchist writer was Fedor Dostoevsky. His road to apologist of the Romanovs was complicated and even dramatic. In 1847 the young Dostoevsky, already a famous writer, joined a socialist circle in St. Petersburg headed by Mikhail Petrashevsky. The police learned of the circle, and its members were arrested in 1849 on orders from Nicholas I. After an intensive investigation, supervised by Nicholas himself, the authorities sentenced twenty-one members of the Petrashevsky circle to hanging, including Dostoevsky.

Dostoevsky later recalled, "We Petrashevskyites stood on the scaffold and heard out our sentence without the slightest repentance . . . almost every condemned man was certain that it would be carried out and we suffered through at last ten horrible, immeasurably horrible minutes awaiting death." At the last moment, there was an announcement that Nicholas had commuted the death sentence to exile and hard labor in Siberia.

In Siberia, "contact with the people, fraternal unity with them in common misery, the understanding that you had become just like them," transfigured Dostoevsky. The writer had not been an atheist ("In our family we knew the New Testament from early childhood"), but in Siberia he became a Russian Orthodox fundamentalist and turned from socialist to monarchist.

When he became tsar in 1855, Alexander II's first act was to pardon the political "state criminals"—the Decembrists and Petrashevskyites, and in late 1859 Dostoevsky was at last allowed to return to St. Petersburg, where he resumed his literary career, publishing the sensational *House of the Dead,* a reportage of his years in Siberia. This was his only work that Tolstoy valued unconditionally.

Dostoevsky remained grateful to Alexander II for his mercy, and Karakozov's assassination attempt in 1866 stunned him. When he learned of it, Dostoevsky, forty-one at the time, a small, lumpy, and unkempt man, rushed to see the poet Maikov, also a monarchist, and shouted in a trembling voice, "They shot at the tsar!"

Prince Meshchersky, the St. Petersburg publisher of the semi-official publication *The Citizen* and fierce opponent of liberal reforms, hired Dostoevsky as editor in 1873 (Dostoevsky started his famous *Diary of a Writer* there), and he recalled that the writer's "soul burned with fiery loyalty to the Russian Tsar . . . I had never seen or met such a total and focused conservative . . . The apostle of truth in everything, major and trifling, Dostoevsky was as strict as an ascetic and as fanatical as a neophyte in his conservatism."[5]

When he heard of the attempt on the tsar's life, Dostoevsky was writing his novel *Crime and Punishment,* which may be his most popular work. The story of the St. Petersburg student Raskolnikov, who killed an old pawnbroker with an ax to prove to himself that he was a superman and could be compared to Napoleon, already posed the quintessential "Dostoevskian" question: "Am I a quaking creature or do I have the *right*?" Karakozov's act of terrorism (which Dostoevsky interpreted in that proto-Nietzschean key) gave the writer the idea to express what "filled my mind and heart" in his 1872 novel, *The Devils.* "I don't care if it turns out to be a pamphlet, I will have my say."

Prince Meshchersky claimed that Dostoevsky hated revolutionaries. Dostoevsky poured out this hatred in *The Devils.* He based it on the trial of a revolutionary group led by the fanatic Sergei Nechaev, who had executed their comrade, accused by Nechaev of being a traitor in 1869.

Dostoevsky avidly followed the trial in the press. The newspapers were, as usual, an important source of inspiration for him in those anxious days. In 1867, Dostoevsky wrote to a friend, "Do you subscribe to any papers? Read them, for God's sake, you can't do otherwise nowadays, not to be fashionable but because the visible connection among all public and private affairs becomes stronger and clearer."

Dostoevsky's marked interest in "despised" newspapers was innovative for Russia. The police blotter created a background for allegedly real, "Dostoevskian" characters with their exalted speechifying and mad deeds in a phantasmagorical atmosphere.

Dostoevsky's prose moves, breathes, pulses like a living organism, pulling the reader into its cruel, paroxysmal world (Dostoevsky was an epileptic). His words, sometimes running off in all directions, then gathering into a thick, sticky mass, form a fabric that yields to translation with difficulty. People who have marveled at the originals of Van Gogh's tightsprung paintings in museums, acutely feeling the bite of each nervous stroke, and then looked at the same works in reproductions, even faithful ones, will understand what I mean. Dostoevsky should be read in Russian.

In early March 1877, the frigate *Svetlana* (named after the popular ballad by the poet Zhukovsky, Alexander II's tutor) sailed into the port of Norfolk, Virginia. On board the ship an eighteen-year-old marine guard was reading Dostoevsky avidly. He began with *The Devils* (which shook him to tears) and then intended to move on to *Crime and Punishment.* His nineteen-year-old cousin had sent him both books, supervising his reading.

The books were not brand-new—*Crime and Punishment* came out eleven years earlier, *The Devils,* six—but they still had far to go to before taking a place in the cultural canon, so the emotionally charged reading by a young naval officer was interesting from a purely sociological point of view. More notably, the young seaman was Grand Duke Konstantin Romanov, grandson of Nicholas I and nephew of the ruling tsar, and his cousin Sergei was Alexander II's son.

Grand Duke Konstantin Konstantinovich Romanov (1858–1915) was a remarkable figure. He was the only Romanov to become a well-known poet (signing his verse K.R.). His father was a liberal and an advocate of Alexander II's reforms. Konstantin grew up a liberal too. He and his cousin Sergei were tall, slender, and handsome, with a dreamy gaze, and they were close friends. But their political views were diametrically opposed, which was probably a sign of the times.

In 1879, Grand Duke Konstantin noted in his diary,

> I argued with Sergei, we talked about what if we have a revolu-
> tion. What will we do, the Romanovs? Would we have to leave
> Russia? That would be the worst disaster for me. I tried to
> expound the idea to Sergei that revolutions bring harm only to
> those against whom they are directed but they have a beneficial
> effect on the country. I gave him France as an example. Sergei was

horrified by my theory and said, "Tu es à plaindre avec de pareilles idées" ("You are pathetic with such ideas").[6]

Subsequently, both cousins became important bureaucrats. Grand Duke Sergei (who married for the sake of decorum but was a homosexual) was appointed Moscow's general governor in 1891 by his brother, Emperor Alexander III, who valued his strict conservative views and administrative zeal. In 1905, Sergei was killed by a terrorist, but few people regretted it, among them Leo Tolstoy, who exclaimed upon learning of the assassination, "A horrible thing!" adding perspicaciously, "And it will be worse."

K.R., a model family man and father of seven children, died mourned by many, as general inspector of the country's military schools and also president of the Imperial Academy of Sciences. He was shattered by the death of his son, Oleg, twenty-three, also a gifted poet, in the First World War.

In 1918, after the victory of the Bolshevik revolution, three of his children who had been exiled to the Urals were executed together with the widow of Grand Duke Sergei (who had become a nun after her husband's assassination): they were thrown down a mine shaft, and then grenades were thrown in after them. The victims did not die right away. Legend has it that even a few days later, feeble sounds of church hymns could be heard coming from the shaft.

In their letters, the great figures of Russian culture who knew him (Tchaikovsky, Fet, Dostoevsky) used the same words—"dear," "charming," "pleasant"—to describe the poetry and personality of K.R. His poems (love lyrics and religious meditations) are professional, traditional, sincere, and easily set to music, which many Russian composers did, including Tchaikovsky.

Amusingly, K.R.'s most famous work today is not his play *King of Judea* (with music by Alexander Glazunov), which he wrote on Tchaikovsky's advice and which was very controversial in its time, nor his translation of *Hamlet,* long considered exemplary, but a simple poem he wrote in 1885, which begins with the words: "He's dead, poor fellow! He lay a long time / In the military hospital . . ."

I remember the doleful song—whose authors no one knew; it was considered a folk song—being sung by Russian veterans begging in trains after World War II. It is still performed today, at tipsy parties, and now there is always some expert to inform the group that the words were written by Grand Duke Konstantin Romanov.

There is a curious episode in the complex history of Dostoevsky's relationship with members of the Romanov family. In early 1878 the writer was visited by Admiral Dmitri Arsenyev, tutor of Alexander II's sons, who came "in the name of the Sovereign, who would like Fedor Mikhailovich to have a beneficial effect with his conversations on the young grand dukes."[7]

There is reason to assume that the flattering visit was prompted by a recent mini-scandal in the royal family. On December 25 the twenty-year-old Grand Duke Sergei recorded the following plaintive lines in his diary: "I recently had a very unpleasant story: Papa accused me of depravity and that Sasha V. aided me in it, and the slander insulted me bitterly. Lord help me! Amen!"[8]

We can only guess what the "unpleasant story" was and whether it was related to Sergei's homosexuality, but it resulted in Alexander II's wish, passed on by Admiral Arsenyev, for Dostoevsky to talk sense to his wayward son. Alexander II—and Alexander III after him—valued Dostoevsky's loyalty to the ideals of autocracy and his oft-expressed idea that young people must be brought up in an Orthodox and highly moral spirit. Dostoevsky, in turn, was happy to influence the views of the Romanovs in a personal conversation.

On March 21, 1878, Dostoevsky had lunch in the Winter Palace with the grand dukes and their tutors. K.R. was present and noted his impressions of the writer in his diary: "This is a sickly looking man, with a thin, long beard and extremely sad and thoughtful expression on his pale face. He speaks very well, as if reading a prepared text."[9]

Judging by subsequent invitations to luncheons and dinners with the Romanov family circle, Dostoevsky's "edifying" conversation with the grand dukes was considered a success. K.R. was delighted: "I love Dostoevsky for his pure, childlike heart, for his profound faith and observant mind."[10]

Dostoevsky told his wife that the grand dukes "have kind hearts and not run-of-the-mill minds and can hold their own in a discussion, sometimes espousing still immature convictions; but they also know how to treat opposing views of their interlocutors with respect."[11]

This idyllic picture, "the great Russian writer instructs members of the ruling dynasty on questions of morality and piety," might not have taken place. While the Romanov family loved Dostoevsky's *The Devils* for its satirical depiction of "nihilists" and revolutionaries, they had read only a radically bowdlerized version.

Dostoevsky was unable to publish the most important chapter of *The Devils* (called "At Tikhon's"), which contained "Stavrogin's confession." The demonic Nikolai Stavrogin, a central character in the novel, confesses a grievous sin to the monk Tikhon that has been tormenting his conscience: he had raped an underage girl.

The conservative Mikhail Katkov, an influential adviser of Alexander II and later of Alexander III, and editor of the journal *Russian Herald*, which published *The Devils* in installments, rejected that chapter as "too real"—the topic and the writing seemed shocking, verging on pornography. We can be sure that if "Stavrogin's confession" had been printed in the journal, Dostoevsky would never have been invited to meet with the young Romanovs—he would have been a scandalous figure.

Dostoevsky was in despair from this literary vivisection at first: the most striking episode of the novel was gone. But then he accepted it, apparently—albeit with pain—and did not include the skipped chapter in a separate edition of *The Devils*. It was never published in his lifetime, appearing for the first time in 1922.

There is a theory that Dostoevsky dropped the chapter that was so dear to his heart because he feared a new wave of talk (there had been whispers for a long time) that the episode with the little girl had autobiographical roots. There is no question that Dostoevsky had a morbid fixation on the topic: there are similar occurrences in other novels—*Crime and Punishment, The Idiot,* and *The Raw Youth.*

It is a very delicate issue. Contemporary Russian specialists speak cautiously about Dostoevsky's possible nymphophilia.[12] His defenders foam at the mouth at this slander and gossip. But that "slander" was discussed by Turgenev and Tolstoy, which makes it at least a fact of the literary discourse of Dostoevsky's era and therefore a fact of cultural history.

Dostoevsky wrote to his confidant, the poet Maikov, "Worst of all, my nature is vile and overly passionate, I always go to the last barrier everywhere and in everything, all my life I have crossed the line." We know that Dostoevsky acknowledged his passion for gambling at roulette as one of his worst vices. He repented in his letters to his wife, Anna, calling himself every possible name: "feckless and base, a petty player"; "I'm worse than a beast"; and so on.

Dostoevsky's "passion" is also recorded in his letters to his wife when it comes to sex. Despite the fact that she carefully excised (with an eraser) the most "indecent" passages when she prepared the letters for publication, a few things remain: "I kiss you every minute in my dreams, all of you, every minute, French kissing. I particularly love that about which was said: 'and he was delighted and enthralled by that thing.' I kiss that thing every minute in every manner and I intend to kiss it all my life."[13]

When he got a letter from his wife with an innocent, even naive hint—"I have the most seductive dreams, and there is a lot in them of one very, very sweet and dear man, whom you know very well—guess who?"—he responded with a hot epistle in which she was later forced to erase twenty-eight lines from one page alone. Dostoevsky concluded his erotic outburst with a confession: "Anna, you can tell just from this page what's happening to me. I'm in a delirium, I'm afraid I'll have a fit. I kiss your hands and palms, and feet, and all of you."[14]

. . .

There is a story that Turgenev told, recorded by the writer Ieronim Yasinsky, that Dostoevsky came to Turgenev once and started "nervously" telling him how he bought sexual favors from a twelve-year-old girl for 500 rubles. Turgenev interrupted him and ordered him from the house immediately, and Dostoevsky allegedly confessed that he had made it up to "amuse" Turgenev.[15]

We know that Turgenev considered Dostoevsky to be the Russian Marquis de Sade from his letter to the writer Saltykov-Shchedrin dated September 24, 1882. Turgenev wrote with disgust that de Sade "insists with particular pleasure on the perverted voluptuous bliss that comes from imposing sophisticated torture and suffering" and added, "Dostoevsky also describes in detail the pleasures of one such connoisseur in one of his novels."[16]

By this Turgenev clearly meant "Stavrogin's confession" from *The Devils*. Turgenev had an account to settle with that novel. Besides the fact that he was caricatured in it as the pathetic Westernizer writer Karmazinov, he was envious of the book's great success.

In 1862, Turgenev published *Fathers and Sons*, in which he first introduced the revolutionary "nihilist" character in his protagonist Bazarov. The author himself and the critics declared Bazarov "the new hero of our times," and he was the subject of endless debate and controversy. This was the peak of Turgenev's topicality for Russian readers.

Dostoevsky conceived his novel in great part as a polemical response to *Fathers and Sons*. Turgenev's Bazarov was described by the author as "a grim, wild, big figure." Dostoevsky's nihilists are petty devils; he wanted to show how the Bazarov type had degenerated in post-reform Russia.

When he presented his *Devils* in 1873 to the future Emperor Alexander III, Dostoevsky explained in the accompanying letter that there was a straight line "from fathers to sons," and that the Westernizers and liberals, like Belinsky and Turgenev, torn "from the native and unique sources of Russian life," engendered contemporary terrorists.

Turgenev apparently was aware of Dostoevsky's court maneuvers. In 1876, when Saltykov-Shchedrin asked why he wasn't the tsarevich's (that is, the future Alexander III's) tutor, Turgenev responded proudly, although perhaps not quite sincerely, that he did not wish to be "the domestic author" of the Romanov family à la Dostoevsky: "You mention teaching the heir; but it was after *Fathers and Sons* that I distanced myself more than ever from the circle in which I basically never did have entrée and writing or working for which I would have considered stupid and shameful."[17]

When Dostoevsky died on January 28, 1881 (a pulmonary artery burst, blood gushing from his mouth), the authorities did not know how to react. The day was saved by Konstantin Pobedonostsev, who in 1880 became high procurator of the Holy Synod (in effect minister of religious affairs) and was one of the closest advisers of Alexander II, and subsequently of Alexander III (whose tutor he was), and even of Nicholas II.

Pobedonostsev, who was described by his enemies as a "clean-shaven bat in eyeglasses and on its hind feet," was a powerful and unique figure. A lawyer by education, Pobedonostsev had a broad cultural outlook, adored the poetry of Tyutchev and Fet, and helped obtain state subsidies for Tchaikovsky.

Pobedonostsev's views were extremely conservative. His lodestar was the ideological triad of the era of Nicholas I (whom he revered as the greatest Russian monarch)—"Orthodoxy, Autocracy, and Nationality." The religious philosopher and critic Konstantin Leontyev, who knew Pobedonostsev well, said, "He is a very useful man; but how? He is like frost: he prevents further rot; but nothing will grow around him."

Pobedonostsev considered democratic ideas and parliamentarism "the great lie of our time." He read the daily press closely and hated it, blaming it for revolutionary ferment. He maintained that in the new era the recently illiterate Russia had suddenly ended up "with newspaper instead of book in hand," which was a "great disaster" for the country, leaving it vulnerable to liberal propaganda.

Dostoevsky considered Pobedonostsev his fellow ideologue and patron, and the latter esteemed the writer as a torchbearer of conservative philosophy; in 1880 he arranged an audience for Dostoevsky with the heir to the throne and his wife.

As soon as he learned of Dostoevsky's death, Pobedonostsev wrote to the heir, "He was a close friend and I am sad that he is gone. But his death is a great loss for Russia, too. Among writers he—perhaps the only one—was a fervent preacher of the basic principles of Faith, Nationality, love of Homeland. Our miserable youth, lost like sheep without a shepherd, trusted him, and his influence was very great and beneficial."[18]

Pobedonostsev asked the heir to request Alexander II to help the Dostoevsky family: "He was poor and left nothing but books." The future Alexander III responded instantly, "I am very, very sorry about the death of poor Dostoevsky, it is a great loss and positively no one can replace him."[19]

With a nudge from Pobedonostsev, the state shifted into full speed in organizing the funeral. On Pobedonostsev's direct orders, the Alexander Nevsky Monastery (the central Russian Orthodox monastery) offered Dostoevsky's widow space for his burial in their prestigious cemetery, the resting place of Karamzin and Zhukovsky, the favorite writers of the Romanovs. For a former state prisoner and convict who had never been in government service, this was unprecedented generosity. The imperial treasury paid for Dostoevsky's funeral.

Dostoevsky's widow received a letter from the minister of finances, which read, "The Emperor on the 30th day of this January beneficently decreed: in view of the services of your late husband to Russian literature, in which he held one of the most honorable places, you, esteemed madam, and your children will receive a pension of two thousand rubles a year."[20] Alexander II also ordered that if the widow wished it, her children's education would be paid for as well. Pobedonostsev became their guardian.

The daily newspapers, which Pobedonostsev so hated, gave enormous coverage to the tsar's munificence. Alexander II was portrayed as the patron of Russian culture who knew, unlike his father, Nicholas I, how to forgive former dissidents. The moves from above coincided with public sentiment, and Dostoevsky's funeral turned into a huge public event, imbued with symbolic meaning.

The coffin, enveloped in gold brocade and covered with wreaths, was borne by pallbearers from Dostoevsky's apartment to the monastery, accompanied by an enormous procession (the newspapers said there were thirty thousand people). The St. Petersburg intelligentsia was present, as were students. The crowd sang the solemn prayer "Holy God" continually; many wept. Pobedonostsev could be satisfied.

The liberal Annenkov, a close friend of Turgenev's, reported sarcastically to France,

> What a pity that Dostoevsky could not see his own funeral—his loving and envious soul and his Christian and angry heart would have been soothed. No one else will ever have such a funeral. He is the only one given to the earth in this way, and before only Patriarch Nikon and Metropolitan Filaret Drozdov got something approximating his send-off. Be joyous, dear shade. You accomplished being added to the list of your predecessors of the holy and Byzantine type. Perhaps soon your relics will be sanctified and my children will hear the prayer, "Saint Fedor, intercede with God on our behalf."[21]

Dostoevsky's widow always said that if he had not died on January 28, 1881, he would have been killed by news of the "villainy of 1 March," when a month after the writer's death the Tsar Liberator Alexander II was assassinated by a bomb thrown by a terrorist. The antimonarchist fanatics, whom Dostoevsky had so feared and hated, had, it seemed, succeeded. Russia was in shock.

But Pobedonostsev was on top of the situation, as always. He knew his former student, the new emperor, Alexander III. He immediately sent him a confidential letter that formulated the policy of the new monarch: "You are receiving a Russia that is bewildered, shaken, swept off course, and thirsting to be led by a firm hand."[22]

CHAPTER 13

Alexander III, the Wanderers, and Mussorgsky

On March 1, 1881, eleven-year-old Alexandre Benois, later a famous painter, heard the persistent ringing of the doorbell in his family townhouse in St. Petersburg. His father was being examined by the boy's older cousin, Dr. Leonty Benois. When the boy answered the door he saw a terrified policeman who shouted, "Is Dr. Benois here? He's wanted! The tsar was just killed! A bomb blew off his legs! The chief of police is wounded! Thirty-four wounds!"[1]

As Benois later recalled, he almost passed out. They didn't want to believe him when he ran into his father's bedroom with the terrible news. "The Lord has spared the tsar so many times, we're sure this time will be all right, too." But the imperial standard had already been lowered to half-staff over the main gates of the royal residence, the Winter Palace, and people were kneeling and weeping on the palace square.

Benois later commented that the attitude toward revolutionaries changed sharply after the murder of Alexander II. Previously, the nihilists were almost trendy, but after the assassination they were roundly condemned both by the general public and by intellectuals.

Photographs circulated throughout Russia of Alexander II, immediately known as the Martyr Tsar, in his coffin. The photograph hung both in the study of Benois's father and in the maid's room. When the impressionable boy looked at the photograph—the tsar was in uniform, covered below the waist—he shivered with horror at the thought that there were only stumps instead of the emperor's legs.

But there were two men who, while condemning the regicide, still dared to appeal to the new emperor to give Christian forgiveness to the terrorists. They were Leo Tolstoy and Vladimir Solovyov, a fashionable religious philosopher, twenty-seven years old.

In his lecture to an audience of over a thousand people, the tall, thin, and pale Solovyov (considered to be the prototype of Dostoevsky's favorite character, Alyosha Karamazov) called on Alexander III to pardon the killers, adding that if the regime rejected the Christian ideal of mercy then society should reject the regime.

Pandemonium followed those "seditious" words. Someone shouted, "You should be executed first, you traitor!" But many of Solovyov's listeners, especially women, wept.

Tolstoy wrote a letter to Alexander III saying that the way to combat terrorists was not with executions but in the spiritual sphere. "There is only one ideal that can be opposed to revolutionary beliefs . . . that is the ideal of love, forgiveness, and responding to evil with good."[2] Tolstoy asked Pobedonostsev to hand his letter to the emperor, but the high procurator of the Holy Synod refused. "Having read your letter, I saw that your faith is one thing and my and the Church's faith is another, and that our Christ is not your Christ."[3]

In the end, Tolstoy's letter was forwarded to Alexander III by his brother, Grand Duke Sergei. In response, the emperor said "that if the attack had been on him, he could have pardoned them, but he did not have the right to forgive the killers of his father." Five terrorists were hanged.

Pobedonostsev, who in his role as spiritual mentor wrote letters to Alexander III almost daily, advised the emperor to lock every door behind him personally, including his bedroom, and to look under tables and bed to see if there were terrorists lurking.

Alexander III, by no means a coward, big and very strong (he could bend iron bars), was so worked up that he mistakenly shot and killed a personal bodyguard when he thought the man was hiding a weapon behind his back. It turned out the poor officer was trying to conceal a cigarette from the tsar, who had entered the room unexpectedly.

The authorities faced a new cultural phenomenon: the accelerating demystification of the traditional image of the omnipotent and invulnerable Father Tsar. No one had been prepared for it, including the imperial security service: the assassination of Alexander II could have been prevented by the use of elementary precautions, nowadays routinely employed to protect every mid-level Russian oligarch.

The "ideological security service" also needed urgent reconstruction, but the Romanovs did not have enough gifted people to implement it. Pobedonostsev and his comrade and rival, the leading conservative journalist of the era, Mikhail Katkov, were intelligent, educated, and energetic, but their program was defensive and protective rather than positive and forward-looking. In addition, neither Pobedonostsev, Katkov, nor their fellow thinker Prince Meshchersky were good writers. They could not compete with the radicals—Nikolai Dobroliubov, Dmitri Pisarev, and Nikolai Chernyshevsky.

Prince Meshchersky admitted as much, complaining in a secret 1882 memorandum to Alexander III, "Whoever has stronger colors and sounds influences the public. For now the colors and sounds of the seditious press are stronger. We have to make every effort to send the public strong conservative sounds and colors."[4]

Meshchersky was asking Alexander for a major subsidy for "sending conservative sounds." The emperor's reaction? "Not a bad idea and I'm not against helping Meshchersky."[5] But the only great Russian writer who was willing to work with Meshchersky—Dostoevsky—was dead by then, and the prince had no other writers of that caliber at his side.

It is no wonder that Alexander III sighed nostalgically for the days when the monarchs were advised by people like the poet Zhukovsky, the tutor of Alexander II: "Such personalities were not rare then, but now they are enormously rare."[6]

Nevertheless, Alexander III and his advisers were certain that a conservative cultural policy would restore order and return the former stability. This was wishful thinking. They thought themselves realists, but in the cultural realm they often behaved like true Romantics, longing for a lost past.

Alexander III and his entourage did a lot to attract cultural figures: they met with writers, composers, and painters, awarded them subsidies and state pensions, and commissioned music, sculptures, and paintings, as well as monumental frescoes in churches. A good example is the friendly, albeit inconsistent, policy Alexander had for the Peredvizhniki, or Wanderers, the members of the 1870 Association of Traveling Art Exhibits.

The roots of the movement go back to 1863, when fourteen of the most talented students of the Imperial Academy of Arts, led by Ivan Kramskoy, refused to take part in the diploma exam and created an independent Art Artel, which functioned as a quasi-socialist commune: the artists rented a large apartment in St. Petersburg and lived and worked there together.

Outrage was the authorities' initial reaction to this bold step. The Academy of Arts was an official institution, under the supervision of the emperor, who personally decided which artists to encourage and which to punish. The rebellion against the academy was therefore seen as rebellion against the monarchy. The "communal" lifestyle also raised suspicions.

The young rebels proved their métier rather quickly, organizing art exhibits independent of the academy and government. The leading Wanderers—Kramskoy, Vassily Perov, Nikolai Ge, Ilya Repin, and Ivan Shishkin—became famous and commercially successful artists. Grand Duke Vladimir, vice-president and then president of the academy, used the carrot-and-stick approach: he would threaten them with official punishments and then try to lure them back into the academy fold.

Still, it was Grand Duke Vladimir, twenty-four years old, curly-haired, handsome, with gray-blue eyes, who commissioned twenty-six-year-old Repin to paint *The Volga Boatmen,* a large work depicting a colorful group of eleven bedraggled muzhiks hauling a barge. This canvas made Repin's reputation as a leading national painter. *Volga Boatmen* hung for many years in the billiard room of Prince Vladimir, who jokingly complained to Repin that he rarely got to see the painting: it was continually on loan to various European exhibitions.

The painting's reception was a vivid illustration of the Wanderers' position in Russian culture. According to Repin, the minister of transportation gave Repin a serious scolding for "showing Europe" the miserable wretches slaving under the broiling sun when "I have reduced that antediluvian method of transport to zero."[7]

The liberals were also certain that Repin's painting was hated "in the highest spheres" for its theme and "exposé" character. But at the same time, the grand duke, in love with the painting, would sometimes act as museum guide for his guests, lovingly explaining the background and psychology of each character in the work.

For all their intuitive preference for order and hierarchy, Alexander III and his entourage gradually realized that the official Academy of Arts, with its outmoded classicist norms, was out of touch with Russian life. The Wanderers, on the other hand, exhibited vivid scenes from provincial life, like Repin's *Procession of the Cross in Kursk Province,* or topical works like Vladimir Makovsky's *Bank Failure,* which revealed the vibrant, motley, and dramatic world of contemporary Russia.

The Wanderers interpreted even traditional religious subjects in a new way. Ge's painting *What Is Truth?,* depicting Christ and Pontius Pilate, projected their conflict onto the contemporary world, so that Tolstoy, for example, saw them as a Russian governor and his prisoner. Conservatives, however, found Ge's works on Christian themes repugnant, because of their excessive naturalism and contemporary allusions.

An indignant Pobedonostsev complained in 1890 to Alexander III,

I cannot avoid reporting to Your Imperial Highness about the general outrage elicited by Ge's painting *What Is Truth?*, exhibited at the Wanderers' show. People are angry not only at the painting but the artist, as well. People of every rank, returning from the exhibition, wonder: how can it be that the government permitted the public exhibition of a blasphemous painting, deeply offensive to religious feeling and at the same time unquestionably tendentious . . . And we must not forget that the traveling exhibition, after St. Petersburg, usually goes around cities in Russia. We can imagine the impression it will make on people and what—I dare to add—censure of the government, since our folk still believe that everything permitted by the government has its approval.

Alexander III, who sympathized with the Wanderers, in this case shared the orthodox emotions of his closest adviser, and wrote his resolution on the memorandum: "The picture is disgusting, write about this to I. N. Durnovo [the minister of internal affairs], I believe that he can ban it from traveling around Russia and remove it now from the exhibit."[8]

The topically oriented Wanderers could not bypass something as sensational as the revolutionary nihilists. Repin devoted a cycle of paintings to them, the best depicting a priest with a cross visiting the prison cell of a condemned terrorist sitting on an iron bed.

His revolutionary refusing final confession is a man of enormous spiritual strength, suffering but righteous. We see a contemporary Jesus Christ, arms crossed, prison jacket open at his sunken chest. This was Repin's response to his fellow Wanderer Kramskoy's controversial painting *Christ in the Wilderness* (1872), where the same question of moral choice was interpreted in a much more conventional vein.

Repin had a complex relationship with the leader of the Wanderers, the charismatic Kramskoy. Kramskoy was both teacher and older comrade. It was Kramskoy who initiated a conversation with Repin one evening about Christ and His temptations: "Almost every one of us has to solve the fateful question, to serve God or mammon."

Repin was stunned by Kramskoy's profoundly personal reaction to the Bible. "Of course, I've read it all before, I even studied it with boredom and listened to it in church, sometimes without any interest . . . But now! Can it be the same book?"[9]

That made all the more bitter Kramskoy's transformation from fiery advocate of artistic independence into a fashionable portraitist, who charged 5,000 rubles for each work and used his newfound fortune to build a luxurious two-story dacha and studio near St. Petersburg with vast grounds, strawberry patches, greenhouse, bathing pool, and a large staff.

Wealth and fame ruined Kramskoy, Repin thought. "Among his friends, Kramskoy had long lost his charm . . . They called his portraits dry, officious, his painting old-fashioned, colorless, and tasteless." It reminded Repin of the sorrowful tale of the fall of an artist, described by Gogol in "The Portrait." Kramskoy gained entrée to the highest government circles, and painted the coronation of Alexander III, but he never could finish the work he had planned ten years earlier, *Rejoice, King of Judea.*

Kramskoy developed an addiction to morphine, aged rapidly, grew gray, and whenever anything upset him, he would clutch his heart, breaking off the conversation, cautiously sinking to his Persian ottoman in his chic St. Petersburg apartment. "Nothing left of the passionate radical,"[10] Repin concluded bitterly. Kramskoy died of a heart attack before reaching fifty, during a portrait session, brush in one hand, palette in the other, without a cry or moan.

Just a month before Kramskoy's death, the composer Alexander Borodin, fifty-three, also succumbed to a heart attack. Borodin was one of the most important members of a group of Russian composers (which also included Modest Mussorgsky, Nicolai Rimsky-Korsakov, Mily Balakirev, and César Cui) dubbed the Mighty Bunch, known in the West as the Mighty Five. The received wisdom was that there was a lot in common between the Mighty Bunch and the Wanderers: both artistic associations were traditionally described as outsiders rebelling against official art and espousing "realism" in their works.

It was more complicated than that. The Wanderers were trained at the Academy of Arts, receiving a superlative professional polish. The Bunch, on the other hand, learned from one another (under the supervision of the strict and suspicious Balakirev). This had a negative effect on their technical prowess and hindered their composing (especially for Mussorgsky and Borodin).

However, freedom from the routine conservatory methods allowed the Bunch to make bold artistic breakthroughs that subsequently influenced Puccini, Debussy, and Ravel, and made their music admired in the West. The Wanderers, on the other hand, remained a local Russian phenomenon.

It is true that both the Wanderers and the Mighty Bunch were nationalists and proponents of social relevance for art. But several of the pillars of the Wanderers (Repin, Vassily Surikov, Victor Vasnetsov, especially in their later years) moved away from the naturalistic approach that originally brought them national fame. The Bunch was always marked by an attraction to fantasy and vivid exoticism. Mussorgsky could even be called a proto-expressionist.

Alexander III was also a nationalist, perhaps the most sincere and consistent of all the Romanovs beginning with Peter I (only two women could rival him in that regard—Elizabeth I and Catherine the Great). Under Alexander III the imperial court, which used to communicate in French and German, suddenly spoke Russian. They stopped drinking French wines, which were replaced, to the dissatisfaction of many courtiers, by "Crimean vinegar."

The continual marriages to German princesses by his predecessors made Alexander III's "Russian" blood rather dubious, but he looked like a fairy-tale folk hero: a broad-shouldered giant with reddish blond hair and a stern look. The Wanderer Surikov considered Alexander III a true representative of the Russian people: "There was something grand about him."[11]

Alexander III created the first museum of national art—today the world-famous Russian Museum in St. Petersburg. It is hard to overestimate the ideological and practical significance of that gesture: it was declared at the summit of authority that Russian art has museum value, not a view shared by many at the time.

The tsar's collection highlighted the works of the Wanderers. He also patronized the great playwright Alexander Ostrovsky, whose delicious comedies of merchant life corresponded to the Wanderer aesthetic. In 1884, Alexander III bestowed an annual pension of 3,000 rubles on Ostrovsky, followed by a "special audience," joking as they met, "I hope you know who I am, and I know you. I am very pleased to see you at the palace."[12]

One would have expected Alexander to support the Bunch as well, but that did not happen. There is a simple explanation. In those days, many connoisseurs disliked the works of the Mighty Bunch: they seemed ugly, vulgar, and crass. Mussorgsky's music was mercilessly mocked by both Turgenev and Saltykov-Shchedrin.

Alexander III loved Tchaikovsky's music. Today it may seem that one can love Tchaikovsky and Mussorgsky both, but back then the two geniuses seemed—to themselves and others—to represent polar opposites in music. The usually gentle and tactful Tchaikovsky exclaimed wrathfully, "I send Mussorgsky's music to the devil with all my heart; it is the most banal and vile parody of music." Mussorgsky responded in kind.

So it comes as no surprise that Alexander III, who had pushed through Tchaikovsky's *Eugene Onegin* into the repertoire of the imperial theaters, would have personally crossed off a new production of Mussorgsky's *Boris Godunov* from the planned season in 1888 of the Maryinsky Theater.

That fact led the Soviet critics to proclaim that the highest authorities had been implacably hostile to Mussorgsky. In fact, Mussorgsky had a patron at the very top: Terty Filippov, who had served more than twenty

years in the State Comptroller's Office (he was its director; in fact, Filippov reported personally to the monarch between 1889 and his death in
1899). Controlling the revenues and expenses of all state and public funds,
Filippov was one of the most powerful officials in the land.

Filippov was a curious and even extravagant character. The illegitimate son (according to gossip) of a provincial postmaster, he made his
fantastic state career thanks to his reputation as an effective manager,
honest and incorruptible—very rare in Russia, both then and now.

Filippov's friends, impressed by his erudition in cultural and religious matters, saw him as a potential minister of education or high
procurator of the Holy Synod. But Pobedonostsev was high procurator
and very wary of Filippov as a possible rival.

The views of both men were similar: they were staunch conservative
defenders of the autocracy and the Orthodox Church. Yet there had been
a time when Filippov was an ardent reader of Belinsky's articles and
George Sand's novels, a "ruthless atheist" and almost socialist. His outlook changed, but traces of his Bohemian youth remained.

Filippov was a music lover, with a pleasant tenor, who enjoyed
singing folk songs and organized a pretty good choir at the Comptroller's
Office. He became a leading expert on Russian antiquity, studying old
manuscripts, icon painting, and church music. This led to a close friendship with the composer Balakirev, the guru of the Mighty Bunch, who
introduced Filippov to Mussorgsky.

Mussorgsky was undoubtedly the most talented member of the
Mighty Bunch, but no one in the group understood it. They treated him
the way a family might a gifted but wayward child, despairing of his
eccentric behavior, intemperate drinking, excessive (in the opinion of
others) self-regard, and inability to work in an organized and concentrated manner (attention-deficit disorder, perhaps). In their correspondence and conversations about Mussorgsky, words like "complete idiot,"
"almost an idiot," and "clouded brain" came up frequently.

When Mussorgsky was composing, people tugged at him from all sides with endless advice and criticism, friendly and otherwise. The press hated him. When his opera *Boris Godunov* (based on Pushkin) was shown for the first time in 1874 at the Maryinsky Theater, the critics were like attack dogs: "ugly monotony," "cacophony in five acts and seven scenes," and "stinking object." They were particularly exercised over the "blasphemous" tampering with the text of Pushkin's tragedy.

Even Cui, a fellow member of the Mighty Bunch, smacked Mussorgsky in print: "There are two main flaws in 'Boris': chopped-up recitative and scattered musical thoughts, making the opera potpourri-like in places." These flaws, in Cui's opinion, were the result of "careless, self-satisfied, and hasty composing."[13]

His friend's hostile attitude bewildered Mussorgsky. "Behind this mad attack, this flagrant lie, I see nothing, as if soapy water had spread in the air."[14]

Not surprisingly, Mussorgsky started his next opera, *Khovanshchina* (or "Khovansky Affair"), about the war the young Peter the Great and his cohort fought against the rebel *streltsy* (musketeers) and Old Believers, in 1682, feeling totally isolated. One of the few who came to his aid then was Filippov.

First Filippov created a sinecure for him in the State Comptroller's Office, and when the composer turned out to be incapable of performing even nominal office duties and fled his job, Filippov (with a few friends) took on paying Mussorgsky a private pension so that he could concentrate on *Khovanshchina*.

Filippov was eager for Mussorgsky to complete the opera also because he was particularly interested in the schism, considering it the epochal event in Russian life. Pobedonostsev viewed the Old Believers as enemies undermining Russian Orthodoxy. His deputy commented, "No one has caused as much harm to the Church in her struggle with the schism as Filippov."[15]

Filippov and Mussorgsky had lively discussions about the schism. The state comptroller provided Mussorgsky with books on its history, including his own writings. The composer read them avidly and used them to write his own original libretto for *Khovanshchina*, but he did not complete the opera, dying in 1881 at the age of forty-two. The funeral took place at the prestigious cemetery at the Alexander Nevsky Monastery in St. Petersburg, arranged by Filippov and Pobedonostsev working together for once. Rimsky-Korsakov completed and orchestrated *Khovanshchina.*

Khovanshchina is perhaps the greatest political opera of all time. It does have a love subplot, but it is clearly secondary. The main thing is the clash of different political forces, expressed in music of such power and passion that the opera comes across as an expressionist thriller.

Mussorgsky conjured up idealists, opportunists, traitors, political pragmatists, and religious martyrs, who lived on the stage like real people. The self-immolation of the schismatics in the finale invariably moves one to tears. This opera will always be timely for Russia, since it probes the secrets of the Russian soul perhaps even more deeply than Mussorgsky's more famous work, *Boris Godunov.*

A comparison of *Khovanshchina* with Glinka's *A Life for the Tsar,* composed in 1834–1836, seems inevitable. Both operas deal with the Romanov struggle for power, but the approach of the two composers is strikingly different. Glinka portrayed the unity of monarch and people; his opera, created under the aegis and with the direct involvement of Nicholas I, instantly became the musical emblem of Russian autocracy. *Khovanshchina* was largely ignored by the Romanovs.

Glinka's enemies of the Russian monarch are foreigners—the Poles; the center of Mussorgsky's opera is the civil war inside Russia. For Glinka, the divine prerogatives of Mikhail Romanov were a given. Mussorgsky's sympathies are with the rebels, even though intellectually he understands the inevitability of Peter's victory.

Glinka's opera is heroic and static, while Mussorgsky's opera is fluid, contradictory, and profoundly tragic. The composer of *Khovanshchina* feels deeply for Russia and mourns its fate. Filippov may have had an idea of how to use it for patriotic propaganda, but it remained a puzzle for Alexander III.

When the Wanderer artist Surikov tackled the schism theme power-fully in his 1887 painting *Lady Morozova,* depicting an Old Believer being driven off into exile while the crowd of onlookers cheer and jeer her, the emperor and his entourage were also ambivalent. Surikov described Alexander's visit to the show. "He came up to the painting. 'Ah, that's the *yurodivy* [holy fool]!' he said. He figured out all the faces. My throat dried up from nervousness: I couldn't talk. The rest, they were like gundogs all over the place."[16]

Most of the Mighty Bunch, unlike many of the Wanderers, came from quite respectable families. But their aesthetic was revolutionary, in the artistic, not political, sense. The Wanderers, as they moved on, became singers of the new, bourgeois Russia. Alexander III is sometimes called the first bourgeois ruler of Russia. And in fact, in cultural issues, the emperor had very bourgeois tastes—and uncountable riches.

Under Alexander's patronage Carl Fabergé flourished; in his St. Petersburg workshops the jeweler set up production of all kinds of expensive trinkets in a gaudy à la Russe style—from tableware to cigarette and cardholders, excessively ornamented in gold, diamonds, emeralds, and rubies.

The peak of this style, which subsequently became so aesthetically attractive to the nouveau riche, were the Easter eggs commissioned by Alexander III (and, after him, by Nicholas II)—essentially tricky jewelry toys with simple but effective "secrets," the better to demonstrate the wealth of royal clients.

The design of the eggs bordered on kitsch. A toy like that—be it a tiny gold chick hidden in a gold egg or a miniature copy of the equestrian statue of Peter I in St. Petersburg, also enclosed in a gold egg encrusted with precious stones—cost between 15,000 and 30,000 rubles (ten of Tchaikovsky's annual pensions).

Fabergé eggs gave Alexander III enormous pleasure, while the music of the Mighty Bunch gave him indigestion. Therefore when the emperor canceled the production of *Boris Godunov* in 1888 at the Maryinsky (*Khovanshchina* had been rejected by the imperial theater administration five years earlier), he also put a question mark next to the planned production of Borodin's opera *Prince Igor*.

Alexander knew absolutely nothing about Borodin's music, but since it came from the camp of the Bunch he considered it suspect. (The opera, unfinished before Borodin's death, was completed and orchestrated by Rimsky-Korsakov and his student Alexander Glazunov.)

It seemed as if *Prince Igor* was going nowhere, at least in the near future. But the St. Petersburg millionaire Mitrofan Belyaev got involved. A good-looking man with an artistic mane of hair and a fashionably trimmed beard (as portrayed by Repin), he was simultaneously typical of the times and unusual. The son of a timber merchant, Belyaev fell in love with music as a child and then, influenced by the personality and compositions of the young Glazunov, decided to found a series of symphonic concerts and a music publishing house that would promote only Russian music.

Belyaev followed the example set by the Moscow merchant Pavel Tretyakov, who used his considerable fortune to gather a unique collection of Russian art, now famous as the Tretyakov Gallery in Moscow. Such generous private support exclusively for national art was still rare in Russia, but it reflected the desire of the new capitalists to assert their taste on the local cultural scene. For Alexander III their activity posed a certain dilemma: he should have hailed their philanthropy, but they were also competing with him, sometimes directly.

At the Wanderer exhibits the emperor would sometimes learn to his chagrin that paintings he liked had already been purchased by Tretyakov. To solve this ticklish hierarchical dilemma, the Wanderers had to compromise: Alexander III got the right of first refusal for all their works.

To get *Prince Igor* onto the Maryinsky Theater stage, Belyaev came up with a complicated gambit in which he was apparently helped by Pobedonostsev, Alexander III's adviser. Belyaev decided to publish the opera score, a very expensive proposition. A memorandum appeared on the emperor's desk, asking for permission to present him a copy of the luxurious edition. The memorandum indicated that the late composer had been a professor at the Imperial Medico-Surgical Academy and an actual state councilor (the civilian equivalent of a major general).

The memorandum went on to explain that Borodin's opera was

based on the *Lay of Igor's Campaign,* a great epic of medieval Russian literature, and that excerpts had been performed with enormous success in Russia and abroad. It concluded with the assurance that Borodin's opera "belongs to the number of those works that bring great honor to our Homeland."[17]

The memorandum, pushing every needed button, succeeded: Alexander III agreed to accept the gift from Belyaev. And that, according to court ritual, was tantamount to the monarch's permission to perform Borodin's opera on the imperial stage.

This unexpected turn of events encapsulated the new relationship between the Russian autocrat and the national capitalist elite, which was trying—cautiously, respectfully, but with growing persistence—to move its cultural values to the forefront.

After Alexander's nod, the wheels of the court machinery spun feverishly. Vast sums were budgeted for the production of *Prince Igor* from the imperial treasury. The prologue, in which the legendary Prince Igor starts his campaign against the nomadic Polovtsian tribes, had 180 people onstage, and the later famous episode with the exotic Polovtsian dances had more than two hundred.

From Central Asia, annexed under Alexander II, the local military governor sent a rich collection of Turkmen weapons, ornaments, and costumes, which were studied and reproduced by the opera's designers. The scenery used motifs from the popular paintings of Vassily Vereshchagin, who had depicted life and landscapes of Central Asia with ethnographic accuracy.

The premiere of *Prince Igor* in October 1890 was a triumph of a Russian opera. The subject—the clash between the ancient Russian prince and Asian tribes—resonated with Russia's recent wars in Central Asia. The authorities had realized at last that the opera of the suspicious Bunch member, if you made the effort, could be used to support the "Orthodoxy, Autocracy, and Nationality" formula.

In the case of *Prince Igor,* the concept was not realized as crude propaganda, but rather through subtle artistic contrasts between the Russian and Polovtsian camps, as represented by the strong and masculine Russian hero and the orgiastic world of the wild Polovtsians (with the show-stopping dances). It was done with such sweep and color and numerous refined and enchanting details that the attractive wrapping made the propaganda filling go down easily, leaving almost no bad aftertaste.

The St. Petersburg press made much of the great love of the "simple" public for *Prince Igor* and—which came as a surprise—of the opera subscribers (that is, higher society). The answer was easy: this unprecedented public unanimity was founded on nationalism.

Nationalism was the common ground that allowed monarchists and traditionalists (who loved the glorification of the unity of people and autocrat) to embrace the opera as much as the Westernizing aesthetes, like Benois, who later swore that before *Prince Igor* he had been mistaken about Russian history: "I thought the ancient Russians were savages or stupid, pathetic slaves of the nomads, not proud and noble masters. Borodin's opera juxtaposed with amazing persuasion the European, Christian world with the Asian one."[18]

It was a new phenomenon, compared to Glinka's *A Life for the Tsar*, which was practically commissioned by Nicholas I. *Prince Igor* had in fact been imposed on Alexander III by a Russian millionaire, an interloper on the cultural scene. The emperor was not very pleased. He would have preferred to set the country's cultural agenda personally, as his grandfather had done for so long.

Nicholas I saw Russian culture as the Neva River, flowing within the granite embankments constructed by autocracy. Its rare and desperate attempts to overflow could and should be blocked. Under Alexander III, Russian culture was a turbulent flow refusing to stay in its allotted bed. By now, it could not be fully controlled by royal command.

CHAPTER 14

Nicholas II and Lenin as Art Connoisseurs

The son of Alexander III, after his father's unexpected death in 1894 from nephritis, took the throne as Emperor Nicholas II, and was the last Romanov to rule the country. Nicholas became emperor at the age of twenty-six, even though he was not ready to lead, as he himself admitted. The new sovereign ruled at an increasingly turbulent time, until 1917, when—faced with a growing revolutionary wave and under pressure of his closest advisers—he was forced to abdicate.

After this revolution (which was to be called the February Revolution), Russia suddenly became the freest democratic republic in the world, and power was in the hands of a coalition of moderate liberals and socialists. But the Provisional Government proved to be really provisional: in the fall of 1917, it was ousted by the Bolsheviks, the radical wing of Russian social democracy headed by Vladimir Ulyanov (his nom de guerre was Lenin). In 1918, the Bolsheviks executed the deposed monarch and his family.

The Bolshevik regime, which many considered ephemeral, turned out to be quite tenacious, lasting—with some mutations—until 1991.

Thus, Nicholas II ended the three-hundred-year-old history of the Romanov dynasty, and Lenin opened the seventy-four-year-old history of the Soviet Union. It is therefore useful to compare the cultural worldview of these two leaders in order to understand how much their cultural baggage influenced their political decisions and fate.

In Soviet times, they tried to present Nicholas II as an underachiever who did not even know the main authors of Russian literature, Turgenev and Tolstoy.[1] On the other hand, Solzhenitsyn in 1989 said of Lenin, whom he hated, "He had little in common with Russian culture."[2] Obviously, both these extremes were dictated by political prejudices.

Nicholas II was two years older than Lenin, one born in 1868, the other, in 1870. Both were well-educated, one at home, the other at a gymnasium (Lenin was the son of the inspector of public schools from the provincial city of Simbirsk). Lenin was an outstanding student, which could not be said of Nicholas II, but both studied conscientiously.

All the Romanovs considered themselves professional military men, therefore the accent in Nicholas's education was on military matters. Lenin got a law degree from St. Petersburg University. But their fundamental cultural baggage was remarkably similar, because in the reign of Alexander III (1881–1894) a unified national cultural canon was formed in Russia.

By that time, the cult of Pushkin as the greatest national poet was established, while the previously sanctioned official reverence for Lomonosov, Derzhavin, Karamzin, and Zhukovsky dimmed significantly. Only the fabulist Krylov remained popular of the old classics. The grand figure of Gogol was no longer controversial, and his greatness was recognized, like Pushkin's, by both the right and the left. Turgenev was making his way to classic status, especially his early prose, *A Sportsman's Sketches*. Ivan Goncharov's novel *Oblomov* was also included in the canon.

The scattered accounts of contemporaries confirm that this cultural canon was strongly ingrained in both Nicholas and Lenin. Moreover, it was received by both explicitly as canon—that is, as mandatory cultural knowledge as necessary for every educated person as brushing teeth and washing hands.

It is noteworthy that neither Nicholas II nor Lenin ever rejected this canon publicly. In Nicholas's case that is understandable: to a great degree the canon was formulated from above and therefore reflected the views of the authorities. Much more curious is Lenin's obvious acquiescence.

It is clear in Lenin's attitude toward Pushkin. For Nicholas, Pushkin was a classic. When he was heir, he played Onegin in a family dramatization of *Eugene Onegin,* and according to the rather patronizing notation in the diary of his uncle, Grand Duke Konstantin (the poet K.R.), "He declaimed Onegin's monologue very sweetly and clearly. Only in his voice could you hear that he was quite nervous."[3] The first official Russian literary prize, instituted under the aegis of the Imperial Academy of Sciences, was called the Pushkin Prize for a reason: the authorities saw his name as the most authoritative.

But Lenin was another matter. Early on, he fell under the influence of revolutionary ideologues, one of whom was Dmitri Pisarev, notorious for his vicious attacks on Pushkin, like this sarcastic pronouncement: "No Russian poet can inspire in his readers such total indifference to the people's suffering, such profound scorn for honest poverty, and such systematic revulsion for honest labor as Pushkin."

While Pisarev's rebuke may sound very "Leninist" in spirit and style today, Lenin himself, albeit a faithful student of Russian nihilists and radicals of the 1860s, never attacked Pushkin in public (nor did he praise him particularly).

We can guess Lenin's real attitude toward Pushkin from a curious incident recounted by Nadezhda Krupskaya, his widow. In 1921, Lenin and Krupskaya visited a Moscow student dormitory to see a daughter of Inessa Armand, the recently deceased love of Lenin's life (and Party comrade). Lenin, Krupskaya, and Armand had a Party ménage à trois for a rather long time.

The students were happy to see Lenin and bombarded him with questions. Lenin, in turn, asked them, "What are you reading? Do you read Pushkin?" The response was, "Oh, no. Pushkin was a bourgeois. We read Mayakovsky." Lenin, who did not like the avant-garde poet Vladimir Mayakovsky, said only, "I think Pushkin is better."

Krupskaya added naively in her account, "After that Ilyich [as the Party comrades called him] was a bit kinder to Mayakovsky," because the name reminded him of "the young people, full of life and joy, ready to die for Soviet power, unable to find the words in contemporary language to express themselves and seeking that expression in the hard-to-understand poems of Mayakovsky."[4]

The blinkered Krupskaya did not notice the grotesqueness of her image of young people "full of life and joy" yet "ready to die," or the ruthlessness of her childless spouse, pleased by the sight of that young cannon fodder. And it's interesting how casually Lenin took the quintessentially nihilist putdown of Pushkin as bourgeois: did he think so, as well, but did not want to say?

Given Lenin's reputation for pitiless debate, his defense of Pushkin from the revolutionary youth seems rather timid. "Pushkin is better than Mayakovsky"? Lenin was devastatingly scathing about Mayakovsky ("nonsense, stupid, double stupidity and pretentiousness"),[5] so that was faint praise indeed. It is obvious that for Lenin Pushkin was merely a name, part of the official canon. He wouldn't get into an argument over Pushkin.

But in one aspect, Pisarev's view of Pushkin as the teacher of "parasites and sybarites" was clearly absorbed by the revolutionary leader: Lenin's disparaging attitude toward ballet and opera.

Pushkin adored the ballet (and ballerinas). For the radical Pisarev that was a readymade target, and he gleefully mocked Pushkin's "useless poetry," attractive only to "those mentally challenged subjects who can be thrilled by ballet poses." Not being "mentally challenged," Lenin resolutely dismissed opera and ballet as a "piece of purely landowner culture."[6]

It is hard to deny a certain logic in Lenin's thinking. Opera and, even more so, ballet, under the personal patronage of the Romanov family, held a special place in the official Russian culture.

The professional theater, including musical theater, began in Russia as court entertainment. Tsar Alexei, father of Peter I, invited musicians from Europe "who know how to play various instruments, such as: organs, horns, pipes, flutes, clarinets, trombones and viola da gambas along with vocal performance, and also other instruments."[7] (The money to support theater and ballet came from the Salt Chancery for many years: the state had the monopoly on the salt trade, and part of the enormous salt income went to actors, singers, dancers, and musicians.)

After various perturbations, the imperial theaters were moved to the Ministry of the Court, which ran (through the Directorate of the Imperial Theaters) the Maryinsky and Alexandrinsky theaters in St. Petersburg and the Bolshoi and Maly theaters in Moscow. In fact, they were the personal theaters of the Romanov family: a display window of their vanity, a platform for elaborating their ideological projects, but also a place for relaxation and merriment and, last but not least, a high-class and exciting harem.

Nicholas I sometimes took over the rehearsals of ballets and liked to hang around backstage, where the ballerinas ran around in tights; Alexander III never missed a dress rehearsal of an opera or ballet, much less the premieres.

Alexander III also introduced the tradition of emperor and family attending the graduation exams of the ballet school. After the performance, the young dancers were presented to the tsar and his wife, and at the dinner that followed, the young grand dukes flirted with their lovely companions.

At one such dinner in 1890, the graduating ballerina seated next to Alexander III was Mathilde Kschessinska, small, dark, muscular, very talented, and incredibly ambitious. She drank tea between the huge, flabby emperor and his miniature heir (who took after his mother), the future Nicholas II, a shy young officer with dreamy gray-blue eyes.

Alexander III told them with a benign smile, "Watch it now, don't flirt too much." The heir timidly spoke to Kschessinska, pointing to the unornamented white mug before her: "You probably don't drink from such plain mugs at home?"[8]

That was the prelude to their famous and stormy affair, which lasted from 1892 until the spring of 1894, when the heir's engagement was announced to Princess Alix Hesse-Darmstadt, who converted to Russian Orthodoxy and took the name Alexandra.

Kschessinska had a brilliant career at the Maryinsky and dictated all her conditions there. Although detractors claimed that her special place at the theater was due to her high connections, the majority of the press and public received her with enthusiasm and considered her among the great stars of the Maryinsky.

Marius Petipa, the great choreographer and creator of *Don Quixote, La Bayadère,* and *Raymonda* (to music by Glazunov) and *The Sleeping Beauty* (Tchaikovsky), worked happily with Kschessinska. She always recalled proudly how Tchaikovsky came to her dressing room after her performance in *Sleeping Beauty* in 1893, praised her, and promised to write a new ballet just for her.

At the turn of the century, the era of Petipa, master of Petersburg classicism in ballet, was closing. Kschessinska, always brazenly chasing after success, befriended innovators, appearing in the experimental ballets of Mikhail Fokine and even traveling to Europe with the Diaghilev troupe, where her partner was the legendary Vaclav Nijinsky. But she lost out to the new stars—Anna Pavlova and Tamara Karsavina. Nevertheless, Kschessinska did not give up, and in 1916, at the age of forty-four, she debuted successfully in *Giselle,* that gem of the Romantic repertoire.

Nicholas II continued acting as her patron all those years. As she later recalled, "[W]henever I had to turn to him, he fulfilled my requests without demur."[9] His beneficence was not affected by the fact that she moved on from him to being the mistress of first one and then another of his cousins, both grand dukes.

The diaries of Nicholas II are peppered with references to attending ballets at the Maryinsky—works by Tchaikovsky, *Don Quixote* and *Daughter of the Pharaoh* ("Pavlova danced divinely").[10] For the tsar these were evenings of great pleasure, a refined mix of aesthetics, nostalgia, and eroticism. Lenin, however, saw nothing but an aristocratic bordello.

. . .

Lenin's theatrical and musical tastes were quite different from the tsar's. In the Soviet Union his comments on Beethoven, recorded by Maxim Gorky, were quoted endlessly:

I know nothing better than the Appassionata, I could listen to it every day. Astonishing, sublime music. I always think with pride, perhaps naïvely: what miracles people can create! . . . But I can't listen to music frequently, it affects my nerves, I want to say sweet nothings and pat people on the head, people who live in a filthy hell but can create such beauty. But today you can't pat anyone on the head—they'll bite your hand off, and they should be beaten on the head, beaten mercilessly, even though we, ideally, are against any violence.[11]

Those are intriguingly frank words, and they are confirmed in other memoirs of how Lenin reacted to music: it "upset," "wearied," "acted too strongly" on him. The musical impressions of Nicholas II, noted in his diaries, are just the opposite—"very beautiful," "a beautiful opera," "marvelous concert."

These were two different ways of perceiving culture: for Nicholas II it was a pleasant entertainment; for Lenin, emotional torture. One was a British gentleman (everyone noted Nicholas's anglicized manner) and the other a typical member of the Russian intelligentsia, absorbing culture intensely, overly so.

Like Nicholas II, Lenin was not tall, not very striking, but a rather sympathetic person. (They both rolled their Rs in a charming way. The choreographer George Balanchine told me about the tsar's Rs; as a young dancer—then called Georgy Balanchivadze—he met Nicholas II in 1916.)[12] But in every other way, Lenin was the complete opposite of Nicholas. He was immeasurably more energetic, persistent, focused, and power hungry.

Nicholas II was a profoundly private and reserved man whom birth and destiny made ruler of a great country at a moment of acute crisis. The obligation to be monarch clearly wearied him; that may be why he abdicated.

Lenin, on the contrary, was a born leader, elbowed his way to power, · grabbed it despite the misgivings of his closest comrades, and held on to it tightly until his physical strength faded. (He died in 1924, at the age of fifty-three. Peter I, with whom Lenin was frequently compared for boundless energy and revolutionary zeal, also died at the age of fifty-three, two centuries earlier.)

Nicholas II was brought up by his family and the imperial court. We do not know for sure whether a work of Russian culture ever wrought a life-changing shock for him. But we do know that about Lenin.

A decisive factor in Lenin's development was *What Is to Be Done?*, the novel by the leading revolutionary author Nikolai Chernyshevsky, written when he was imprisoned at the Peter and Paul Fortress in St. Petersburg and somehow passed by the censors for publication in 1863, in the most popular magazine of the time, *Contemporary*. Lenin admitted that Chernyshevsky's novel "plowed me up profoundly."

Lenin's reaction was not unique. The revolutionary youth of the 1860s saw the novel as a revelation. What was the secret of its success? In our day the work seems rather flat and boring, despite the author's clumsy attempt to enliven a preachy treatise with a naive, semi-detective plot. *What Is to Be Done?* appeared in the right place at the right time. Tectonic cultural shifts occurred in Russia after the emancipation of the serfs in 1861: education spread, the press grew livelier, and moral values were debated fiercely.

The old ways of life were discredited, and new ideals had not yet taken root. In that situation, the young generation thirsted for a "life textbook." For some, Chernyshevsky's novel became that textbook.

Chernyshevsky wrote his novel as a polemic against Turgenev's recently published *Fathers and Sons*. He felt that Turgenev had caricatured revolutionaries as "nihilists." So Chernyshevsky gave them another name—"new people"—and, most importantly, elaborated a detailed encyclopedia of everyday life for anyone who wanted to become a "new person": the right way to live, work, love, eat, and rest.

Essentially, it was a reference work masquerading as a novel, a method. (Chernyshevsky disarmingly believed that he had written a poetic and entertaining novel, similar to works of Dickens and *The Count of Monte Cristo,* by Alexandre Dumas.)

His enemies ridiculed him, but the novel's impact was just what the author wanted: the story of how an emancipated "new woman," while setting up a quasi-socialist sewing factory, develops progressive amorous relations with two young "new men" became the bedside reading of Russian radicals for decades, replacing the once-popular novels of George Sand.

Lenin was most influenced by another character from the novel, Rakhmetov, who trains for underground activity: he lives ascetically, not drinking wine, or touching women, or eating white bread (just black), doing without sugar, reading only necessary books and meeting only necessary people, and preparing physically and mentally (he even sleeps one night on a bedding filled with nails) for the coming revolution. Gorky later noted that the intense Lenin cultivated self-imposed restraints that were akin to "self-torture, self-mutilation, Rakhmetov's nails."[13]

Lenin first read *What Is to Be Done?* at the age of fourteen, and he did not like the novel then. (He was enthralled by Turgenev, Chernyshevsky's antipode, and he could quote long passages from Turgenev's novels by heart.) But it was a favorite book of Lenin's older brother, Alexander, a student at St. Petersburg University.

Alexander Ulyanov joined an underground student group that plotted to assassinate Alexander III. The police arrested them in 1887; five of the prisoners who refused to plead guilty and ask for pardon were hanged, including Alexander. This stunned Lenin. He reread *What Is to Be Done?* and decided to become a professional revolutionary, a "new man."

Going from soft and poetic Turgenev to stern and dogmatic Chernyshevsky was a dizzying transformation, and Lenin achieved it not without considerable effort. Certainly along the way there were doubts and regrets. Just how difficult that road was is evinced by Lenin's painfully conflicting attitude toward music. Actually, it is the only window into the young Lenin's soul and its agonies.

Lenin could have repeated the words of the protagonist of Tolstoy's *Kreutzer Sonata:* "And really, music is a strange thing . . . They say that music elevates the soul—nonsense, lies! . . . It doesn't elevate or debase the soul, it irritates it . . . In China music is a state affair. And that is how it should be. A person cannot be permitted to hypnotize someone or many people and then do what he wants with them."

There are accounts of Tolstoy listening to music and weeping, his face reflecting "something like horror" as he wept. The writer Romain Rolland commented that "only with such richness of spirit as Tolstoy's, music can become threatening to a person."[14] Rolland was referring to heightened emotional arousal, present in complex personalities, of which Lenin clearly was one.

For Lenin, music had both sweet and tormenting associations. Beethoven's *Moonlight* Sonata reminded him of his childhood: it had been played frequently by his mother and his beloved younger sister, Olga, who died of typhus when she was only nineteen.

Beethoven was also associated with his deepest love: in 1909 Lenin began his affair with Inessa Armand, thirty-five, a Russian revolutionary of French descent, a beautiful and independent woman, an accomplished pianist. Inessa idolized Beethoven, and Lenin often listened to her play his sonatas. He particularly liked Inessa's interpretation of the *Pathétique,* which he said he could listen to "ten, twenty, forty times . . . and each time it captivates me and delights me more and more."[15]

Abroad as a revolutionary émigré, Lenin lived in a classic ménage à trois with his wife, Nadezhda Krupskaya, and Inessa Armand. This union, based as much on emotions as on the commonality of interests and ideology, was undoubtedly inspired by Chernyshevsky's ideas on married life, as expressed in *What Is to Be Done?*

This is another reason why Lenin blew up at a Party comrade who said the novel was primitive and without talent. "This is a work that gives you a charge for your entire life. Works without talent do not have that kind of influence,"[16] Lenin said. Obviously, Lenin defended Chernyshevsky much more energetically than he had Pushkin.

Inessa Armand died of typhus in 1920; she was buried by the Kremlin Wall. Her death was a terrible blow to Lenin and hastened his own death. He could no longer listen to Beethoven without emotional pain: the sounds reminded him of too much. Lenin, a true follower of Chernyshevsky, firmly decided that listening to music was "an unproductive waste of energy."[17] (I heard about this statement of Lenin's in 1994 in Oslo from ninety-eight-year-old Maria Dobrowen, widow of the pianist Issai Dobrowen, who had played for Lenin.) Like a real "new man," Lenin squashed his emotions. The politician in Lenin won over the private person. Nicholas II was just the opposite.

Lenin's attitude toward dramatic theater was complicated, as it was toward music. We know about it from Krupskaya's reminiscences. "Usually we'd go to the theater and leave after the first act. The comrades laughed at us, for wasting money."

Krupskaya explained that it was not because Lenin was bored at the theater. On the contrary, he followed the action onstage with too much intensity and agitation, and therefore "the mediocrity of the play or falseness of the acting always jangled Vladimir Ilyich's nerves."

But when a production touched him, he could weep. There is evidence of this from a friend of Lenin's abroad. In Geneva, at a play starring the celebrated Sarah Bernhardt, he was astonished to see Lenin furtively wiping away his tears: "The cruel, heartless Ilyich was weeping over *La Dame aux camélias.*"[18]

Lenin liked the Art Theater founded in 1889 in Moscow by Konstantin Stanislavsky and Vladimir Nemirovich-Danchenko, although he did not become a habitué. For him this theater was part of the canon of topical "realistic" art—along with the Wanderers' paintings, Tchaikovsky's music, and the works of Chekhov. Here the tastes of Nicholas and Lenin were identical: for both of them it was the same mainstream cultural paradigm.

Nemirovich-Danchenko's archives contain a draft of his letter dated April 19, 1906, to Count Sergei Witte, then chairman of the Cabinet of Ministers, with a request to inform Nicholas II that the Art Theater was on the brink of financial collapse and needed a state subsidy. Nemirovich-Danchenko "most respectfully" pointed out that the theater's recent tour in Europe was a great artistic success and was seen as evidence "of the power of Russia's spiritual strengths."[19]

The Art Theater was saved then by an eccentric Moscow millionaire, and the letter to Count Witte was never sent. But after the 1917 Bolshevik revolution, when Lenin became leader of the new Russia, the Art Theater faced financial disaster again and applied to Lenin for help. Lenin agreed instantly to give them money. "How else? If there is a theater that we must rescue and preserve from the past at any cost, then it is of course the Art Theater."[20] (As we know, Lenin was not so generous toward opera and ballet.)

This was part of Lenin's cultural strategy: he felt that in Communist Russia the place of religion as "opium for the masses" should be taken by theater, and in his opinion, the Art Theater was best suited for that role. But precisely because Lenin understood the theater's importance in the political and cultural upbringing of the people, he reacted so aggressively to its "errors."

For Lenin, one such "error" was the Art Theater's production in 1913 of a stage version of Dostoevsky's *The Devils*. A scandal broke out over the play, elicited by an open letter in the popular newspaper *The Russian Word* from Maxim Gorky, the most famous Russian writer of the time, calling Dostoevsky the "evil genius" of Russian literature and *The Devils* a slanderous mockery of the revolution.

Gorky maintained that staging Dostoevsky in the current tense political situation was "a dubious idea aesthetically and certainly harmful socially" and called on "everyone who sees the need for healing Russian life to protest against the production of Dostoevsky's novels in theaters."[21]

Gorky's anti-Dostoevsky letter created a sensation. Dostoevsky's name was taking on the status of cultural symbol then. His rejection of revolution, expressed with such anger in *The Devils,* made the late writer a topical and controversial political figure whom conservative forces were pushing into the national cultural canon, against the fierce resistance of the progressive camp. For the Romanov family, Dostoevsky was "their" author, having expressed vividly their innermost thoughts on the Orthodox Church and autocracy being organic for Russia and on the harm of atheistic and socialistic ideas, spread by revolutionary "devils."

Many noted writers of the period attacked Gorky, blaming him for daring to defame Dostoevsky, the new "literary saint." Only Lenin and the Bolsheviks defended Gorky. Their newspaper accused the writers ganging up on Gorky of "going with the reactionaries against the proletariat— that is the main reason for the forgiveness of Dostoevsky and his reactionary writing and of the anger against Gorky."[22]

Lenin called *The Devils* genius but "disgusting." When angry, Lenin called Dostoevsky "archterrible," but in other moments admitted that his novels had "lively pictures of reality,"[23] a rare example of his ambivalence. Lenin would remind people that Nicholas I had condemned Dostoevsky to death, "pardoned" him only after a humiliating preparation for hanging, and then exiled him to hard labor. Lenin considered *The House of the Dead* Dostoevsky's best book; as we remember, so did Tolstoy.

It is telling that Nicholas II never met a single great Russian writer, which he could have easily done. One of Nicholas's favorite ways to relax was to read aloud in the evening from a novel (in Russian, English, or French) to his wife and children. He read them Tolstoy and Chekhov, but never tried to talk to the authors. Why? Maybe because of his famous reticence, which some attributed to his shyness and others characterized as secretiveness, hypocrisy, and slyness?

Apparently, Nicholas II did not like to argue and did not know how to do it. In conversations, he never contradicted others, but invariably remained true to his own convictions. It is clear that a meeting with Tolstoy would inevitably lead to confrontation. But Nicholas II preferred not to meet even with Chekhov, known for his delicacy and tact.

He certainly would not have wanted to meet Gorky, even though the writer was very popular, not only in Russia, but in the West. Gorky declared himself a socialist early on—yet his works continued to be published in mass printings. He had a romantic biography, working numerous exotic jobs (dishwasher on ships, student in an icon-painting studio, night watchman at a railroad station, extra in the theater), and walking all around Russia—which made him the idol of the public.

The paradox is that Gorky's grandfather had been a wealthy man (who went bankrupt) while Chekhov's grandfather had been a serf. Still, the literary roots of both writers were in the mass literature of the times.

Chekhov started out in pulp fiction magazines of the 1880s with names like *Grasshopper, Alarm Clock,* and *Shards,* where he was paid a few kopecks a line and published not only short stories but also jokes, parodies, theater reviews, and courtroom reports.

His early, "funny" pieces were Nicholas II's favorites. The tsar was also a great fan of Chekhov's early comedies, like *The Bear* and *The Marriage Proposal.* Lenin was more interested in the late, "serious" Chekhov.

Gorky also had a "lowbrow" literary ancestry. One of the most popular heroes of mass literature in Russia then was the fearless "bandit Churkin," the local Robin Hood. The stories of his adventures were read until the ink wore off. The protagonists of Gorky's early stories were tramps and rebels, similar to the heroes of the "bandit" stories. But Gorky, unlike Chekhov, was a political radical. By 1889, when he was twenty-one, Gorky was arrested for revolutionary activity.

A writer like that naturally would not find approval from Nicholas II, and the tsar was upset to learn in March 1902 that Gorky was elected an honorary member of the Imperial Academy of Sciences. Nicholas II learned about it in *The Citizen,* Prince Meshchersky's conservative publication (he read every issue from front page to last), where the selection—which took place under the aegis of Nicholas's uncle, Grand Duke Konstantin (the poet K.R.), president of the academy—was described as "a challenge directed at all educated Russia of Pushkin and Karamzin, all of loyal Russia."[24]

Nicholas II demanded an explanation from the minister of internal affairs and wrote "More than original" on his memorandum. He was outraged by the fact that they made an honorary academician of a writer under investigation: "In today's confused times, the Academy of Sciences permits itself to elect such a man into its milieu."[25]

The academy backtracked immediately, declaring Gorky's election "invalid." This must have put Grand Duke Konstantin in an awkward position, yet he could not disobey the sovereign.

Nicholas intended "to sober up at least a bit the state of the minds in the Academy." But what he got instead, as it often happens, was a greater scandal. Among the protests, his favorite writer Chekhov, who previously avoided political gestures, refused his title as honorary academician, which had been awarded him earlier.

Chekhov's letter to the academy was characteristic of the new situation, when public reputation and independence were more important to a writer, artist, or actor than the government's approval. In his letter, Chekhov recalled that he was the first to congratulate Gorky on his honorary title: "I congratulated him sincerely, and now for me to recognize the election as invalid—that contradiction does not fit in my mind and my conscience."[26]

All the leading papers wrote about the scandal, fueling Gorky's popularity. Here it was, a clear sign of crisis of power: the tsar tried to punish a writer, but instead only increased his appeal.

In the final analysis, Nicholas II lost this small skirmish with Gorky. But, naturally, he did not even notice his defeat—it was about some "despicable tramp." The revolution of 1917 was fifteen years away.

· · ·

On Stalin's order, the legend about the great friendship between Lenin and Gorky was created in the Soviet Union, based on several cleverly cropped quotes from Lenin's writings on and to Gorky. But a close reading of the texts reveals a much more complex picture. It was not a friendship of equals. Lenin, who was two years younger, nevertheless behaved like a strict, demanding teacher dealing with his talented but errant student.

Lenin never stopped lecturing and chastising Gorky. In one letter, we find: "Why are you behaving so badly, chum? You're overworked, tired, nerves on edge. This is unacceptable . . . No one to supervise you and you've let yourself go?" In another, "What are you doing? It's terrible, really!"[27] And so on.

In one of his articles, Lenin quotes Gorky as telling him, with an "inimitably sweet smile" in private conversation, "I know I'm a bad Marxist. We artists are all slightly irresponsible." Lenin comments sarcastically, "It's hard to argue with that . . . but then why does Gorky take on politics?"[28]

Lenin scolded Gorky before the Bolshevik revolution for his "ideological vacillation" and propaganda of "incorrect" (from Lenin's point of view) philosophical theories; after the revolution, when Lenin was leader of Russia, he was irritated by Gorky's endless attempts to save intellectuals who had offended the Bolsheviks and were threatened with prison or execution. He learned that Gorky divulged Lenin's confidential views, expressed in private conversations with the writer, to the "counterrevolutionaries."[29] That was too much.

Their relationship ended with the Bolshevik leader pushing Gorky out of Russia in 1921, writing, "Leave, get treatment. Don't be stubborn, I'm asking you." As one of his Party comrades said of Lenin, "Ilyich loved anyone the party needed. Tomorrow, if that comrade should take the wrong position, Ilyich would drop all relations with him, and he would be ruthless toward him."[30]

Lenin never really praised Gorky by using the lofty words he found for Leo Tolstoy or even Chernyshevsky. Gorky reluctantly admitted that.

In his memoirs, quoting Lenin's reaction to his political novel *The Mother* ("A very timely book"), he added, "That was the only, but extremely valued, compliment from him."[31]

Lenin wrote, "Literary work should become *part* of the whole proletarian movement, 'a cog and wheel' of the one and only, great social-democratic machine." For Lenin, culture was a political instrument. "Writers must certainly join party organizations. Publishing houses and warehouses, stores and reading rooms, libraries and various book dealers—all that must belong to the party."

Lenin formed this politicized utilitarian view of culture early and retained it throughout his life. Gorky tried many a time to persuade him that this was a mistake. He was the only major writer Lenin knew well, and Lenin valued the opportunity to talk with him, but he never yielded on any point.

Gorky took his revenge for Nicholas II's persecution with his pamphlet *Russian Tsar* (1906), where he described the tsar this way: "A miserable soul, a despicable soul, inebriated by the blood of the hungry people, sick with fear, a small, greedy soul."

Gorky settled his accounts with Lenin, too, but in a different way, writing a seemingly loving essay after his death; in fact, it was a polemic against Lenin. It is Gorky's masterpiece, on which he worked for almost ten years.

For Gorky, Lenin was a politician par excellence ("while I have an organic revulsion for politics," noted Gorky). Earlier, when Lenin was alive, Gorky spoke even more frankly about him in the press: "A talented man, he has all the qualities of a leader as well as the requisite absence of morality and ruthless attitude toward the life of the masses."

In his memoirs, Gorky analyzes Lenin in a more nuanced way. His Lenin admits, "I know little of Russia." Nevertheless, he believes that he has a very good understanding of the Russian people: "The Russian masses have to be shown something very simple, very accessible. Soviets and communism are simple."

Gorky's Lenin is secretive ("He, like no one else, knew how to keep quiet about the secret storms of his soul") and cruel: "'What do you want?' he would ask in surprise and anger. 'Is humanity possible in such an unprecedented, fierce fight? Where is there room for soft-heartedness and magnanimity?'"

Gorky stressed Lenin's "untrusting, hostile" attitude toward intellectuals. For Gorky, Lenin is a "strict teacher," and the leader's words remind him of "the cold sparkle of iron filings." Then Gorky makes an about-face and, commenting on Lenin's hidden pride in Russia and Russian art, which he had noticed, calls Lenin a "great child." The errant student finally put his late teacher in his place. The writer had the last word.

Gorky's unusual portrait of Lenin is the only psychologically perceptive depiction of the revolutionary leader made from life. It is worth comparing it to the no less unusual portrait of Nicholas II painted by one of the great Russian artists, Valentin Serov, in 1900.

Like Gorky, Serov was a masterful portraitist. His picture of Nicholas is important because of the artist's unprecedented closeness to the model: for the first time in the history of the Romanov dynasty, the monarch posed obediently for many hours and days, fulfilling all the painter's demands. (In 1920, the artist Natan Altman spent 250 hours in the course of six weeks in the Kremlin, sculpting Lenin's bust while the Bolshevik leader worked, mostly ignoring Altman.)[32]

Serov was called prickly, capricious, and mean—both as a man and as a portraitist. Stocky, clumsy, hands always in pockets, Serov occasionally interrupted his grim silence to utter a gloomy aphorism through gritted teeth clenching a smoldering cigar.

His habits and looks did not keep Serov from becoming the favorite portraitist in prerevolutionary high society, and for almost a decade (1892 to 1901) he was the unofficial court painter of the Romanovs.

Serov was feared for his outspokenness, but he was respected for his honesty and sure mastery. A contemporary noted, "Patience and meekness were needed by anyone wanting to be painted by Serov."[33]

Nicholas II ordered his "private" portrait as a gift for Empress

Alexandra. In it, he is seated, leaning forward, his hands clasped wearily on the table, gazing quietly. He wears a shabby military tunic. (Nicholas II was known for wearing old, patched clothing at home.) It depicts Nicholas as a person sympathetically, even as it underscores his main political liability: the lack of energy and leadership.

Both Lenin and Gorky liked to talk—they had verbal diarrhea. While Serov and Nicholas II were famously taciturn, their relationship during work on the portrait turned into a mini-play.

Serov, who hated asking for anything, found himself requesting a subsidy for the art journal *The World of Art,* published by his friend Sergei Diaghilev. Even more unexpectedly, Nicholas (who, like Lenin, disliked the "decadents," considering Diaghilev chief among them) agreed to give 15,000 rubles of his personal funds to support the journal. Nicholas later extended the subsidy for another three years.

The sovereign agreed to yet another request from Serov: he ordered the release from prison of Savva Mamontov, a railroad magnate and patron of the arts, who was under investigation for alleged embezzlement. However, the emperor and the artist found themselves in conflict over Serov's work.

Empress Alexandra, who considered herself a fair painter, came in during one of the sessions and started telling Serov how to improve the portrait. In response the artist, infuriated by this inappropriate art lesson, handed her his palette with the words, "Well, then, Your Majesty, you should do the painting, since you draw so well!"

Alexandra blew up, turned on her heel, and left; Nicholas, caught in the middle, ran after her and returned with an apology: the empress "went a bit overboard."

The scene was unpleasant and humiliating for all the participants. Serov announced that he would no longer continue as court artist and demanded 4,000 rubles for the portrait, double the amount Nicholas had offered.

Nicholas had a courtier scold Serov for "taking advantage of the situation and setting a too high fee," basically calling him a rip-off artist. Insulted, Serov asked for an apology.

Nicholas retreated and paid the demanded sum, but after that privately referred to the artist as "terribly insolent." This was yet another farcical situation, not at all commensurate with previous ideas of what the relationship between monarch and subject should be in Russia.

The subsequent story of the painting was telling. In a surprise for everyone, Serov's "private" portrait was exhibited with the *World of Art* group in St. Petersburg in January 1901. The painting was presented without any particular pomp. Traditionally in Russia, all depictions of monarchs were controlled diligently: the Ministry of the Imperial Court handled these matters.[34] That this unprecedentedly "domestic" portrait of the sovereign was shown publicly and presented with marked modesty was a sign of the times. The emperor even visited the show the day before it opened. Yes, he wanted people to see and love him this way: simple, quiet, gentle.

The initial effect was what Nicholas had intended. Everyone said (and wrote) that the sovereign in Serov's portrait "looks into your soul." But Serov's later commentary was quite different: "Yes, yes, childlike pure, honest, kind eyes. Only executioners and tyrants have them."[35]

Serov's contempt for Nicholas II was fixed on January 9, 1905: on that fateful day, army troops in St. Petersburg shot at a peaceful workers' demonstration for better wages. Serov happened to observe the shooting and was horrified.

In a wrathful letter to his friend Repin, Serov, as an artist, vividly described the tragic event:

What I saw from the windows of the Academy of Arts on 9 January I will never forget—the restrained, majestic, unarmed crowd walking toward the cavalry attack and rifle scope—a horrible vision. What I heard afterward was even more incredible in its horror. Did the fact that the sovereign did not deign to come out to the workers and receive their petition mean they must be attacked? And who had decided on that attack? No one and nothing can remove that stain.[36]

Serov's portrait of Nicholas II is one of the few outstanding works that embody the perception of the Romanov dynasty in the mirror of Russian culture. The first was the equestrian statue of Peter the Great, Falconet's Bronze Horseman, erected by Catherine the Great and still considered St. Petersburg's calling card.

The Bronze Horseman—a dynamic Peter on a rearing steed that is Russia—was immortalized by Pushkin and remains in the Russian mind as the image of a forward-looking ruler. The work radiates energy, joy, and grandeur.

Another symbolic sculptural depiction of a Romanov, which immediately elicited comparisons with the Bronze Horseman, was the statue of Alexander III, erected in 1909 by Nicholas II. The sculptor was Prince Paolo Trubetskoy, of Russian heritage but in fact, like Falconet, a foreigner: he was born in Italy to an American mother, he grew up and was educated there, and came to Russia already an accomplished master, spending even less time there than Falconet.

Trubetskoy was an eccentric: he refused to read newspapers or books (and was proud of it) and was a fanatical vegetarian, even training the wolf and bear that lived in his studio to stick to a vegetarian diet.

Trubetskoy did a bust of Leo Tolstoy (also a vegetarian) that delighted the writer, so Tolstoy gave him his books. When the sculptor forgot them in the hallway when he left, Tolstoy was amused. (Nicholas II also liked Trubetskoy's apparent naïveté.)

Trubetskoy spoke Russian poorly and knew nothing about Russian history or politics, but he studied Falconet's monument closely and considered his statue of Alexander III to be in competition with it. His portrait of a Romanov is a polar opposite of Falconet's work: Trubetskoy depicted the tsar as a "fat-assed martinet," to use Repin's description, squashing beneath him a heavy, stubborn horse—symbol of a different Russia.

None of the higher officials wanted to have this monument in the imperial capital—its satirical overtones were painfully obvious—but the work pleased Alexander III's wife: "Looks like him." When the statue was unveiled at the square in front of the railroad station (like Falconet, Trubetskoy had left St. Petersburg before the event), everyone gasped. While people were awed by the statue of Peter I, they "laughed and wept inside" over the statue of Alexander III (as the essayist Vassily Rozanov described the reaction of Russian intellectuals).

The artist Benois, who had observed Alexander III up close, was a great admirer of his. Benois claimed that the prerevolutionary flourishing of Russian culture that is sometimes ascribed to the patronage of Nicholas was in fact primed by the reign of his father. If that giant had lived another twenty years, Benois went on, "The history of not only Russia but the world would have been different and certainly better."[37] But even Benois described Trubetskoy's work as "a monument characteristic of a monarchy doomed to destruction."

An acute observer, Benois felt that even though Nicholas II was "a nice man," he fatally "lacked those special gifts that allow one to play with dignity the role of head and leader of a gigantic state."[38] Serov demonstrated that in his portrait, which thus became the final piece in the trinity of notable portrayals of Romanov rulers: from tsar-as-leader to tsar-as-keeper to "non-tsar."

While the Bolsheviks never tampered with the Bronze Horseman, they tagged the statue of Alexander III with a mocking epigram caption by the proletarian poet Demyan Bedny:

> My son and my father were executed in my lifetime
> While I reaped the fate of posthumous ignominy,
> I stand here as a cast-iron scarecrow for the country
> That threw off the yoke of autocracy forever.

In 1937, Trubetskoy's work was concealed in the courtyard of the Russian Museum (founded by Alexander III). Now, the monument-caricature stands outside the Marble Palace of St. Petersburg.

The fate of Serov's portrait of Nicholas II was even more dramatic. During the capture of the Winter Palace in 1917, the revolutionary soldiers found the portrait in the family's private quarters and dragged it out to Palace Square, stabbing it with their bayonets, trying to tear it into pieces.

A few young artists were nearby and they appealed to the soldiers, telling them it was the work of the famous Serov and should be preserved for the museum. The soldiers, surprisingly amenable, gave up the portrait they had been attacking so furiously (they had already poked out both eyes). In that piteous state, the portrait was given to the Russian Museum. Fortunately, the Tretyakov Gallery in Moscow retained an unharmed author's copy of Serov's masterpiece.

A politician's cultural baggage may be his weapon and capital, but it can turn into a huge weight around his neck. Lacking natural political instincts, Nicholas II came to dubious conclusions while reading Russian literature. His diaries suggest that he read like an ordinary consumer of culture.

Lenin, on the contrary, read Russian literature with a political scalpel in his hand—that was the way his mind worked. He may have consciously deprived himself of the "culinary" pleasure (in Bertolt Brecht's phrase) of reading, but his pragmatic approach to culture worked better from a political point of view and fed his revolutionary activity.

These contrasting approaches resulted in contrary readings of Tolstoy by Nicholas and Lenin. For Nicholas II, Tolstoy was primarily a patriotic military writer. Nowadays that may seem incongruous, since we know the late Tolstoy as a man who passionately rejected all forms of violence and hated war. Also, in his later years, Tolstoy often repeated Samuel Johnson's aphorism about patriotism being the last refuge of a scoundrel. This did not mean that he did not consider himself a Russian patriot. But official patriotism as an instrument of state policy sickened him.

These positions coupled with his rejection of official Russian Orthodoxy brought Tolstoy into conflict with Russian autocracy. He wrote
harsh accusatory letters to Alexander III and to Nicholas II. His works
were strictly censored and often banned. But that had not always been the
case.

Tolstoy made his name as a war writer. After his first novellas (*Childhood* and *Adolescence*), the works that had the greatest impact on the
Russian public were his *Sevastopol Stories,* about the defense of Sevastopol in 1854–1855, during the Crimean War against the British and
French.

Alexander II particularly liked one of the stories, "Sevastopol in
December," and he gave orders to keep Tolstoy out of the line of fire. Tolstoy's first book, which included the Sevastopol tales, was simply called
War Stories. Tolstoy was planning to publish a special magazine for soldiers, *Military Leaflet,* to inculcate patriotic feelings, but Nicholas I did
not approve the idea.

In general, the young Tolstoy treated his military service with great
enthusiasm and ardor, and until the end of his life, despite his rejection of
violence and war, he continued to consider himself a military man. In
that particular sense, he and Nicholas II were on the same wavelength.

Nicholas II read Tolstoy's *War Stories* to his heir, eight-year-old
Alexei, not only about Sevastopol but also "The Raid" and "The Wood
Felling" (early stories about the war in the Caucasus, where Tolstoy also
fought). Apparently, the emperor used those tales as edifying material—
for he saw his son (despite his hemophilia) as a future brave officer: a true
Romanov simply could not be a civilian.

War and Peace is Tolstoy's most celebrated work, but when it was first
published in a magazine in 1865–1866, it was first of all perceived as a
highly controversial account of the war against Napoleon and was
roundly criticized from that point of view.

Tolstoy was a historical determinist. Therefore, in describing Russia's battles with Napoleon in 1805–1807 and then the Patriotic War of 1812, he insisted that their outcome and the course of historic events in general did not depend on emperors or military leaders or their orders, as was traditionally believed: "In order for the will of Napoleon and Alexander (the people on whom events seemed to depend) to be executed, a coincidence of endless circumstances was necessary."

For Tolstoy, both Napoleon and Alexander I were just puppets who thought that they were puppeteers; they were only "the unconscious weapon for the achievement of historical universal goals."

According to Tolstoy, Napoleon and Alexander I considered themselves to be national leaders, practically demigods, and therefore the writer presented them in a caricatured way in the novel. Tolstoy's sympathy was with the phlegmatic Russian commander Kutuzov, who "understands that there is something more powerful and significant than his will—it is the inevitable course of events."

For him, Kutuzov's highest wisdom was his historical fatalism. Viktor Shklovsky, a Tolstoy biographer, commented that the real Kutuzov was no fatalist, he was merely an aging man who husbanded his strength.[39] But Tolstoy turned him into the spokesman of his idea, and now we see Kutuzov through the prism of *War and Peace*.

Despite irritated reviews by military experts who accused the writer of distorting historical facts, Tolstoy's interpretation of Commander Kutuzov found resonance with Nicholas II, who was a religious fatalist. When he was twenty-six, he wrote to his mother, "God alone wills all, He does everything for our good, and we must accept His holy will with prayer!" His invariable calm response to the apocalyptic predictions and moaning of his officials and entourage was "It's all God's will."

His identification with Kutuzov as depicted in *War and Peace* is obvious here. When, in 1915, Nicholas took on the command of the Russian army that was waging war against the Germans, he behaved exactly like Tolstoy's Kutuzov: he didn't interfere in tactical decisions, concerning himself mainly with improving the morale of soldiers and officers. He earnestly believed that would guarantee victory in the war.

Nicholas II thought he understood the Russian people, understood his soldiers, and knew how they would behave in a difficult moment. He was sure they all shared his profound faith in God and supported the emperor's divine right to rule Russia.

His mistaken belief was created in part by his perception of Tolstoy's *War and Peace*.

Every reader of *War and Peace* remembers its protagonists: the delightful Natasha Rostova and her noisy, silly, and charming family; Natasha's fiancé, the ambitious and brave Prince Andrei Bolkonsky, and his eccentric father; the fat, clumsy, and kind Pierre Bezukhov. Tolstoy's creations remain with you forever as you go through life.

But one of the most memorable characters (despite the relatively few pages devoted to him) is a peasant soldier, Platon Karataev, whom Pierre Bezukhov befriends while in French captivity. For Tolstoy, Karataev is a symbol of the Russian people: he is pious, patient, and gentle. No trials or temptations can confuse his clear mind and Christian soul.

Nicholas II imagined that the Russian nation and the Russian army consisted of millions of peasant Karataevs, who, he was sure, would never fall for the antimonarchist propaganda of a bunch of revolutionary "devils." Lenin also read Tolstoy and also drew political conclusions, but they were directly opposite.

According to Lenin's analysis, Tolstoy was predicting a successful Russian revolution. In an article written in 1908 on the occasion of the writer's eightieth birthday, "Leo Tolstoy as a Mirror of the Russian Revolution," Lenin maintained that even though "Tolstoy's ideas are a mirror of the weakness and inadequacies of our peasant rebellion," the situation was changing every day: "The old pillars of peasant economy and peasant life, pillars that have held up for ages, are breaking down with extraordinary speed."[40]

Lenin admitted that Tolstoy was "an artist of genius who gave us not only incomparable pictures of Russian life but first-rate works of world literature." But Lenin, a cynical professional politician, did not fall under the magical spell of Tolstoy's "realism," and did not confuse the literary characters with actual people.

Also, Lenin saw in Tolstoy's novels what Nicholas II preferred not to notice—"mountains of hatred, anger, and desperate determination," felt by the peasants who were already prepared, in Lenin's opinion, "to sweep out the official church, and the landowners, and the landowner government."

The February Revolution of 1917 occurred almost spontaneously, without plan, organization, or leadership. During those days Russia's capital overflowed with crowds of revolutionary soldiers and sailors—the main force of the rebellion. Some historians, then and now, characterized the crowd as a gathering of "devils." This is hardly an objective assessment. But it is also unlikely that there were many Platon Karataevs from *War and Peace* among the rebels.

One of the most remarkable descriptions of the February Revolution came from its witness Vassily Rozanov, a perceptive essayist. Rozanov was one of the first to be struck by how quickly Imperial Russia collapsed, in just two, at most three, days. "The remains of the police crawled out of the attics and surrendered. The troops rolled over like an avalanche to the side of the rebellion, and attempts to return power by military force to the old hands looked like attempts to weave a knout out of sand. Everything was falling apart."[41]

Rozanov was amazed to hear of an old peasant declaring that "the former tsar should be skinned strip by strip."[42] Rozanov was shocked: there's your holy Russian muzhik, there's your Dostoevsky and Tolstoy and *War and Peace*.

According to Rozanov, the Russian revolution was fed and prepared by Russian culture: "There is no doubt that Russia was killed by literature. Of the 'corrupters' of Russia, there is not a single one without a literary background."[43] And the last Russian tsar, lamented Rozanov, turned out to be inadequate, and broke down.

There has been a fatal "rift between the monarchy and literature,"

Rozanov concluded bitterly. And as a result, "Literally, God spat and blew out the candle."[44] The vast empire slipped out of the Romanovs' hands, and with it, its biggest treasure—the great Russian culture.

Yet the Romanovs will remain forever in the history of that magnificent culture, where Catherine the Great quarrels and makes up with Derzhavin and Nicholas I with Pushkin, Karamzin mentors Alexander I, Zhukovsky brings up the future Alexander II, Alexander III listens attentively to Tchaikovsky's *Swan Lake,* and Nicholas II reads Tolstoy's stories to his son.

Notes

INTRODUCTION

1. Konstantin Pleshakov, *Sv. iskusstvo* [Sacred art] (Moscow, 2003), p. 15.
2. Viktor Shklovsky, in conversation with the author.

CHAPTER 1
The First Romanovs: From Tsar Mikhail to Peter I

1. *Russkii arkhiv,* 1910, vol. 2, p. 377.
2. Vadim Kozhinov, *Tiutchev* (Moscow, 1994), p. 218.
3. Quoted from *M. I. Glinka, Issledovaniia i materialy* [Research and materials] (Moscow and Leningrad, 1950), p. 16.
4. Quoted from *Russkii biograficheskii slovar'* [Russian biographical dictionary], vol.: Suvorov-Tkachev (St. Petersburg, 1912), p. 177.
5. *M. I. Glinka,* p. 26.
6. *Letopis' zhizni i tvorchestva M. Glinki* [Chronicle of the life and work of M. Glinka], in two parts, part 1 (Leningrad, 1978), p. 88.

7. M. Glinka, *Literaturnye proizvedeniia i perepiska* [Literary works and corre-spondence], vol. 1 (Moscow, 1973), p. 268.

8. Ibid., p. 266.

9. Ibid., p. 267.

10. Ibid.

11. Quoted from V. A. Sollogub, *Povesti. Vospominaniia* [Novellas, reminis-cences] (Leningrad, 1988), p. 576.

12. Quoted from T. Livanova, Vl. Protopopov, *Glinka,* vol. 1 (Moscow, 1955), p. 176.

13. V. F. Odoevskii, *Izbrannye muzykal'no-kriticheskie stat'i*[Selected musical criticism] (Moscow-Leningrad, 1951), p. 31.

14. Glinka, vol. 1, p. 275.

15. Quoted from A. Gozenpud, *Russkii opernyi teatr XIX veka (1836-1856)*[Rus-sian opera of the nineteenth century (1836–1856)] (Leningrad, 1969), p. 37.

16. Ibid., p. 69.

17. Quoted from V. S. Kliuchevskii, *Sochineniia* [Works], in nine volumes, vol. 3 (Moscow, 1988), p. 62.

18. Ibid., p. 308.

19. *Zhitie Avvakuma i drugie ego sochineniia* [Avvakum's *Life* and other works] (Moscow, 1991), p. 62.

20. Ibid.

21. Ibid., p. 52.

22. Ibid., p. 54.

23. Ibid., p. 396.

24. Ibid.

25. Quoted from N. B. Golikova, *Politicheskie protsessy pri Petre I po materialam Preobrazhenskogo prikaza* [Political processes under Peter I from materials of the Preobrazhensky office] (Moscow, 1957), p. 169.

26. Quoted from *Utverzhdenie dinastii. Istoriia Rossii i doma Romanovykh v memuarakh sovremennikov XVII–XX vv.* [Assertion of the dynasty: The his-tory of Russia and the House of Romanov in the memoirs of contempo-raries, XVII–XX centuries] (Moscow, 1997), p. 288.

27. Kliuchevskii, vol. 3, p. 264.

28. N. A. Dobroliubov, *Polnoe sobranie sochinenii* [Complete collected works], in six volumes, vol. 3 (Moscow, 1936), p. 195.

29. Quoted from I. E. Berenbaum, *Knizhnyi Peterburg* [Literary St. Petersburg] (Moscow, 1980), p. 12.

30. *Podlinnye anekdoty o Petre Velikom, sobrannye Yakovom Shtelinym* [True anecdotes about Peter the Great, collected by Jacob Staehlin], part 1, 2nd ed. (Moscow, 1820), p. 208.

31. Abram Efros, *Dva veka russkogo iskusstva* [Two centuries of Russian art] (Moscow, 1969), p. 38.

32. Quoted from *Pervye khudozhniki Peterburga* [First artists of St. Petersburg] (Leningrad, 1984), p. 98.

33. Ibid., p. 123.

34. Ibid., p. 126.

35. *Panegiricheskaia literatura petrovskogo vremeni* [Panegyric literature of the Petrine era] (Moscow, 1979), p. 279.

36. Quoted from Solomon Volkov, *Istoriia kul'tury Sankt-Peterburga s osnovaniia do nashikh dnei* [History of the culture of St. Petersburg from its founding to the present] (Moscow, 2001), p. 9. English translation: *St. Petersburg: A Cultural History* (New York, 1995).

CHAPTER 2

Kantemir, Lomonosov, and Barkov

1. V. A. Zhukovskii, *Estetika i kritika* [Aesthetics and criticism] (Moscow, 1985), pp. 204, 206.

2. Quoted from Antiokh Kantemir, *Sobranie stikhotvorenii* [Collected poems] (Leningrad, 1956), p. 31.

3. Quoted from Evgenii Lebedev, *Lomonosov* (Moscow, 1990), p. 28.

4. Ibid., p. 99.

5. I. S. Barkov, *Polnoe sobranie stikhotvorenii* [Complete collected poems] (St. Petersburg, 2005), p. 31.

CHAPTER 3

Catherine the Great and the Culture of Her Era

1. I. S. Barkov, *Polnoe sobranie stikhotvorenii* [Complete collected poems] (St. Petersburg, 2005), p. 563.

2. M. N. Pokrovskii, *Izbrannye proizvedeniia v chetyrekh knigakh* [Selected works in four volumes], vol. 3 (Moscow, 1967), p. 115.

3. See A. Kamenskii, *Pod seniiu Ekateriny . . .* [Under the protection of Catherine . . .] (St. Petersburg, 1992), p. 122.

4. *Zapiski imperatritsy Ekateriny Vtoroi* [Notes of Empress Catherine II] (St. Petersburg, 1907), pp. 233–34.

5. Quoted from A. Kaganovich, *"Mednyi Vsadnik": Istoriia sozdaniia monumenta* ["The Bronze Horseman": History of the making of a monument] (Leningrad, 1975), p. 94.

6. P. A. Viazemskii, *Stikhotvoreniia. Vospominaniia. Zapisnye knizhki* [Poems, memoirs, notebooks] (Moscow, 1988), p. 252.

7. Quoted from V. F. Levinson-Lessing, *Istoriia kartinnoi galerei Ermitazha (1764–1917)* [History of the Hermitage picture gallery, 1764–1917] (Leningrad, 1985), p. 61.

8. Ibid., p. 74.

9. I. E. Barenbaum, *Knizhnyi Peterburg* [Literary St. Petersburg] (Moscow, 1980), p. 32.

10. Ibid., p. 74.

11. Quoted from Kamenskii, p. 397.

12. Quoted from N. Eidel'man, *Mgnoven'e slavy nastaet* [The moment of glory is upon us] (Leningrad, 1989).

13. *Russkie memuary. XVIII vek* [Russian memoirs, eighteenth century] (Moscow, 1988), p. 133.

14. Quoted from G. R. Derzhavin, *Stikhotvoreniia* [Poetry] (Leningrad, 1957), p. 32.

15. *Russkie memuary,* p. 151.

16. Ibid., p. 162.

17. Quoted from V. Khodasevich, *Derzhavin* [Derzhavin] (Moscow, 1988), p. 143.

CHAPTER 4

Paul I and Alexander I; Karamzin and Zhukovsky

1. *A. S. Pushkin v vospominaniiakh sovremennikov* [Reminiscences of A. S. Pushkin by his contemporaries], in two volumes, vol. 2 (Moscow, 1974), p. 196.

2. N. M. Karamzin, *Pis'ma russkogo puteshestvennika* [Letters of a Russian traveler] (Leningrad, 1984), p. 20.

3. Quoted from Viktor Afanas'ev, *Zhukovskii* [Zhukovsky] (Moscow, 1986), p. 7.

4. *Dnevniki V. A. Zhukovskogo* [Journals of V. A. Zhukovsky] (St. Petersburg, 1901), p. 27.

5. Quoted from M. I. Bogdanovich, *Istoriia tsarstvovaniia imperatora Aleksandra I i Rossiia v ego vremia* [History of the reign of Emperor Alexander I and the Russia of his time], vol. 1 (St. Petersburg, 1869), pp. 18–19.

6. *Russkie memuary. XVIII vek* [Russian memoirs, eighteenth century] (Moscow, 1988), p. 165.

7. Quoted from *V bor'be za vlast'. Stranitsy politicheskoi istorii Rossii XVIII veka* [Struggle for power: Pages from the political history of eighteenth-century Russia] (Moscow, 1988), p. 323.

8. Ibid., pp. 363–64.

9. N. M. Karamzin, *Zapiska o drevnei i novoi Rossii v ee politicheskom i grazhdanskom otnosheniiakh* [The memoir on ancient and modern Russia in political and civic aspects] (Moscow, 1991), p. 46.

10. Quoted from S. F. Platonov, *Lektsii po russkoi istorii* [Lectures on Russian history] (Moscow, 1993), p. 649.

11. See Andrei Zorin, *Kormia dvuglavogo orla . . . Literatura i gosudarstvennaia ideologiia v Rossii v poslednei treti XVIII—pervoi treti XIX veka* [Feeding the double-headed eagle . . . Literature and official ideology in Russia from the last third of the eighteenth century to the first third of the nineteenth] (Moscow, 2001).

12. *Istoriia russkoi zhurnalistiki XVIII–XIX vekov* [History of Russian journalism in the eighteenth and nineteenth centuries] (Moscow, 1973), p. 101.

13. Karamzin, p. 48.

14. Quoted from Afanas'ev, p. 131.

15. *I. A. Krylov v vospominaniiakh sovremennikov* [Reminiscences of I. A. Krylov by his contemporaries] (Moscow, 1982), p. 242.

CHAPTER 5

Alexander I, Zhukovsky, and Young Pushkin

1. Andrei Zorin, *Kormia dvuglavogo orla . . . Literatura i gosudartstvennaia ideologiia v Rossii v poslednei treti XVIII—pervoi treti XIX veka* [Feeding the double-headed eagle . . . Literature and official ideology in Russia from the last third of the eighteenth century to the first third of the nineteenth] (Moscow, 2001), p. 269.

2. Ibid., p. 272.

3. Quoted from *Russkie memuary. Izbrannye stranitsy. 1800–1825 gg.* [Russian memoirs: Selected pages, 1800–1825] (Moscow, 1989), pp. 453, 471.

4. Quoted from Viktor Afanas'ev, *Zhukovskii* [Zhukovsky] (Moscow, 1986), p. 175.

5. *Perepiska A. S. Pushkina.* [Correspondence of A. S. Pushkin], in two volumes, vol. 1 (Moscow, 1982), p. 379.

6. *A. S. Pushkin v vospominaniiakh sovremennikov* [Reminiscences of A. S. Pushkin by his contemporaries], in two volumes, vol. 1 (Moscow, 1974), p. 77.

7. Ibid., p. 88.

8. Ibid., p. 91.

9. T. J. Binyon, *Pushkin: A Biography* (New York, 2002), p. 31.

10. B. Tomashevskii, *Pushkin*, vol. 2 (Moscow, 1990), p. 61.

11. Ibid., p. 11.

12. Quoted from N. Ia. Eidel'man, *Tvoi XVIII vek. Prekrasen nash soiuz . . .* [Your eighteenth century, How splendid is our union . . .] (Moscow, 1991).

13. Solomon Volkov, *Dialogi s Iosifom Brodskim* [Dialogues with Joseph Brodsky] (Moscow, 1998), p. 307.

14. Quoted from S. F. Platonov, *Lektsii po russkoi istorii* [Lectures on Russian history], p. 668.

15. Quoted from *Rossiiskie samoderzhtsy. 1801–1917* [Russian tsars, 1801–1917] (Moscow, 1994), p. 75.

16. *A. S. Pushkin v vospominaniiakh sovremennikov,* vol. 2, p. 134.

17. Ibid., p. 98.

18. Ibid., p. 103.

19. Ibid., p. 208.

20. Ibid., pp. 221–22.

21. Quoted from *Rossiiskie samoderzhtsy,* p. 83.

22. See G. Vasilich, *Imperator Aleksandr I i starets Fedor Kuz'mich* [Emperor Alexander I and the elder Fedor Kuzmich] (Moscow, 1911); Grand Duke Nikolai Mikhailovich, *Legenda o konchine imperatora Aleksandra I v Sibiri v obraze startsa Fedora Kuz'micha* [Legend of the death of Alexander I in Siberia under the identity of the elder Fedor Kuzmich] (St. Petersburg, 1907); K. V. Kudriashov, *Aleksandr I i taina Fedora Kuz'micha* [Alexander I and the mystery of Fedor Kuzmich] (Petrograd, 1923); L. Liubimov, *Taina imperatora Aleksandra I* [Mystery of Emperor Alexander I] (Paris, 1938); N. Ia. Eidel'man, *Iz potaennoi istorii Rossii XVIII–XIX vekov* [From the secret history of Russia of the eighteenth and nineteenth centuries] (Moscow, 1993); K. V. Chistov, *Russkie narodnye sotsial'no-utopicheskie legendy XVII–XIX vv.* [Russian popular utopian legends of the seventeenth to the nineteenth centuries] (Moscow, 1967); *Dva monarkha* [Two monarchs] (Moscow, 1991); Aleksandr Arkhangel'skii, *Aleksandr I* [Alexander I] (Moscow, 2000).

CHAPTER 6

Nicholas I and Pushkin

1. Quoted from the collection *14 dekabria 1825 goda i ego istolkovateli* [14 December 1825 and its exponents] (Moscow, 1994), p. 332.

2. Ibid., p. 336.

3. *Perepiska A. S. Pushkina.* [Correspondence of A. S. Pushkin], in two volumes, vol. 1 (Moscow, 1982), p. 112.

4. Quoted from Leonid Vyskochkov, *Nikolai I* [Nicholas I] (Moscow, 2003), p. 125.

5. Quoted from N. Eidel'man, *Pushkin. Iz biografii i tvorchestva. 1826–1837* [Pushkin: From his biography and works, 1826–1837] (Moscow, 1987), p. 9.

6. Ibid., pp. 33, 35.

7. *A. S. Pushkin v vospominaniiakh sovremennikov* [Reminiscences of A. S. Pushkin by his contemporaries], in two volumes, vol. 2 (Moscow, 1974), p. 122.

8. Eidel'man, *Pushkin*, p. 62.

9. Ibid., p. 63.

10. On this, see Solomon Volkov, *Shostakovich i Stalin: Khudozhnik i tsar'* (Moscow, 2004), pp. 59–79. English translation, *Shostakovich and Stalin: The Extraordinary Relationship Between the Great Composer and the Brutal Dictator* (New York, 2004).

11. A. V. Anikin, *Muza i mamona. Sotsial'no-ekonomicheskie motivy u Pushkina* [Muse and Mammon: Socioeconomic motifs in Pushkin] (Moscow, 1989), p. 180.

12. *Perepiska Pushkina*, vol. 2, p. 120.

13. N. I. Grech, *Zapiski o moei zhizni* [Notes on my life] (Moscow and Leningrad, 1930), p. 704.

14. *Literaturnoe nasledstvo* [Literary heritage], vols. 16–18 (Moscow, 1934), pp. 101, 105.

15. *Pisateli-dekabristy v vospominaniiakh sovremennikov* [Reminiscences of the Decembrist writers by their contemporaries], vol. 2 (Moscow, 1980), p. 247.

16. Iu. M. Lotman, *Aleksandr Sergeevich Pushkin. Biografiia pisatelia* [Alexander Sergeevich Pushkin: Biography of a writer] (Leningrad, 1981), p. 135.

17. T. J. Binyon, *Pushkin: A Biography* (New York, 2002), p. 546.

18. *Novoe literaturnoe obozrenie*, 40 (1999), p. 84.

19. *Pushkin v vospominaniiakh sovremennikov,* vol. 2, p. 192.

20. Anna Akhmatova, in conversation with the author.

21. Quoted from R. G. Skrynnikov, *Pushkin. Taina gibeli* [Pushkin: The mystery of his death] (St. Petersburg, 2005), p. 319.

22. Eidel'man, *Pushkin*, p. 400.

CHAPTER 7
Lermontov and Briullov

1. *A. S. Pushkin v vospominaniiakh sovremennikov* [Reminiscences of A. S. Pushkin by his contemporaries], in two volumes, vol. 1 (Moscow, 1974), p. 122.

2. Quoted from *V. A. Zhukovskii—kritik* [V. A. Zhukovsky, critic] (Moscow, 1985), p. 246.

3. Ibid., pp. 251–52.

4. See the collection *Rossiiskie konservatory* [Russian conservatives] (Moscow, 1997), p. 105; and the collection *Kontekst—1989. Literaturno-teoreticheskie issledovaniia* [Context 1989: Studies in literary theory] (Moscow, 1989), pp. 10, 38.

5. Aleksandr Vasil'evich Nikitenko, *Zapiski i dnevnik* [Notes and journal], in three volumes, vol. 1 (Moscow, 2004), p. 362.

6. *M. Iu. Lermontov v vospominaniiakh sovremennikov* [Reminiscences of M. Iu. Lermontov by his contemporaries] (Moscow, 1989), p. 18.

7. Alla Marchenko, *S podorozhnoi po kazennoi nadobnosti. Lermontov: Roman v dokumentakh i pis'makh* [With travel papers on official business. Lermontov: The novel in documents and letters] (Moscow, 1984), p. 233.

8. *M. Iu. Lermontov v vospominaniiakh sovremennikov,* p. 486.

9. Ibid.

10. See Emma Gershtein, *Sud'ba Lermontova* [Lermontov's fate] (Moscow, 1964), p. 98.

11. Quoted from ibid., p. 101.

12. Ibid.

13. See M. Iu. Lermontov, *Izbrannoe* [Selected works] (Moscow, 1953), p. 11.

14. Quoted from *Lermontov v vospominaniiakh sovremennikov,* pp. 342, 470.

15. Quoted from Gershtein, p. 112.

16. Ibid., p. 113.

17. Quoted from V. Turchin, *Epokha romantizma v Rossii. Istoriia russkogo iskusstva pervoi treti XIX stoletiia. Ocherki* [The Romantic era in Russia: A history of Russian art in the first third of the nineteenth century. Essays] (Moscow, 1981), p. 80.

18. Quoted from Galina Leont'eva, *Karl Briullov* (Leningrad, 1976), p. 319.

19. Quoted from ibid., p. 192.

20. Quoted from A. V. Kornilova, *Karl Briullov v Peterburge* [Karl Briullov in St. Petersburg] (Leningrad, 1976), p. 105.

21. Leonid Vyskochkov, *Nikolai I* [Nicholas I] (Moscow, 2003), p. 570.

22. See *Literaturnoe obozrenie,* 11 (1991).

23. Quoted from Kornilova, p. 131.

24. Quoted from Alla Marchenko, *S podorozhnoi po kazennoi nadobnosti. Lermontov: Roman v dokumentakh i pis'makh* [With travel papers on official business. Lermontov: The novel in documents and letters], pp. 101–02.

25. Quoted from *Lermontov v vospominaniiakh sovremennikov,* p. 206.

CHAPTER 8

Gogol, Ivanov, Tyutchev, and the End of the Nicholas I Era

1. Quoted from Vikentii Veresaev, *Gogol' v zhizni* [Gogol in life] (Moscow, 1990), p. 183.

2. Quoted from P. V. Annenkov, *Literaturnye vospominaniia* [Literary memoirs] (Moscow, 1983), p. 59.

3. Quoted from Veresaev, p. 184.

4. Quoted from Igor' Zolotusskii, *Gogol'* [Gogol] (Moscow, 1979), p. 193; *Nikolai Pervyi i ego vremia* [Nicholas I and his times], vol. 2 (Moscow, 2000), p. 278.

5. Quoted from Annenkov, p. 355.

6. R.-M. Rilke, *Vorpsvede. Ogiust Roden. Pis'ma. Stikhi* [Worpswede, Auguste Rodin, letters, poetry] (Moscow, 1971), p. 389.

7. Annenkov, p. 49.

8. Ibid., p. 401.

9. *Nikolai Pervyi i ego vremia,* vol. 2, p. 208.

10. Quoted from Iu. Mann, *V poiskakh zhivoi dushi* [In search of the living soul] (Moscow, 1984), p. 125.

11. Quoted from Aleksandr Vasil'evich Nikitenko, *Zapiski. Dnevnik* [Notes and Journal], in three volumes, vol. 1 (Moscow, 2004), p. 561.

12. Quoted from Kirill Pigarev, *F. I. Tiutchev i ego vremia* [F. I. Tiutchev and his times] (Moscow, 1978), p. 124.

13. Quoted from *Sovremenniki o F. I. Tiutcheve. Vospominaniia, otzyvy i pis'ma*

[F. I. Tiutchev in the words of his contemporaries: Memoirs, reviews, and letters] (Tula, 1984), p. 14.

14. Quoted from F. I. Tiutchev, *Lirika* [Lyric poetry], vol. 2 (Moscow, 1965), p. 361.

15. Quoted from Vadim Kozhinov, *Tiutchev* (Moscow, 1994), p. 319.

16. N. Ia. Eidel'man, *Gertsen protiv samoderzhaviia. Sekretnaia politicheskaia istoriia Rossii XVIII–XIX vekov i vol'naia pechat'* [Herzen vs. autocracy: The secret political history of Russia in the eighteenth and nineteenth centuries and the independent press] (Moscow, 1984), p. 10.

17. Quoted from Vyskochkov, *Nikolai I* [Nicholas I], pp. 605–06.

CHAPTER 9

Alexander II, Tolstoy, Turgenev, and Dostoevsky

1. Quoted from the collection *Aleksandr Vtoroi: Vospominaniia. Dnevniki* [Alexander II: Memoirs and diaries] (St. Petersburg, 1995), p. 76.

2. Quoted from E. P. Tolmachev, *Aleksandr II i ego vremia* [Alexander II and his times], in two volumes, vol. 1 (Moscow, 1998), p. 79.

3. D. V. Grigorovich, *Literaturnye vospominaniia* [Literary memoirs] (Moscow, 1987), p. 133.

4. Ibid., p. 294.

5. Ibid.

6. A. Ia. Panaeva (Golovacheva), *Vospominaniia* [Memoirs] (Moscow, 1986), p. 210.

7. Ibid., p. 212.

8. Quoted from G. A. Bialyi and A. B. Muratov, *Turgenev v Peterburge* [Turgenev in St. Petersburg] (Leningrad, 1970), p. 69.

9. Panaeva, p. 115.

10. *I. S. Turgenev v vospominaniiakh sovremennikov* [Reminiscences of I. S. Turgenev by his contemporaries], in two volumes, vol. 2 (Moscow, 1969), pp. 175, 178.

11. Ibid., p. 319.

12. Quoted from B. Ia. Bukhshtab, *A. A. Fet. Ocherk zhizni i tvorchestva* [A. A. Fet: A study of his life and work] (Leningrad, 1974), p. 33.

13. A. L. Ospovat, *"Kak slovo nashe otzovetsia . . ." O pervom sbornike Tiutcheva* ["Not ours to know the impact of our words": On the first collection of Tiutchev] (Moscow, 1980), p. 46.

14. *Turgenev v vospominaniiakh sovremennikov,* vol. 2, p. 153.

15. Ibid., p. 197.

16. F. M. Dostoevskii and A. G. Dostoevskaia, *Perepiska* [Correspondence] (Leningrad, 1976), p. 347.

17. Quoted from *L. N. Tolstoi v vospominaniiakh sovremennikov* [Reminiscences of L. N. Tolstoy by his contemporaries], in two volumes, vol. 1 (Moscow, 1978), p. 281.

18. Quoted from *Perepiska I. S. Turgeneva* [Correspondence of I. S. Turgenev], in two volumes, vol. 2 (Moscow, 1986), p. 483.

CHAPTER 10

Herzen, Tolstoy, and the Women's Issue

1. Quoted from Kirill Pigarev, *F. I. Tiutchev i ego vremia* [F. I. Tiutchev and his times] (Moscow, 1978), p. 165.

2. See Marshall Berman, *All That Is Solid Melts into Air: The Experience of Modernity* (New York, 1982), p. 232.

3. P. V. Annenkov, *Literaturnye vospominaniia* [Literary memoirs] (Moscow, 1983), p. 314.

4. *Literaturnoe nasledstvo* [Literary heritage], vol. 62 (Moscow, 1955), p. 381.

5. Quoted from V. Prokof'ev, *Gertsen* [Herzen] (Moscow, 1979), p. 32.

6. A. Ia. Panaeva (Golovacheva), *Vospominaniia* [Memoirs] (Moscow, 1986), p. 139.

7. Annenkov, pp. 288–89.

8. *Literaturnoe nasledstvo* [Literary heritage], vol. 64 (Moscow, 1958), p. 298.

9. *Perepiska I. S. Turgeneva* [Correspondence of I. S. Turgenev], in two volumes, vol. 2 (Moscow, 1986), p. 557.

10. Ibid.

11. Quoted from B. Ia. Bukhshtab, *Literaturovedcheskie rassledovaniia* [Investigations in literary criticism] (Moscow, 1982), p. 105.

12. Ibid., p. 103.

13. P. A. Kropotkin, *Zapiski revoliutsionera* [Memoirs of a revolutionary] (Moscow, 1966), p. 240.

14. G. A. Tishkin, *Zhenskii vopros v Rossii: 50–60–e gody XIX v.* [The women's issue in 1850s and 1860s Russia] (Leningrad, 1984), pp. 213–14.

15. Prince Meshcherskii, *Vospominaniia* [Memoirs] (Moscow, 2001), p. 332.

16. L. N. Tolstoi, *Perepiska s russkimi pisateliami* [Correspondence with Russian writers], in two volumes, vol. 1 (Moscow, 1978), p. 464.

17. Anna Akhmatova, in conversation with the author.

18. Ibid.

19. Quoted from Aleksei Zverev and Vladimir Tunimanov, *Lev Tolstoi* [Leo Tolstoy] (Moscow, 2007), p. 443.

20. M. Gor'kii, *Literaturnye portrety* [Literary portraits] (Moscow, 1983), p. 155.

21. Ibid., p. 199.

22. Quoted from Zverev and Tunimanov, p. 466.

23. Ibid., p. 465.

24. L. L. Sabaneev, *Vospominaniia o Taneeve* [Reminiscences of Taneev] (Moscow, 2003), pp. 65–66.

25. Gor'kii, p. 168.

CHAPTER 11

Tchaikovsky and Homosexuality in Imperial Russia

1. P. I. Chaikovskii, *Perepiska s. N. F. von Mekk* [Correspondence with Nadezhda von Meck], vol. 2 (Moscow and Leningrad, 1935), p. 63.

2. P. I. Chaikovskii, *Pis'ma k rodnym* [Correspondence with family], vol. 1 (Moscow, 1940), p. 268.

3. Chaikovskii, *Perepiska*, p. 63.

4. *Dnevniki P. I. Chaikovskogo. 1873–1891* [Tchaikovsky journals, 1873–1891] (Moscow and Petrograd, 1923), p. 209.

5. Quote from A. Shol'p, *"Evgenii Onegin" Chaikovskogo. Ocherki.* [Tchaikovsky's *Eugene Onegin*: Essays] (Leningrad, 1982), p. 15.

6. P. Chaikovskii, *Polnoe sobranie sochinenii. Literaturnye proizvedeniia i perepiska* [Complete collected works: Literary works and correspondence], vol. 6 (Moscow, 1961), p. 100.

7. Quoted from *Lev Tolstoi i muzyka. Khronika. Notografiia. Bibliografiia* [Leo Tolstoy and music: Chronicle, bibliography of musical scores, bibiliography] (Moscow, 1977), pp. 149–50.

8. L. Tolstoi, *Perepiska s russkimi pisateliami* [Correspondence with Russian writers], p. 185.

9. Ibid., p. 187.

10. M. Chaikovskii, *Zhizn' Petra Il'icha Chaikovskogo* [Life of Peter Ilich Tchaikovsky], in three volumes, vol. 2 (Moscow, 1997), p. 232.

11. G. A. Larosh, *Izbrannye stat'i* [Selected articles], part 2 (Leningrad, 1975), p. 104.

12. See, for instance, interview with Mikhail Buianov, president of the Moscow Academy of Psychotherapy, "Was Tchaikovsky a Homosexual?" in *Argumenty i fakty,* 49 (2003), p. 20.

13. Richard Taruskin, *On Russian Music* (Berkeley, Los Angeles, and London, 2009), p. 98.

14. M. Chaikovskii, *Zhizn',* vol. 2, p. 11.

15. Théodule-Armand Ribot, *Volia v ee normal'nom i boleznennom sostoianii* [The will in its normal and diseased state] (St. Petersburg, 1894), p. 121.

16. *Vospominnaniia o P. I. Chaikovskom* (Reminiscences of P. I. Tchaikovsky] (Moscow, 1979), p. 399.

17. Ibid., p. 400.

18. Ibid., pp. 130–31.

19. P. I. Chaikovskii, *Al'manakh* [Anthology], part 1 (Moscow, 1995), p. 127.

20. Aleksandr Poznanskii, *Samoubiistvo Chaikovskogo: Mif i real'nost'* [Suicide of Tchaikovsky: Myth and reality] (Moscow, 1993), p. 40.

21. E. Feoktistov, *Za kulisami politiki i literatury. 1848–1896* [Behind the scenes of politics and literature, 1848–1896] (Moscow, 1991), p. 238.

22. See, for instance, A. Suvorin, *Dnevnik* [Diary] (Moscow, 1992), pp. 371, 374, 376–77; A. Bogdanovich, *Tri poslednikh samoderzhtsa* [The last three autocrats] (Moscow, 1990), pp. 104, 161, 178, 299.

23. See *Novyi mir,* 5 (1999), pp. 189–90.

24. Quoted from K. K. Rotikov, *Drugoi Peterburg* [The other Petersburg] (St. Petersburg, 1998), p. 407.

25. *Novyi mir,* 5 (1999), p. 189.

26. Quoted from *Neizvestnyi Chaikovskii* [The unknown Tchaikovsky] (Moscow, 2009), p. 19.

27. Chaikovskii, *Al'manakh,* part 1, p. 123.

28. Ibid.

29. See Truman Bullard, "Tchaikovsky's *Eugene Onegin:* Tatiana and Lensky, the Third Couple," in *Tchaikovsky and His Contemporaries: A Centennial Symposium* (Westport, Conn., and London, 1999), pp. 157–66.

30. George Balanchine, in conversation with the author.

31. Igor' Glebov (Boris Asaf'ev), *Chaikovskii: Opyt kharakteristiki* [Tchaikovsky: Essay of a characterization] (St. Petersburg and Berlin, 1923), p. 45.

CHAPTER 12

Dostoevsky and the Romanovs

1. P. Chaikovskii, *Polnoe sobranie sochinenii. Literaturnye proizvedeniia i perepiska* [Complete collected works: Literary works and correspondence], vol. 5 (Moscow, 1959), pp. 106–07.

2. *Zapiski P. A. Cherevina* [Memoirs of P. A. Cherevin] (Kostroma, 1918), pp. 4–5.

3. Aleksandr Vasil'evich Nikitenko, *Zapiski i dnevnik* [Notes and journal], in three volumes, vol. 2 (Moscow, 2004), pp. 244-45.

4. Ibid., pp. 302, 304.

5. Prince Meshcherskii, *Vospominaniia* [Memoirs] (Moscow, 2001), p. 307.

6. Quoted from Igor' Volgin, *Koleblias' nad bezdnoi: Dostoevskii i russkii imperatorskii dom* [Hovering over the abyss: Dostoevsky and the Russian imperial house] (Moscow, 1998), pp. 271–72.

7. A. G. Dostoevskaia, *Vospominaniia* [Memoirs] (Moscow, 1971], p. 326.

8. Quoted from Volgin, p. 302.

9. *Literaturnoe nasledstvo* [Literary heritage], vol. 86 (Moscow, 1973), p. 135.

10. Ibid., p. 136.

11. Dostoevskaia, p. 327.

12. See, for instance, *Novyi mir,* 5 (1999), pp. 195–215.

13. F. M. Dostoevskii and A. G. Dostoevskaia, *Perepiska* [Correspondence] (Leningrad, 1976), p. 293.

14. Ibid., pp. 285, 291.

15. See *Sredi velikikh: Literaturnye vstrechi* [Among the greats: Literary encounters] (Moscow, 2001), pp. 355–57.

16. *Perepiska I. S. Turgeneva* [Correspondence of I. S. Turgenev], in two volumes, vol. 2 (Moscow, 1986), p. 305.

17. Ibid., p. 294.

18. Quoted from Igor' Volgin, *Poslednii god Dostoevskogo* [Dostoevsky's last year] (Moscow, 1986), p. 486.

19. Quoted from *Konstantin Petrovich Pobedonostsev i ego korrespondenty* [Konstantin Petrovich Pobedonostsev and his correspondents], in two volumes, vol. 1 (Minsk, 2003), p. 34.

20. Quoted from Volgin, *Poslednii god Dostoevskogo*, p. 487.

21. Quoted from B. Bursov, *Lichnost' Dostoevskogo* [Dostoevsky the person] (Leningrad, 1974), p. 131.

22. Quoted from K. P. Pobedonostsev, *Velikaia lozh' nashego vremeni* [The big lie of our time] (Moscow, 1993), p. 340.

CHAPTER 13

Alexander III, the Wanderers, and Mussorgsky

1. Aleksandr Benua, *Moi vospominaniia* [My memoirs], in five volumes, vols. 1–3 (Moscow, 1980), p. 382.

2. Quoted from *Lev Tolstoi i russkie tsari* [Leo Tolstoy and the Russian tsars] (Moscow, 1995), p. 23.

3. Quoted from Aleksei Zverev and Vladimir Tunimanov, *Lev Tolstoi* [Leo Tolstoy] (Moscow, 2007), p. 359.

4. Quoted from Iu. B. Solov'ev, *Samoderzhavie i dvorianstvo v kontse XIX veka* [Autocracy and nobility in the late nineteenth century] (Leningrad, 1973), p. 90.

5. Ibid.

6. *Konstantin Petrovich Pobedonostsev i ego korrespondenty* [Konstantin Petrovich Pobedonostsev and his correspondents], in two volumes, vol. 1 (Minsk, 2003), p. 246.

7. I. E. Repin, *Dalekoe blizkoe* [Far and near] (Leningrad, 1982), p. 293.

8. *Pobedonostsev i ego korrespondenty*, vol. 2, pp. 498–99.

9. Repin, p. 152.

10. Ibid., p. 185.

11. Vasilii Ivanovich Surikov, *Pis'ma. Vospominaniia o khudozhnike* [Letters, memoirs] (Leningrad, 1977), p. 187; Maksimilian Voloshin, *Liki tvorchestva* [The faces of creativity] (Leningrad, 1988), p. 343.

12. Quoted from V. Lakshin, *Aleksandr Nikolaevich Ostrovskii* [Alexander Nikolaevich Ostrovsky] (Moscow, 1976), p. 504.

13. Quoted from A. Orlova, *Trudy i dni M. P. Musorgskogo. Letopis' zhizni i tvorchestva* [Works and days of M. P. Mussorgsky: Chronicle of his life and work] (Moscow, 1963), p. 360.

14. Modest Petrovich Musorgskii, *Pis'ma, biograficheskie materialy i dokumenty* [Letters, biographical materials, and documents] (Moscow, 1971), p. 176.

15. Quoted from A. Gozenpud, *Russkii operny teatr XIX veka. 1873–1889* [Russian opera of the nineteenth century, 1873–1889] (Leningrad, 1973), p. 107.

16. Surikov, Pis'ma. *Vospominaniia*, p. 187.

17. Quoted from A. Gozenpud, *Russkii operny teatr na rubezhe XIX-XX vekov i F. I. Shaliapin. 1890–1904* [Russian opera at the turn of the twentieth century and F. I. Chaliapin, 1890–1904] (Leningrad, 1974), p. 28.

18. Benua, *Moi vospominaniia*, vols. 1–3, p. 650.

CHAPTER 14

Nicholas II and Lenin as Art Connoisseurs

1. See, for instance, M. K. Kasvinov, *Dvadtsat' tri stupeni vniz* [Twenty-three steps down] (Moscow, 1978), pp. 82, 128.

2. Aleksandr Solzhenitsyn, *Publitsistika* [Essays on society and politics], in three volumes, vol. 3 (Yaroslavl, 1997), p. 332.

3. *Teatr*, 12 (1992), p. 127.

4. Quoted from the collection *V. I. Lenin o literature* [V. I. Lenin on literature] (Moscow, 1971), p. 226.

5. Quoted from *Literaturnoe nasledstvo* [Literary heritage], vol. 65 (Moscow, 1958), p. 210.

6. A. V. Lunacharskii, *Vospominaniia i vpechatleniia* [Memoirs and impressions] (Moscow, 1969), p. 195.

7. Quoted from S. K. Bogoiavlenskii, *Moskovskii teatr pri tsariakh Aleksee i Petre* [Muscovite theater under Tsars Alexis and Peter] (Moscow, 1914), p. 19.

8. Matil'da Kshesinskaia, *Vospominaniia* [Memoirs] (Moscow, 1992), p. 29.

9. Ibid., p. 48.

10. Nicholas II, *Dnevniki* [Journals] (Moscow, 2007), p. 13.

11. M. Gor'kii, *Literaturnye portrety* [Literary portraits] (Moscow, 1983), p. 40.

12. George Balanchine, in conversation with the author.

13. Gor'kii, p. 37.

14. Quoted from *Lev Tolstoi i muzyka. Khronika. Notografiia. Bibliografiia* [Leo Tolstoy and music: Chronicle, bibliography of musical scores, bibliography] (Moscow, 1977), p. 22.

15. Quoted from A. G. Latyshev, *Rassekrechennyi Lenin* [Lenin declassified] (Moscow, 1996), p. 291.

16. *V. I. Lenin o literature* [V. I. Lenin on literature] (Moscow, 1971), p. 254.

17. Maria Dobrowen, in conversation with the author.

18. Quoted from the collection *Prometei* [Prometheus], vol. 8 (Moscow, 1971), p. 61.

19. See L. Freidkina, *Dni i gody V. I. Nemirovicha-Danchenko* [Life of V. I. Nemirovich-Danchenko] (Moscow, 1962), p. 219; I. Solov'eva, *Nemirovich-Danchenko* [Nemirovich-Danchenko] (Moscow, 1979), pp. 211–12.

20. Quotes from Simon Dreiden, *Spektakli. Roli. Sud'by* [Plays, roles, and destinies] (Moscow, 1978), p. 22.

21. Quoted from M. N. Stroeva, *Rezhisserskie iskaniia Stanislavskogo. 1898–1917* [Directorial pursuits of Stanislavsky, 1898–1917] (Moscow, 1973), p. 304.

22. Quoted from *Literaturnoe nasledstvo* [Literary heritage], vol. 72 (Moscow, 1965), p. 539.

23. *Lenin o literature*, p. 263.

24. *Grazhdanin*, 3 March 1902.

25. Quoted from *Letopis' zhizni i tvorchestva A. M. Gor'kogo* [Chronicle of the life and work of A. M. Gorky], part 1 (Moscow, 1958), p. 372.

26. Quoted from *Russkaia literatura kontsa XIX–nachala XX v. 1901–1907* [Russian literature at the turn of the twentieth century: 1901–1907] (Moscow, 1971), p. 373.

27. *Lenin o literature,* pp. 148, 150.

28. Ibid., pp. 157–58.

29. See *Bol'shaia tsenzura: Pisateli i zhurnalisty v Strane Sovetov. 1917–1956* [Censorship on a grand scale: Writers and journalists in the Soviet Union, 1917–1956] (Moscow, 2005), p. 29.

30. *Prometei* [Prometheus], vol. 8, p. 61.

31. M. Gor'kii, *V. I. Lenin* (Moscow, 1974), p. 7. (Quotations hereafter taken from this edition.)

32. Natan Altman, in conversation with the author.

33. Abram Efros, *Profili* [Profiles] (Moscow, 1994), p. 15.

34. See S. I. Grigor'ev, *Pridvornaia tsenzura i obraz Verkhovnoi vlasti (1831–1917)* [Court censorship and the image of the Crown, 1831–1917] (St. Petersburg, 2007).

35. Quoted from *Valentin Serov v vospominaniiakh, dnevnikakh i perepiske sovremennikov* [Valentin Serov in the memoirs, diaries, and correspondence of his contemporaries], vol. 2 (Leningrad, 1971), p. 296.

36. *Valentin Serov v perepiske, dokumentakh i interv'iu* [Valentin Serov in correspondence, documents, and interviews], vol. 2 (Leningrad, 1989), pp. 6–7.

37. Aleksandr Benua, *Moi vospominaniia* [My memoirs], in five volumes, vols. 1–3, p. 634.

38. Ibid.

39. Viktor Shklovsky, in conversation with the author.

40. This and subsequent quotations from V. I. Lenin, *Lev Tolstoi, kak zerkalo russkoi revoliutsii* [Leo Tolstoy as a mirror of the Russian Revolution] (Moscow, 1970).

41. Quoted from the collection *Pod sozvezdiem topora: Petrograd 1917 goda—znakomyi i neznakomyi* [Under the sign of the ax: Petrograd, 1917—the familiar and the unknown] (Moscow, 1991), p. 50.

42. Ibid., p. 56.

43. V. V. Rozanov, *Nesovmestimye kontrasty zhitiia. Literaturno-esteticheskie raboty raznykh let* [Life's incompatible contradictions: Literary-aesthetic works of various dates] (Moscow, 1990), p. 553.

44. Ibid., p. 546.

Index

A NOTE ON THE TYPE

This book was set in Minion, a typeface produced by the Adobe Corporation specifically for the Macintosh personal computer, and released in 1990. Designed by Robert Slimbach, Minion combines the classic characteristics of old-style faces with the full complement of weights required for modern typesetting.

Composed by Creative Graphics
Allentown, Pennsylvania

Printed and bound by Berryville Graphics
Berryville, Virginia

Designed by Soonyoung Kwon